# DEVIANT MODERNISM

*Sexual and textual errancy in T. S. Eliot,
James Joyce, and Marcel Proust*

This original study re-evaluates central texts of the modernist canon – Eliot's early poetry including *The Waste Land*, Joyce's *Ulysses*, and Proust's *Remembrance of Things Past* – by examining sexual energies and identifications in them that are typically regarded as perverse. According to modern cultural discourses and psychosexual categorizations, these deviant desires and identifications feminize men or tend to render them homosexual. Colleen Lamos's analysis of the operations of gender and sexuality in these texts reveals conflicts concerning the definition of masculine heterosexuality which cut across the aesthetics of modernism. She argues that canonical male modernism, far from being a monolithic entity with a coherently conservative political agenda, is in fact the site of errant impulses and unresolved struggles. What emerges is a reconsideration of modernist literature as a whole and a recognition of the heterogeneous forces that formed and deformed modernism.

Colleen Lamos is Associate Professor in the Department of English at Rice University in Texas and has taught at the Ohio State University and the University of Saarland in Germany. She has published widely on fiction, modernism, and gender studies in journals and edited collections of essays, and is co-editor of a special issue of the *European Joyce Studies Annual* on "Joycean Masculinities."

# DEVIANT MODERNISM

*Sexual and textual errancy in*
*T. S. Eliot, James Joyce, and Marcel Proust*

COLLEEN LAMOS

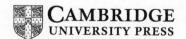

CAMBRIDGE
UNIVERSITY PRESS

PUBLISHED BY THE PRESS SYNDICATE OF THE UNIVERSITY OF CAMBRIDGE
The Pitt Building, Trumpington Street, Cambridge CB2 1RP, United Kingdom

CAMBRIDGE UNIVERSITY PRESS
The Edinburgh Building, Cambridge CB2 2RU, United Kingdom   http://www.cup.cam.ac.uk
40 West 20th Street, New York, NY 10011–4211, USA   http://www.cup.org
10 Stamford Road, Oakleigh, Melbourne 3166, Australia

First published 1998

Printed in the United Kingdom at the University Press, Cambridge

Typeset in Baskerville MT 11/12½ [SE]

*A catalogue record for this book is available from the British Library*

*Library of Congress cataloguing in publication data*
Lamos, Colleen.
Deviant modernism: sexual and textual errancy in T. S. Eliot, James Joyce, and
Marcel Proust / Colleen Lamos.
p.   cm.
Includes bibliographical references and index.
ISBN 0-521-62418-5
1. Eliot, T. S. (Thomas Stearns), 1888–1965 – Criticism and
interpretation.   2. Proust, Marcel, 1871–1922. A la recherche du
temps perdu.   3. Joyce, James, 1882–1941. Ulysses.   4. Sexual
deviation in literature.   5. Gender identity in literature.
6. Masculinity in literature.   7. Modernism (Literature)   8. Sex in
literature.   9. Men in literature.   I. Title.
PS3509.L43Z69174   1998
820.9'353 – dc21   98-16594 CIP

ISBN 0 521 62418 5

*To Dominique*

# Contents

# Acknowledgments

My deepest and happiest debt is to Dominique Groeneveld, to whom this books is dedicated with gratitude for her sustaining love. These pages testify to her unswerving confidence, her astute advice, her generosity, and, above all, her inspiration.

Vicki Mahaffey and Joseph Valente have given me years of warm friendship and provocative intellectual exchange that, along with their insightful observations on portions of this book, contributed immeasurably to its writing. I am indebted to Barbara Herrnstein Smith for her steadfast support and rigorous teaching, which helped me to hone my ideas and my prose; the imprint of her instruction is everywhere in this book. Christine van Boheemen insisted that I read Joyce ten years ago and has since been a thoughtful critic of my work, for which I am grateful. Elisabeth Ladenson's wit and scholarly acumen played an important role in my thinking about Proust. For their encouragement and advice on various aspects of my work, I thank Marilyn Reizbaum, Kim Devlin, Margot Norris, Patrick McGee, and Eve Kosofsky Sedgwick. I am especially obliged to my editor, Josie Dixon, for her commitment to this project, which she has guided judiciously through many difficult moments. Terry Munisteri provided invaluable assistance in the production of the manuscript. My parents and Sharon, Susan, and David have been unflagging in their enthusiasm for this book, which I profoundly appreciate.

Madame Brassaï has graciously granted permission to reproduce a photograph by her late husband. I am also grateful for permission to reprint portions of this book that originally appeared in *Joyce in Context*, published by Cambridge University Press, and in the *James Joyce Quarterly*. Research grants from Rice University have aided me in my work.

# Abbreviations

ASG   T. S. Eliot. *After Strange Gods: A Primer of Modern Heresy*. New York: Harcourt, Brace and Co., 1934.

AVP   T. S. Eliot. *Ara Vos Prec*. London: Ovid Press, 1920.

CC    T. S. Eliot. *To Criticize the Critic and Other Writings*. 1965. Reprint, Lincoln and London: University of Nebraska Press, 1991.

CPP   T. S. Eliot. *The Complete Poems and Plays: 1909-1950*. New York: Harcourt, Brace and World, 1971.

CW    James Joyce. *The Critical Writings of James Joyce*. Ed. Ellsworth Mason and Richard Ellmann. New York: Viking, 1959.

D     James Joyce. *Dubliners*. New York: Penguin, 1976.

F     T. S. Eliot. *The Waste Land: A Facsimile and Transcript of the Original Draft including the Annotations of Ezra Pound*. Ed. Valerie Eliot. New York: Harcourt Brace Jovanovich, 1971.

FW    James Joyce. *Finnegans Wake*. New York: Viking, 1939. References are to page and line number.

I     T. S. Eliot. *Inventions of the March Hare: Poems 1909-1917*. Ed. Christopher Ricks. New York: Harcourt, Brace and Co., 1996.

ICS   T. S. Eliot. *The Idea of a Christian Society* and *Notes toward a Definition of Culture*. New York: Harcourt, Brace and Co., 1949.

L     T. S. Eliot. *The Letters of T. S. Eliot*. Vol. 1 (1898-1922). Ed. Valerie Eliot. New York: Harcourt Brace Jovanovich, 1988.

LJ    James Joyce. *Letters of James Joyce*. Vol. 1, ed. Stuart Gilbert. New York: Viking 1957, 1966. Vols. 2 and 3, ed. Richard Ellmann. New York: Viking, 1966.

OPP   T. S. Eliot. *On Poetry and Poets*. New York: Farrar, Straus and Cudahy, 1957.

*ORR*        Marcel Proust. *On Reading Ruskin*. Tr. and ed. Jean Autret,
             William Burford, and Phillip J. Wolfe. New Haven: Yale
             University Press, 1987.
*P*          James Joyce. *A Portrait of the Artist as a Young Man*. Ed.
             Chester G. Anderson. New York: Viking, 1964.
*PE*         James Joyce. *"Poems" and "Exiles."* Ed. J. C. C. Mays.
             Harmondsworth: Penguin, 1992.
*R*          Marcel Proust. *Remembrance of Things Past*. Tr. C. K. Scott
             Moncrieff and Terence Kilmartin. 3 vols. New York:
             Random House, 1982. References are to volume and page
             number.
*SE*         T. S. Eliot. *Selected Essays*. 1951 3rd. edn. Reprint, London:
             Faber and Faber, 1991.
*SL*         James Joyce. *Selected Letters of James Joyce*. Ed. Richard
             Ellmann. New York: Viking, 1975.
*SP*         T. S. Eliot. *Selected Prose*. Ed. Frank Kermode. New York:
             Harcourt Brace Jovanovich, 1975.
*SW*         T. S. Eliot. *The Sacred Wood*. 1920. Reprint, London:
             Methuen, 1960.
*U*          James Joyce. *Ulysses: The Corrected Text*. Ed. Hans Walter
             Gabler with Wolfhard Steppe and Claus Melchior. New
             York: Random House, 1986. References are to chapter and
             line number.
*UPUC*       T. S. Eliot. *The Use of Poetry and the Use of Criticism*. 1933.
             Reprint, Cambridge: Harvard University Press, 1986.
*V*          T. S. Eliot. *The Varieties of Metaphysical Poetry*. Clark and
             Turnbull Lectures. Ed. Ronald Schuchard. London: Faber
             and Faber, 1993.

# Introduction

This book had its beginning some years ago when, confronted by the lingering authority of T. S. Eliot's poetry and prose, I wondered where he went wrong – that is, where he strayed from his stated purposes. In the course of my research I discovered an early poem, "Ode," which Eliot had suppressed, that opened a series of doors for me onto the vagrant tendencies of his work as a whole and that offered an entirely different view of Anglo-American modernism. It became clear that his creative and critical works were engaged in a struggle against identifications and desires that he considered perverse yet that found symptomatic expression within his own texts. Subsequent investigation of the writings of James Joyce and Marcel Proust led me to ask the questions to which this book is the answer. I wondered how our understanding of canonical male modernist authors and of so-called high modernism would be different if we were to examine the ways in which their texts swerve from their explicit or implicit intentions. What if the errant elements in their works were given a central place in the assessment of their position as the defining authors of modern literature? How would Eliot, Joyce, and Proust appear if we viewed them in terms of the ways in which they go astray; specifically, how would they look when seen through the lens of the gender anxieties and homosexual desires that pervade their works, yet which they displaced or disavowed?

The primary aim of this study is to analyze the significant effects of sexual energies and identifications that, for male subjects, were (and are) coded as deviant according to modern cultural discourses and psychosexual categorizations, in the works of writers who are widely regarded as the major figures of literary modernism. These desires and identifications fall under the heading of perversion inasmuch as they are believed to feminize or homosexualize men. My purpose is not to uncover the genuine sexual orientations or gender identities of these authors or their fictional characters but to examine the operations of the gender and sexuality in their texts, including the contradictions among the inter-related forces at work within them. The perversity of their writings is not a repressed libidinal truth but the effect of larger, cultural conflicts concerning the definition of masculine heterosexuality with which their texts are fully engaged. The latter both reflect and importantly contributed to early twentieth-century debates concerning the meaning of gender difference and sexual desire, and thus they intersect in complex ways with contemporary social, political, and scientific discourses, including feminism, sexology, psychology, anthropology, and others. A broader implication of this study is thus that canonical male modernist texts, far from composing a monolithic entity, are the site of unresolved struggles. An examination of the heterogeneous impulses and divagations within the texts of Eliot, Joyce, and Proust may contribute to a reconceptualization of modernist literature as a whole and to a recognition of the multiple, centrifugal forces that formed and deformed it, inasmuch as these texts are representative instances of it.

Modernism, as the dominant literary movement in Western Europe and America from, roughly, 1900 to 1940, has come under sharp attack in recent years from feminist critics who charge that the modernist canon was constructed as an exclusively male club centered primarily and even obsessively upon Eliot, Joyce, and Proust. Broadly speaking, feminist theorists have taken two, divergent approaches to literary modernism.

First, observing that the received narrative of the emergence and triumph of modernism relies upon the promotion of certain aesthetic values such as irony, self-reflexivity, formal experimentation, textual autonomy, and so forth,[1] some critics have concluded that these values are linked, either contingently or necessarily, to a set of politically conservative, masculine cultural values.[2] The omission of writings by women and ethnic minorities from the traditional modernist canon, the devaluation of genres, like melodrama, that are associated with women and popular culture, and the denigration of affects culturally defined as feminine, such as sentimentality, in modernist manifestos and critical discourses, have resulted in the now common judgment of "high" modernism as a reactionary cultural movement.[3] This assessment intersects (and diverges) at some points with Marxist accounts of modernity as dominated by commodity fetishism and an ideology of instrumental reason and autonomous subjectivity,[4] as well as with psychoanalytic accounts of the constitution of adult male subjectivity as purchased at the price of the repression of feminine affects and pre-oedipal desires. Clinching this critique of modernism are the facts that some leading modernist figures openly espoused fascist and racist political beliefs and that the consolidation of modernism as a cultural discourse, institutionalized in academia, took place under the auspices of New Criticism, led in the United States by members of the southern Agrarian school. As a consequence, many feminist scholars have directed their attention elsewhere, to women writers of the period, and have successfully delineated a rich, alternative female canon.[5]

However, some feminist critics have taken an opposed tack on modernism, stressing the ways in which the fragmentation of language in modern writing introduces a dehiscence within language as well as subjectivity, a difference culturally designated as feminine. Drawing upon Derridean deconstruction and Lacanian psychoanalysis, for instance, Cixous's notion of *écriture féminine* aligns femininity with the textual gaps and flows characteristic of modernist writing. Her work, along with that of Julia Kristeva and Luce Irigaray, has contributed to an understanding of modernism as a crucial site for investigating the subversion of psycholinguistic discursive structures. While Eliot is typically cited as the bad example by the first group of critics, Joyce often appears as the exemplary "good" male writer in what Eugene Jolas called the modern "revolution of the word."[6]

My own view of modernism is indebted to both of these strands of feminist theory and to the works of scholarship they have produced, although my aim is different. By choosing Eliot, Joyce, and Proust as objects of study, I do not intend to reinstate them as the reigning triumvirate of modernism, nor do I consider them as inherently privileged figures representing their age. Rather, I have selected them in order to dismantle the putatively unified entity in which they have been accorded a privileged, paradigmatic place. Moreover, my examination of them focuses upon the errant elements in their writings and thus, in a sense, upon the ways in which they fail the modernist program. Yet aesthetic programs, in my judgment, are necessarily constituted by divergent elements and have differential, multivalent effects. It is therefore not a question of deciding whether Eliot, Joyce, and Proust are, in truth, conservative or subversive writers, or if modernism in general was reactionary or transgressive. A more useful approach to canonical modernist writers is, I believe, to attend carefully to the particular complexities of their texts in order to gain an understanding of the larger crisis of gender and sexual definition in the early twentieth century.

From another quarter, modernism has come under fire for its aesthetic ideology, that is, for idealizing works of art as incarnations of aesthetic value allegedly transcending – but in fact obfuscating – the material conditions of which they are the product.[7] Accused of promoting a bourgeois vision of the literary work as a sacred icon that rises above the messy chaos of the real world, modernism is thus guilty not only of political conservatism but of rank dishonesty. Indifferent or even hostile to contemporary social problems, modernist writers are reproached for indulging in reactionary nostalgia for a precapitalist past, concomitant with a longing for a totalitarian future order.[8] Extreme versions of this view hold that modernist, post-Kantian aesthetics ultimately leads to fascism, while, in more charitable versions, modernism signals a retreat into a sterile formalism whose works offer a spurious consolation for the disintegration of modern culture or, at best, a mirror of its dissolution, what Lukács called the "tattered surface" of capitalism.[9] Additionally, modernism is denounced as complicit with the aims and ideology of British imperialism or blamed for denigrating popular culture as feminine and, hence, serving the interests of cultural elites.[10]

Given the extent and volume of these attacks, my choice of Eliot, Joyce, and Proust as the subjects for an interpretation of modernism may seem perverse. While many of these accusations clearly merit thoughtful attention, the wholesale assault on modernism has had the effect of obscuring – indeed, of promoting a militant blindness to – the aberrant forces at work in modernist texts. Examining the fissures in its canonical monuments can do more to shake the belief in their authority, including their presumptively reactionary politics, than sweeping condemnations. The academic discourse that for much of this century constructed the image of the modernist canon is simply reproduced, in inverted form, in the many rejections of it. For instance, Terry Eagleton's attack on modernist aesthetic ideology, while offering him the opportunity to prosecute with evidently satisfying vigor his indictment of it, reiterates the conventional terms of post-Kantian aesthetics, reversing its valence but without troubling to inquire with precision into its specific relevance for modernist texts. Although many modernist writers played upon – and off – the idealization of the literary work as, in Yeats's words, an autotelic "artifice of eternity," and of the artist as a godlike "artificer of the world," in Stevens's phrase, modernist writings are thoroughly riven by political conflicts, taken in a broad sense.

The burden of this book is to address the gender and sexual contradictions that preclude modernist works from serving as mere mouthpieces for patriarchal authority or of what Monique Wittig calls the "heterosexual contract." The conferral of such an authoritative and authoritarian status has everything to do with competing interests and discursive strategies for the investment of literary and cultural value, legitimating and delegitimating, in a complex manner and for diverse reasons, the modernist canon.[11] Neither a radical nor a reactionary ideology issues naturally from any text – assuming that we understand the difference between progress and regress – which is not to assert that all texts, literary or otherwise, are undecidable but that such decisions are the products of necessarily interested interpretations, including not only the deliberate intentions of certain groups of readers for particular, assignable purposes but, more often, their unconscious and less easily determined ends, or simply the unintended consequences of reading. Similarly, Astradur Eysteinsonn argues that "'modernism' is not a concept that emanates directly from literary texts; it is a construct created by the critical inquiry into certain kinds of texts."[12] Although an analysis of the institutionalization of the modernist canon lies outside the purview of this study, its clear implication is that celebrations of and attacks on modernism are strikingly transferential activities which, by and large, ignore the sexual and gender dynamics of that transference. My approach is neither to affirm nor to discredit the modernist canon but to investigate the waywardness of gender identifications and sexual desires within the construction of works by prominent modernist male authors, particularly insofar as those errant identifications and desires inform and deform their declared aesthetic aims.

A typical strategy of revisionist critics of modernism is to introduce heretofore marginal works and so to reverse the relation between the canon and its periphery. The laudable and necessary attention paid to works by women, ethnic and sexual minorities, and colonial and post-colonial writers must, however, confront the knotty problem of the binary opposition between center and margin. As the canon wars of recent years attest, this theoretical dilemma is not resolved by simply reversing the hierarchal relation between the canon and its outcasts. For instance, the works of feminist critics, such as Sandra Gilbert and Susan Gubar's multivolumed *No Man's Land*, amply demonstrate the pivotal role that women played in Anglo-American modernism, yet they retain the structure and values of canonicity. By contrast, a critique targeted at the interior dehiscence of canonical modernist texts may explicate and dismantle the assumptions upon which canonical authority rests. Specifically, the difference between what these texts say they do and what they inadvertently express, between their coherent programs and their vagrant practices – in short, their errancy – not only exposes the buried pilings that found the canonical edifice but also offers a quite different view of modernism. Neither an imposing, hegemonic monument dominating the landscape of twentieth-century literature nor a caricaturized straw man or whipping boy, the texts of heretofore canonical male writers may be understood in terms of the fruitfulness of their failures.

The writings of canonical male modernists were generated and inflected by homoerotic energies that they largely denied and by feminine identifications whose proximity to male self-constitution evoked both fantasies of escape from the strictures of masculinity and fears of same-sex desire. The Grishkins, Albertines, Brett Ashleys, Clara Daweses, and Molly Blooms who populate the texts of male writers in this period testify to their profound ambivalence toward women's sexual and sociopolitical agency, an equivocal fascination with and revulsion from femininity. This ambivalence was lodged within the masculine psyche in the potential for male femininity, a possibility broached by sexology as a catastrophic potential in the form of sexual inversion. The convergence in the early twentieth century of women's socioeconomic independence, of feminist political agitation, and of the discourses of sexology, psychology, and anthropology, among others, meant that women could be neither simply rejected nor elevated as absolutely "other" to man but that femininity and masculinity became mutually implicated, even imbricated within each other. The much-noted and oft-decried virilization of women at the time had as its more disquieting corollary the effeminization of men which, after the trial of Oscar Wilde, implied the homosexualization of same-sex male affection and bonds.

This project of dismantling the supposedly seamless unity of modernism has been undertaken by Michael Levenson, who aims at "undermining . . . the homogeneity of modernist doctrine" by pointing out its "conflicting currents," especially the divergence between two strands of early modernist thought. Before the First World War, "English modernism [was] divided between Fordian and Hulmean principles," the former advancing an "egoist" agenda, its claims to realism grounded in the truth of subjective impressions, while the latter promoted a classical, antihumanist aesthetic based upon objective, formalist abstractions.[13] Although there was considerable confusion and overlap between these distinct impulses, Levenson's scrupulous scholarship corrects the mistaken belief in the homogeneity of modernism and alludes to, without rendering explicit, the gender dynamics at work in this dichotomy. The convergence of these two currents, after 1914, in Pound's imagist program ensured that the mainstream of Anglo-American modernism would favor a formally precise, sculpted art along the lines of Lewis's vorticism and Marinetti's futurism, opposed to what the latter denounced as the "effeminacy" and "sentimentality" of contemporary English art.[14] The ambiguity of futurism's relation to modernity is paralleled by Pound's paradoxical insistence upon an elite artistic vanguard while exploiting advertising techniques and the low-brow lingo of mass culture to propagandize for it.[15] Moreover, the ambiguity in modernism between an impressionist aesthetics, evident in Proust, Woolf, and much contemporary philosophy, and the objective, abstract aesthetics advanced by Pound, Lewis, and others reflects a persistent tension between literary values gendered as feminine and masculine.

This gendering of literary styles served certain polemical purposes at the time and overlapped numerous other oppositions, including Jew/gentile and homo-/heterosexuality, sometimes in conflicting ways. The eponymous hero of Lewis's *Tarr* draws an evolutionary line between "lower" and "higher" forms of life; "everything beneath that line was female," consisting of a "jellyfish diffuseness" spreading and oozing everywhere.[16] Bonnie Kime Scott points out that both Tarr and Stephen Dedalus in Joyce's *Portrait of the Artist as a Young Man* "place the female at the bottom of their conceptual hierarchies, with mud, vegetative material, and animals."[17] Although in this imaginary scheme women are mired in a primordial muck, they also represented, for Lewis, Eliot, Pound, Lawrence, and many other modernists, an effete, overly refined literary culture that, according to Lewis, reduces art to a "pleasant tea-party."[18] If women are at once too primitive and too cultured, his vigorous efforts to de-aestheticize art, Lewis's "blasting and bombardiering" assault on the prevailing bourgeois aesthetic ideology, took the form of asserting the virility of art. Far from embracing an idealized vision of art as an escape from distressing social realities, such attacks were made in the name of brutal honesty and were therefore endorsed by some feminists who likewise advocated a tough and austere art. Rebecca West, for instance, decried the fact that poetry had become "the occupation of learned persons given to soft living." No longer "the beautiful stark bride of Blake, it has become the idle hussy hung with ornament kept by Lord Tennyson . . . and is now supported at Devonshire Street by the Georgian school."[19]

Modernist writers, male and female alike, framed aesthetic concerns in terms of sexual difference that inscribe its historical contradictions, often in ways that bizarrely echo current debates in feminist theory. Pound's belief, expressed in canto 29, that "the female / Is an element, the female / Is a chaos / An octopus / A biological process," resonates peculiarly with Kristeva's notion of the feminine chora and Irigaray's claims concerning female fluidity.[20] To be sure, Pound was, in his own words, "yet to be convinced that any women ever invented anything in the arts,"[21] envisioning the brain as a "great clot" of sperm and, hence, as a "presenter of images." While woman is allotted an "accumulation of hereditary aptitudes," man is given "the 'invention,' the new gestures, . . . because in him occurs the new up-jut, the new bathing of the cerebral tissues in the residuum, in *la mousse* of the life sap." Man is "the phallus or spermatozoid charging, head-on, the female chaos," just as Pound "felt it, driving any new idea into the great passive vulva of London."[22] Despite his unabashed, archaic phallocentrism, Pound sought to incorporate that feminine chaos within himself. In a letter to Marianne Moore (1 February 1919), Pound wrote that "The female is a chaos, / the male / is a fixed point of stupidity"; he changes places with Moore, who is a "stabilized female," while "I am a male who has attained the chaotic fluidities."[23] Pound's representation of himself as androgynous is quite in keeping with the notion of the male artist as grafting femininity onto a masculine nature; indeed, the idea has a long history and a certain prestige upon which, for instance, Joyce plays.[24]

The lure of crossing the boundary of gender and participating in women's "jellyfish diffuseness" immediately raises the dangerous possibility, for modern men, of homosexuality. Pound's contempt for "Bloomsbuggers" is matched by the fear of the charge of effeminacy of which E. M. Forster, himself a queer Bloomsbury fellow, was so chary. Forster, whose erotic ideal was "a strong, young man of the lower classes," is careful to make the hero of his self-suppressed *Maurice* a man's man, a middle-class stockbroker who is normal in every way but one, although Clive, the effete intellectual who disavows homosexual love, is the author surrogate in the novel.[25] Forster's queasiness concerning male femininity, his eroticization of working-class masculinity, and, even more, the cross-gender identifications of men like Joyce, Pound, and Lawrence suggest that certain fantasies are, in Christopher Lane's phrase, "unamenable" to the purposes of Britain's empire or to the aims of modernist aesthetics as they are typically conceived. Lane suggests that "we uncouple sexuality from hydraulic definitions of desire, in which sexual repression appears amenable to political service," in order to focus on "the failures of self-mastery, [and] the insufficiency and over-abundance of drives to colonial sublimation."[26] Rather than under-standing sexual desire as a smoothly oiled component of bourgeois aesthetic ideology, its psychical as well as historical inutility disrupts both political and aesthetic programs, leading us to consider them as hetero-geneous fields in which multiple and conflicting forces are at work. The failure of "classical" modernist works to embody the genderized aes-thetic norms that they are supposed to promote or to sublimate desires into functionalist, normative heterosexuality calls for a radically different reading of modernism as a whole in terms of its errant inscriptions.

In this book, I argue that the writings of Eliot, Joyce, and Proust are compelled and shaped by the contemporary turmoil in male gender and sexual identity and by disputes over masculine authority. Although their works manifest diverse responses to this dilemma – ranging from Eliot's reassertion of traditional authority to Joyce's flirtation with femininity to Proust's interrogation of the epistemology of sexuality – all of these writers confronted the modern challenge to normative understandings of manhood and paternal authority. Typically, this issue took the form of a preoccupation with femininity. They share the modern problem of a loss of confidence in the status and meaning of masculinity, and con-sequently of what one might call male hysteria; they share a fear and resentment of female power, often representing that power as deadly or hysterical; and, finally, they share a peculiarly modern version of homo-phobia that is linked to a dread of feminization. In their works, women appear as the other of masculine values and hence as simultaneously threatening and attractive.

Rather than collapsing Eliot, Joyce, and Proust into a generalized metanarrative of modern male gender anxiety, though, I wish to stress the specificity of their works by attending to their individual nuances and local contexts. The stories they tell are different in many ways, owing in no small part to the fact that one was an Anglo-identified American, another was an expatriate Irishman, and the third, a Jewish Frenchman. While all three writers were profoundly affected by shifting constructions of gender and sexuality, their responses are significantly related to national and racial concerns. For instance, Eliot disavows his gender and sexual anxieties, like his Americanness, subsuming them within a European, patriarchal and anti-Semitic literary tradition; abjuring fem-inine and queer alterity, he positions himself as the adoptive heir of his self-appointed fathers. By contrast, Joyce subsumes these anxieties, like his Irishness, within a putatively transnational and transgendered perspective; his Jewish, "womanly man," Leopold Bloom, ambivalently incorporates feminine and homosexual alterity. Proust plays a double game, the hero of his *Remembrance of Things Past* poised both inside and outside the secret universe of Jews and queers, resolutely and snobbishly French yet sharing the hidden, shameful otherness of those whom he disdains.

The response to the "woman question" by male modernists in general took two, complementary forms. In the first instance, they were alarmed by the increasing popularity and economic power exercised by women in the literary marketplace at the turn of the century as well as by the disturbing assertion of overt female sexual desire. Eliot's public and private writings attest to the challenge posed by female agency to male literary, cultural, and sexual authority. In the second instance, femininity appeared as a means of evading the constraints of those authorities. By identifying with and trying to gain access to the secrets of women, modernist writers like Joyce attempted to harness the errant impulses that others, such as Eliot, sought to contain. Yet in both cases, whether as salvational or as damning, women functioned as the other to a masculine norm. Indeed, these two views sometimes converged, as in Nietzsche's ironic and reversible claim that "truth is a woman" in its deceptive and feminine (dis)simulation of itself.[27] In a similar fashion, the hero of Proust's *Remembrance of Things Past* engages in an endless search to learn the duplicitous truth of Albertine's sexual desires. Consequently, femininity is commonly represented in male modernist texts as a site of errancy, at once externalized as an alternatively dangerous or utopian alterity and internalized as the exciting possibility of freedom from restrictive masculine norms. Such a freedom, however, also implied the potential of a feminizing sexual inversion, the famous formula for which was *anima muliebris virili corpore inclusa* – a female soul lodged in a male body. Becoming woman for modern male figures, like Eliot's Tiresias or Joyce's Bloom, promised a way out of the rigid confines of gender yet broached the discovery of a latent femininity – even homosexuality – within one's self. The potential of a feminine interiority thus assumed a particular urgency for men at the time with the articulation of the concept of homosexuality by sexologists and the emergence of homosexuality as a social role, epitomized by Wilde.

The modern characterization of same-sex desire as a sickness had particularly troubling effects for male sexual self-understanding. The uncertainty of the boundaries between heterosexuality and homosexuality and the anxiety with which the latter was and remains shrouded means that homosexual desire occupies an occluded place at the heart of male subjectivity. The possibility that same-sex relations could be contaminated by a hidden pathology has significant implications for Eliot's account of male literary relations, including the intergenerational transmission of literary authority and, with it, the conception of the literary tradition as a homosocial, patriarchal affair between "fathers" and "sons," as well as intragenerational relations among male writers. While Joyce is somewhat ambivalent, Proust plumbs in exacting detail the depths of the epistemological confusion generated by the emergence of homosexuality. Modernist literature is profoundly affected by what Proust calls "the sudden inadequacy of a definition," including the definitions of male and female and of heterosexual and homosexual, as well as the edifice of literary authority that has been built upon the presumed solidity of such formulations.

The challenges to the distinction between masculinity and femininity in the early twentieth century are bound up with the problem of distinguishing between same- and cross-gendered desire and same- and cross-gendered identification. Joyce's work, like that of Eliot and Proust, bears witness to the blurring, in the twentieth century, of the distinction between desire and identity. So-called normal masculine subjectivity requires, on the one hand, erotic desire for but a clear-cut disidentification with women and, on the other hand, a nonerotic, identificatory alliance with other men. Modernism is the moment in our culture when this configuration of male subjectivity became both necessary yet impossible. Since then, masculine identity has been potentially implicated in pathologized erotic desire (of a man for another man) while, in turn, cross-gender desire (of a man for a woman) has possibly feminizing effects. The split between heterosexuality and homosexuality is thus both a symptom of and a defense against the erosion of the difference between desire for and alliance with one's own and with the other sex. As Eve Kosofsky Sedgwick has shown, the fear of homosexuality, or "homosexual panic," so pervasive in our culture enforces that distinction along with normative gender and sexual roles.[28]

These vexed, intertwined issues of erotic desire and gender definition typically condense around the figure of the mother in male modernist texts. One of their distinguishing yet disturbing features is the representation of maternal identification and matricidal fury as collaborative impulses. The profusion of murdered and murderous mothers and the coherence of these images point to a common, intertextual imagination among their works, which draw upon matriarchal myths prevalent in modern anthropology, psychology, and Western cultural discourses at large.[29] A brief examination of the fantasy of *mors matris* in the texts of Joyce, Eliot, and Proust shows its psychosexual and cultural operations.

In *Molloy*, Samuel Beckett's eponymous hero remarks, "I am in my mother's room. It's I who live there now . . . I sleep in her bed . . . I have taken her place. I must resemble her more and more." Later, he admits, "I had been bent on settling this matter between mother and me, but had not succeeded."[30] Molloy's monologue could serve as an epigraph for the works of many male writers of the period who, confronting the specter of the dead, but undead, mother, tried to "settle this matter" by taking her place. To take someone else's place is also to take it over. The occupation of maternal space may be understood as an act of appropriation, or a double gesture of incorporation and abjection. Having moved into the mother's room and coming to resemble her, the modernist writer qua Molloy seems to be on his way to becoming mother. This move has sometimes been read as manifesting a desire for a pre-oedipal union or a longing for the lost paradise of primary narcissism, a move celebrated by Kristeva in her claim that Joyce reinstates "maternal territory in language"; however, this fantasy of merging also unleashes and licenses powerful aggression.[31] Molloy's dream of "settling matters" with mother thinly veils a death wish – settling matters once and for all – while the death of the mother also implies death by mother, that is, her fatal agency, often figured as poisonous maternal nurturance.

Mother love is famously idealized by Stephen Dedalus in *Ulysses*: "*Amor matris*, subjective and objective genitive, may be the only true thing in life" (*U* 9:843, 2:165–66). Although he has buried his mother, May Dedalus refuses to stay in the ground and returns to haunt him because he has, fantasmically speaking, killed her through his apostasy. Bloodied by guilt, Stephen cannot rid himself of the pale corpse despite his denials of culpability. Moreover, evocations of maternal affection quickly reverse into vengeful resentment. Stephen's reference to *amor matris* is immediately followed by the memory of his mother's impoverished nourishment: "With her weak blood and wheysour milk she fed him" – or, rather, starved him. When she subsequently appears as a ghost and tells him to get his sister to cook him the boiled rice that she used to feed him, it is clear that she is a vampire who has sucked out his life. Stephen's savior (she offers him her prayers) is his destroyer, and her womb is his tomb; thus, her death implies his own. "Nother dying come home father," the tellingly erroneous telegram to Paris reads (*U* 3:199). May Dedalus's lethal nourishment resembles, in an ascetic fashion, the feeding practices of the mother of Proust's hero in the *Remembrance*. Although Mrs. Dedalus is more inclined to stuff Stephen with prayers than with madeleines, she, like the narrator's mother, gives him too much yet too little food. Finally, the maternal image in *Ulysses* assumes greater complexity in the figure of Molly Bloom as well as in Joyce's other works, yet Stephen's flight from the mother, notably in his dream of the artist usurping her procreative power through his literary creations, starkly delineates the longing and aversion for an imaginary maternal origin common to male modernist writers, an ambivalence that is imbricated with homophobia.[32]

The displacement of matricidal fantasies onto a murderous mother is the compulsively enacted scenario of Eliot's early poetry. A cursory review of his poems from "Prufrock" through *The Waste Land* produces an inventory of fatal Cleopatras, poisonous Belladonnas, sadistic salon matrons, and rapacious whores. Correspondingly, these texts are littered with the corpses of young men, many of whom have drowned in a lethal, uterine element. Like Joyce's Stephen and Proust's narrator, becoming an author for Eliot entailed an ambivalent struggle against and identification with maternal authority. Charlotte Sterns Eliot urged her son to become the famous poet she had aspired to be. Taking her place, Tom nonetheless kept trying to kill off incarnations of her in his poetry and *The Family Reunion*. If, as I argue, abjecting the mother is the aim of Eliot's early poetry, the impossibility of doing so and, hence, of becoming a fully masculinized subject is that writing's condition of possibility. Despite his resistance to his mother's power, represented in sometimes violent poetic fantasies, Eliot's very success as a poet returned him to his mother's room. In a gesture that is the symmetrical opposite of Joyce's attempt to write in a fluid, feminine voice in the "Penelope" episode of *Ulysses*, Eliot referred in a denigrating fashion to his own poetry as the effluvia of childbirth. By contrast, in his official writings, Eliot imagined becoming a writer as becoming the son of self-designated fathers, and his essays on literary history are proclamations of filiation with patriarchal authorities. Yet even in these gestures he resembled his mother, who, like her son, was fond of paternal genealogies. Mrs. Eliot's history of her husband's family and her letters to Bertrand Russell, proudly informing him of Tom's descent from an ancient English family, are domestic versions of her son's literary essays, similarly announcing and instituting a patrilineage. Eliot's writings reiterate his mother's erasure of her matrilineage – like her, he dreams that he had no mother – yet they covertly reinforce her power.

Proust's *Remembrance* is openly obsessed with maternal authority. Among the many ways in which the cult of the mother is enacted in the novel are countless dinner parties and eating rituals in which food is a weapon of power. The most prominent example of the latter are the two madeleine scenes, one involving the real mother and the other, Aunt Léonie. As Serge Doubrovsky points out, the madeleine serves a double function in the hero's struggle with the mother.[33] In the first scene, his mother feeds him the cake and thus exerts her control, while the second eating of the madeleine produces his epiphanic, involuntary memory of Combray and prompts the writing of the book. In short, the madeleine signifies both the hero's unwilling submission to maternal power and his triumph over it by giving birth to his own book and thus becoming his own mother. Having been read to by his mother, he now writes his own book in which he purports to write himself. Superseding his mother, he effectively eliminates her by becoming her; in other words, by eating the cake he likewise consumes – kills and incorporates – her and so produces a book that testifies to his ambivalent love and hatred.[34]

The matricidal fantasies that form the obverse of maternal identification in these works and others by modern male writers, such as D. H. Lawrence, for instance, call for a revision of psychoanalytic accounts – themselves issuing from the modernist milieu – that consign the mother to a presymbolic realm. Becoming mother in these texts, far from manifesting an urge to unite with a pre-oedipal breast, is more usefully examined in terms of historically specific divisions within the cultural constitution of male subjectivity. The matricidal representations in modernist texts are fully implicated with the twentieth-century crisis in sexual and gender definition in which becoming mother was linked to the potential for same-sex desire. The homophobic construction of homosexuality in Western culture around the turn of the century rendered identificatory love for the mother an irresolvable dilemma for men. Just as Molloy tries to reach his mother by crawling back to her backwards, queerly inverting himself, so modernist male writers understood their ambivalence toward femininity in terms of fantasies of gender and sexual inversion associated with homosexuality. To sleep in her bed, like Molloy, might mean sleeping with father. Yet the denaturalization of gender in the modern era, in which femininity and masculinity became detached from male and female sexed bodies, was also a tantalizing prospect. In Joyce, it takes the form of Bloom's androgyny; in Proust, hermaphrodism, represented by the "men-women" of Sodom and Gomorrah; and, in Eliot, the bisexual Tiresias. Following their lead, some critics, such as Gilles Deleuze, have claimed that the fragmentation of the modern male sexual subject allows for the incorporation of feminine alterity.[35] However, the *mors matris* fantasy suggests that such appropriative wishes are equally defensive gestures that attest to the violent consequences of the modern disavowal of same-sex desire.

Contemporary critics of modern culture typically regarded homosexuality as a symptom of decadence, signifying the feminization of men and the virilization of women. In the logic of sexologists, notably Havelock Ellis and Richard von Krafft-Ebing, same-sex desire was a manifestation of sexual inversion resulting from and producing a concomitant inversion of gender role, so that to be a homosexual was to forfeit one's proper identity as a man or woman.[36] Radclyffe Hall's widely read *Well of Loneliness* also promulgated the notion that same-sex desire issues from an inherently reversed gender; her heroine is a man trapped in the body of a woman. Moreover, the discourse of sexual inversion was indebted to an older, classical understanding of sodomy that differentiated subjects according to penetrator and penetrated, or active and passive sexual positions. To complicate matters, the representation of female same-sex desire has had a largely independent history and divergent form. On the one hand, the modern image of the lesbian as sadistic and seductively wicked was influenced by Baudelaire's *femmes damnées* and informs Proust's novel and Eliot's early poetry. On the other hand, the feminine, schoolgirl sapphism of late Victorian British and American literature, in which female friendship and desire are blurred, continued to influence modernist writers, especially Woolf. These various modernist versions of homosexuality remain significant for queer theory in our day. Indeed, the fact that the modern crisis of sexual definition was (and is) interpreted as a sign of social decay by conservative commentators such as Otto Weininger and Max Nordau, who linked homosexuality to the perverse influence of Jews and feminists, has given queer theory much of its revolutionary appeal. Jeffrey Weeks thus argues that the feminization and pathologization of male same-sex desire reflect a disturbing and on-going upheaval in socioeconomic relations between the sexes.[37] In a world turned upside down by male effeminacy and female virility, sexual inversion became, and remains, a powerfully charged symbol of social disorder.

The unifying thread of this book is error, conceived as a multifaceted figure that connects moral, perceptual, cognitive, scribal, and hermeneutic lapses. To fumble, sin or forget, to fall into illusions or false beliefs, or to commit misprints or lies – these forms of erring resonate with the archaic sense of errancy as a wandering from the true path. By linking them, I aim to show the bivalence of error as a transgressive mistake and a mistaken transgression in the works of modernist writers for whom transgression was intimately bound up with the violation of gender and sexual norms. Moreover, such errant desires are complexly related to error on other levels of literary discourse, ranging from flaws in the composition of a text and the mistakes that arise in its production and transmission to the seemingly infinite number of ways in which readers go wrong. My initial focus is on the various conceptions of error advanced by Eliot in his critical prose. As the great prescriber – and pro-scriber – of modernism, setting its canon and issuing magisterial injunc-tions as to its proper interpretation, his critical writings are an appropriate place to begin an inquiry into the errors against which he wished to guard. In the account outlined here, Eliot is the straight man of modernism, Joyce is its "ladies' man," and Proust is its queer fellow.

Error possesses a seemingly endless allure. The prospect of straying from the bounds of authority appears to offer freedom, even if such errancy returns one, at last, to the fold. This impulse was fundamental to the way modernist writers saw themselves and their literary project of "making it new." As a departure from inherited literary norms, modern-ism was bound up with the idea of subversive innovation, responding not only to the explosion of technologies and commodities but to radi-cally novel gender and sexual arrangements. The modernist impulse toward the transgression of literary norms was engaged in various and conflicting ways with these changes in gender and sexual definition. The object of this study is to specify the manner in which three of the most prominent figures of the modernist movement came to terms with the provocations of error.

# CHAPTER I

# Straightening out literary criticism: T. S. Eliot and error

Most of us are somewhat impure and apt to confuse issues; hence the justification of writing books about books, in the hope of straightening things out.

T. S. Eliot, *Selected Essays*

Every emission of speech is always . . . under an inner compulsion to err.

Jacques Lacan, *Seminar*

T. S. Eliot's critical writings are a consistent, sustained attempt to identify and weed out error from the practice of literary criticism and to establish normative criteria for English poetry and poetic drama. In his words, Eliot was always trying to "straighten things out," yet his own works are energized by errant tendencies that are bound up in various ways with the norms which they violate. Although Eliot rarely hints at sexual perversion, the types of error that he censures are closely implicated with errant sexuality and, more broadly, with transgressions of social order. In many instances, Eliot wanted his readers to infer the larger moral, political, social, and even sexual significance of his literary criticism. Indeed, gender and sexual errancy are crucial to his judgments of error, even those that seem purely aesthetic.

Eliot's often local assessments of the mistakes of poets and critics possess a general, theoretical coherence. In order to demonstrate their systematic character as well as their larger ramifications, I have grouped Eliot's judgments of literary error in his critical prose into four categories which I term *perversion, inversion, impure mingling,* and *dissemination.* By proposing these general headings, I aim both to follow Eliot's intentions and to tease out the unintended implications of his own arguments. The kinds of error that typically concern Eliot are (1) perverse egotism or "emotionalism," as opposed to the properly "impersonal" character of poetry; (2) inversions of a literary or natural order, including linguistic, poetic, social, and sexual hierarchies; (3) the impure mingling of categories, especially epistemological and aesthetic ones; and (4) the dispersion of what should be a unified whole, whether a text, an author's oeuvre, or a social body – even the dissipation of literary value in general. This chapter is organized around these four kinds of error, with individual sections devoted to each type.

The problem of error in Eliot's critical writings is engaged in a paradoxical economy. Like the Judeo-Christian theodicy that underlies it, this economy is driven by the demand to exclude impurities and, hence, is engaged in continually separating and expelling errors. Yet because error arises from within and masks itself as truth, it is an ever-present, inherent possibility, making the task of correction an endless struggle toward a transcendent goal. Eliot's persistent attempts to differentiate good from bad poetry and to determine the appropriate limits and functions of literary criticism thus rest upon his assumption of a prelapsarian poetic ideal as well as upon his belief in a standard of taste.

The economy of error in Eliot's criticism is marked by its recursivity. Inasmuch as the mistakes that he tries to root out of the works of others appear in his own, the truth of his corrective discourse is bound up with the desires and practices that he wishes to cast out. In short, Eliot's critical texts are grounded in a disavowal of the very forces that energize them. His literary judgments depend upon the exclusion of what he believed were violations of gender and sexual norms as well as guard against the impure motives of authors and readers and the relativization of literary value. These exclusions return within his own work as fructive tendencies; far from occasional blunders on his part or exceptions to the rule, Eliot's own errors are constructive and, indeed, constitutive of his critical enterprise. Specifically, Eliot's corrective project is driven by the denial of a host of related psychosexual forces whose power derives from their negation. Rather than simply claiming that Eliot's work is motivated by repressed sexual desires, though, I argue that those desires are constituted as such, in their dangerous potency, through repeated disavowals such as those we see in Eliot's texts.

Eliot's continual attempts to purify poetry and criticism hinge upon the symbolic distinction between inside and outside, between interior integrity and exterior errancy. However, because error necessarily maintains a negative relation to that from which it has been abjected, the former inevitably reappears within the body of Eliot's text. According to Jacques Derrida, "the possibility of the negative . . . is in fact a structural possibility" of every argument so that "failure is an essential risk," yet philosophers typically try to "exclude that risk as accidental [and] exterior . . . [to] the phenomenon being considered." "On the contrary," Derrida asks, "is this risk rather its internal and positive condition of possibility? Is that outside its inside, the very force and law of its emergence?"[1] Similarly, Eliot's attempt to exclude error from literary discourse confirms and draws strength from the errant impulses that he denounces.

Eliot's remedial project is also an effort to assert his critical authority by means of a self-validating, self-citational rhetoric whose success depends upon that indispensable error, tautology. His aim in demarcating error is to establish literary authority, especially the canon of the English literary tradition as he saw it, and to define the norms of literary criticism. Both of these goals implicitly call for a justification of his own authority. When Eliot comes face-to-face with the problem of the validity of his judgment, he resorts to Humean and Kantian claims for taste, buttressed by the supposed necessity of aesthetic value as a regulative ideal. Despite – or perhaps because of – the circular nature of such arguments, Eliot's rhetoric was remarkably successful. By implying what is defined (the normative value of poetry as he saw it) within the terms of the definition, Eliot performatively authorizes the very norms that he seeks to establish. Likewise, Eliot produces the effect of his own authority by means of this reiterative practice, citing as the basis of his authority the literary norms and canonical texts that his critical practice also defines and regulates.[2] Far from being an anomalous "error," Eliot's tautological claims for literary value and the validity of his literary judgments conform precisely to what Judith Butler, expanding on Derrida's concept of citationality, describes as the inevitable constitution of juridical authority through repeated attributions of power or enactments of it. The law of literature is, in Butler's phrasing, "fortified and idealized as the law only to the extent that it is reiterated as the law, produced as the law . . . by the very citations it is said to command."[3] Eliot's use of poetic allusions, which I will examine in chapter 2, is thus closely allied to the logic and rhetoric of his critical prose, both of which rely for their performative effects upon specific exclusions.

Eliot's tireless determination to separate truth from error, to set the boundaries of criticism, to distinguish, in his words, "genuine" from "sham" poetry, and to rank poets in their proper order founders on the bivalence of every discourse on truth. The opposition between truth and error, like other binarisms such as good/evil and pure/impure, depends upon the absolute exclusion of the inferior term, yet the excluded term must also be presupposed as a deficiency – as a pathological, depraved, or aberrant version of the true, the good, or the pure. In other words, the operation of the true/false binary requires, on the one hand, the abjection of the false from the realm of the true (e.g., "genuine poetry") and, on the other hand, the continued existence of the false as a flaw within that realm. The asymmetrical, hierarchical opposition between truth and error in Eliot's conceptual framework demands the ongoing purgation of errors that arise within literary discourse – an infinite inquisition. The boundary demarcating the interior of truth from its contaminating exterior must be constantly redrawn because error springs from within, as an internal alien, a fifth column, or, as in William Cowper's "The Progress of Error," an "insinuating worm" who "successfully conceals her loathsome form."[4] Error seems perversely fecund, constantly breeding new errors as though it were a female monster. Indeed, error has often been imagined as such in English poetry. Like Cowper's "serpent error," Spenser's "Foul Error" in *The Faerie Queene* is an "ugly monster,"

> Half like a serpent horribly display'd,
> But th'other half did woman's shape retain,
> Most loathsome, filthy, foul, and full of vile disdain.
> . . . of her there bred
> A thousand young ones, which she daily fed,
> Sucking upon her pois'nous dugs.     (1.lines 14–15)[5]

Insofar as any error is a crippling deviation from a proper norm, it is also an enabling waywardness, opening the possibility of multiple, alternative versions, or of what Michel Foucault calls "reverse discourses."[6] This polyvalence of error is inscribed in its tangled etymological roots. The word *error* entered English from the Old French *errer*, which meant both "to rove or wander, especially in search of adventure," and "to stray from what is right." Margaret Soltan points out that "the cultural values attached to the general metaphor of errancy have always been dramatically gender-linked," so that "the errant man errs in search of truth and goodness, while the errant woman errs into evil."[7] The former sense is retained in the modern English term *errantcy* which, according to *Webster's Third International Dictionary*, means "wandering, especially in quest of knightly adventure," and is differentiated from *errancy*, as "a state, practice, or instance of erring." However, the ambiguity is preserved in *errant*, which signifies both "traveling" and "straying outside the proper bounds" or "deviating from a standard, erring."[8]

This etymological confusion reflects the longstanding suspicion that straying from the path of truth might possibly lead to better knowledge, a suspicion that Eliot would have classified as a romantic mistake but which constitutes a persistent dilemma in Christian theology – specifically, the problem of the nature and origin of evil. Jonathan Dollimore has offered a cogent analysis of Augustinian theodicy, focusing on the twin paradoxes that sin originates within the divine order that it subverts and that man is created desiring that which is sinful.[9] Dollimore traces these paradoxes through John Milton, for whom good and evil, in Milton's words, "grow up together almost inseparable; and the knowledge of good is so involv'd and interwoven with the knowledge of evil and in so many cunning resemblances hardly to be discern'd"; indeed, "we know good only by means of evil."[10]

Eliot's attempts to distinguish truth from error are involved in a similar dilemma. Dollimore's term for this quandary is the "paradoxical perverse," which he argues is a phenomenon not restricted to theology but which pervades Western thought and culture, especially concerning sexuality. The "paradoxical perverse" embraces two paradoxes: first, that perversion is "rooted in the true . . . while being . . . the utter contradiction of the true," and, second, that perversion is "often perceived as at once utterly alien to what it threatens, and yet, mysteriously inherent within it" (121). These paradoxes produce what Dollimore calls a "perverse dynamic" with the potential "to destabilize [or] to provoke discoherence" within a social or epistemological field (121). The problem of error in Eliot's critical prose manifests contradictions whose (il)logic is similar to the paradoxes outlined by Dollimore. For instance, in "What Is a Classic?" Eliot claims that the heterogeneity of the English language is an essential flaw, preventing it from ever producing a classic work of literature, yet that defect is also the source of its fruitful production of nonclassic texts.

In this chapter I will examine the full range of Eliot's literary criticism, including his early, uncollected journalism and the recently published Clark and Turnbull Lectures. While respecting the particular contexts of Eliot's essays, this study is organized around the concepts of error employed therein and, hence, does not offer a chronological or developmental narrative. Despite the occasional nature of much of his critical production, Eliot's assessments of literary error possess a systematic coherence.[11] Although there are all sorts of ways in which a poet or critic may go wrong, those ways fit into certain logical and rhetorical patterns. To put it in another fashion, Eliot's various judgments of error share

important "family resemblances." The four "families" or general categories I have identified – perversion, inversion, impurity, and dissemination – are a heuristic construction designed to show that the problem of
error in Eliot's critical oeuvre forms a web of intersecting and sometimes
contradictory but nonetheless interconnected sets of issues. These categories, each of which I will treat in turn, are themselves clusters of
related, overlapping ideas whose boundaries are permeable.

The typology of error I am proposing selects and foregrounds certain
patterns among Eliot's recurrent aesthetic, religious, social, political, and
sexual concerns. Specifically, I argue that Eliot's literary norms are fully
implicated with sexual norms and, thus, that textual and sexual erring
in his critical discourse are mutually constitutive. Perversion, inversion,
impurity, and dissemination are significant nodes in the network of error
that traverses Eliot's critical texts, condensing potent yet disavowed,
errant energies. Finally, an analysis of these ways of going astray enables
us to situate the conceptual structure of Eliot's writings within the larger,
historical context of twentieth-century political and cultural discourses,
and is especially relevant for current debates concerning Eliot's conservatism and anti-Semitism.

PERVERSION

Eliot's early essays are preoccupied with what I am calling perversion,
following the traditional definition of the term as "a turning aside from
truth or right, a diversion to an improper use" (*OED*). Poets and critics
whose attention is drawn away from the poetry itself to the personality
or the emotions of the poet have, in his view, perverted poetry's true
purpose. Egotistical indulgence in "self-expression" or "emotionalism"
on the part of poets is "impure," in Eliot's words, as are the practices of
critics such as A. G. Swinburne, Arthur Symons, and Walter Pater, who
read poetry in order to savor their own feelings and "impressions" (*SW*
3, 13).

Eliot sometimes uses the term "perversion," as in "Tradition and the
Individual Talent" where he describes the "perverse" effects of the
pursuit of novelty in poetry. Here, I employ it to designate a type of
error, repeatedly criticized by Eliot, characterized by a straying from the
object of poetry to the subjective interests of readers and writers.
Among the cognate terms for perversion are thus deviation, diversion,
digression, and wandering. Perversion also typically implies an inversion
of natural or instituted hierarchies, yet it has a specific significance in

Eliot's criticism as a deflection from the proper aims of poetry in favor of the poet's or critic's personal desires. The effects of such perversion include effeminate decadence, moral vice, egotistical pride, and ethical relativism.

The diversion of poets and critics from their rightful goal, turning instead toward nonpoetic topics or dwelling excessively upon their feelings rather than "working them up into poetry," bears a striking resemblance to Freud's concept of perversion. In *Three Essays on the Theory of Sexuality*, Freud claims that "perversions are sexual activities which either (a) extend, in an anatomical sense, beyond the regions of the body that are designed for sexual union, or (b) linger over the immediate relations to the sexual object which should normally be traversed rapidly on the path towards the final sexual aim."[12] In the first instance, this extension or transgression involves the choice of an "inappropriate" sexual object, such as the foot or someone of the same sex. The poets and critics whom Eliot censures may be said to have chosen the wrong object, such as the personality of the poet, or to "linger over . . . immediate" pleasures at the expense of the development of their taste. He argues, in the "Note on the Development of 'Taste' in Poetry," that while, as youthful readers, we may feel a passionate attachment toward certain poetry, "absorbed" as we are in our own "delightful feelings," the "mature stage of enjoyment of poetry comes when we cease to identify ourselves with the poet we happen to be reading" and are able "to distinguish between the genuine and the sham" in poetry (*UPUC* 26). Freud's ideal of mature, reproductive sexuality and Eliot's ideal of mature, objective taste share a teleological structure in which error is figured as dalliance or waywardness.

The locus classicus of Eliot's condemnation of this error is "Tradition and the Individual Talent," where he formulates his famous "impersonality theory of poetry." Eliot's claim that "the progress of an artist is a continual self-sacrifice, a continual extinction of personality" (*SE* 17), has been subjected to countless critiques, many of which reflexively apply Eliot's criteria for "genuine poetry" and "honest criticism" back upon himself, discovering that Eliot commits the very mistakes that he decries. Thus, for instance, Maud Ellmann argues that "in the second half [of the essay] he rehabilitates the personality that he had humbled in the first."[13] Moreover, later in life, Eliot occasionally admitted the autobiographical impulse in his poetry, notably and perhaps disingenuously in the remark attributed to him that *The Waste Land* "was only the relief of a personal and wholly insignificant grouse against life" (*F* 1).

The impersonality thesis seems designed to fail, and the artist's or critic's mask of self-abnegation seems to invite exposure of the seething and possibly seedy demands of the personality beneath. The success of Eliot's theory may reside not in the efficacy of its prohibition but in the sense of a temptation barely escaped and of overwhelming desires scarcely contained. Just as Eliot's poet-critic acquires authority through ostensible self-effacement, so, too, he dallies with egotistical lusts through renouncing them. In short, the disavowal of the expression of one's feelings may be another way of indulging them, through the act of renunciation. If the denial of a pleasure is, in effect, a negative affirmation, Eliot's essay perversely attests to the allure of precisely what it rejects.

Among the several moments in "Tradition and the Individual Talent" in which Eliot criticizes the improper treatment of emotions in poetry, the following passage is a representative instance as well as an especially telling example of Eliot's rhetoric.

One error, in fact, of eccentricity in poetry is to seek for new human emotions to express; and in this search for novelty in the wrong place it discovers the *perverse*. The business of the poet is not to find new emotions, but to use the ordinary ones and, in working them up into poetry, to express feelings which are not actual emotions at all. (*SE* 21; emphasis mine)

The terminological slippages in this quotation render the relation between "feeling" and "emotion," in Stephen Clark's words, "permanently insoluble."[14] Yet it is precisely such slippages that have made passages like this persuasive to many of Eliot's readers, along with his rhetorical habit of building an argument not by logical syllogism but by the repetition and accretive heightening of the same point until the aggregate force of his assertion makes it seem self-evident.[15] Thus, Eliot writes, "one error . . . of *eccentricity* . . . is to seek for *new* human emotions," the newness of these emotions restating and reinforcing their errant eccentricity. Eliot piles on the eccentricity by adding that such a poet searches "for *novelty in the wrong place*," although, in his pursuit of novelty, the eccentric poet is already wayward. It thus comes as no surprise that the eccentric poet "discovers the *perverse*," which is another term for the eccentric, for that which has turned away from the normal or "ordinary." Eliot's assertion here is, strictly speaking, tautological, yet his rhetorical error promotes the putative truthfulness of his claim by means of its performative reiteration.

Many of Eliot's essays subsequent to "Tradition and the Individual

Talent" continue his critique of perversion as a swerve from what he believed was the proper object of poetry – the poem as an aesthetic object – toward the expression of the poet's personality. Among the instances of such perversity in Eliot's critical prose is John Donne. Although Donne is usually remembered as the exemplar of what Eliot called the "unified sensibility" of the early seventeenth century, in whose poetry "there is a direct sensuous apprehension of thought, or a recreation of thought into feeling" (*SE* 286), in an essay published only five years after "The Metaphysical Poets," Eliot offers him as an example of "personality" gone awry. In "Lancelot Andrewes" (1926), Eliot compares Donne's sermons unfavorably to those of Andrewes, and he describes the pernicious effects of Donne's rhetoric upon his audience.

Donne is a "personality" in the sense in which Andrewes is not: his sermons, one feels, are a "means of self-expression." He is constantly finding an object which shall be adequate to his feelings; Andrewes is wholly absorbed in the object and therefore responds with the adequate emotion . . . Donne . . . belonged to the class of persons . . . who seek refuge in religion from the tumults of a strong emotional temperament which can find no complete satisfaction elsewhere. He is not wholly without kinship to Huysmans . . . He is dangerous only for those who find in his sermons an indulgence of their sensibility, or for those who, fascinated by "personality" in the romantic sense of the word – for those who find in "personality" an ultimate value – forget that in the spiritual hierarchy there are places higher than that of Donne. (*SE* 351–52)

The force of Eliot's condemnation of Donne is striking and explicitly links personal "self-expression" to moral vice, fin-de-siècle French decadence, and even sorcery.[16] "About Donne there hangs the shadow of the impure motive . . . He is a little of the religious spellbinder, the Reverend Billy Sunday of his time, the flesh-creeper, the sorcerer of emotional orgy" (*SE* 345).

Eliot's scathing criticism of Donne underscores what he saw as the danger of indulging in emotions at the expense of rational, objective religious belief, an indulgence that stems from ethical relativism and that leads to sexual depravity. In *After Strange Gods*, published in the following year, Eliot argues that, when each man is his own moral authority, "*personality* becomes a thing of alarming importance" (58). Thomas Hardy is an "example of a powerful personality uncurbed by any institutional attachment or by submission to any objective beliefs"; "unhampered" by moral "restraint," Hardy, like Donne, is not a "wholesome or edifying" influence (59). The perverse sexual implications of the writer's gratification of his "feelings" are further evident when Eliot turns to feminine – and effeminate – writing.

The historically overdetermined, even banal association of women with the expression of emotions is tacit in Eliot's essays, unlike those of his male contemporaries such as T. E. Hulme, Wyndham Lewis, and Ezra Pound. With the exception of his elegy on Marie Lloyd, the beloved music-hall entertainer, Eliot very rarely mentions women in his critical work, and women writers even less.[17] Perhaps the clearest sense of what Eliot considers "feminine" art is his remark in *After Strange Gods* on Katherine Mansfield's story "Bliss". Her story is

brief, poignant, and . . . slight . . . The story is limited to [the wife's] sudden change of feeling, and the moral and social ramifications are outside [its] terms of reference. As the material is limited in this way . . . it is what I believe would be called feminine. (*ASG* 38; emphasis Eliot's)

In a word, feminine writing is "limited" to emotions. Although in his critical prose Eliot is circumspect, his letters exhibit a frankly hostile attitude toward literary women, including scattered vituperations against female literary authority and the "feminization of modern society" in general.[18] Writing to Pound (15 April 1915), Eliot complains of the feminization of literary study in American universities, where it is reduced to the contemplation of

How to Appreciate the Hundred Best Paintings, the Maiden Aunt and the Social Worker. Something might be said . . . about the Evil Influence of Virginity on American Civilization . . . [L]iterature has rights of its own which extend beyond Uplift and Recreation. Of course it is imprudent to sneer at the monopolisation of literature by women. (*L* 96)

As we will see in the following chapter, Eliot's sneer at powerful literary women is especially pertinent in regard to his relationship to his mother, herself a poet and dramatist, and contrasts sharply with his published remarks concerning the slightness of feminine writing. In his "London Letter" to the *Dial* of July 1921, Eliot compares strong male artists, such as James Joyce, to "a more feminine type [which] . . . makes its art by feeling and by contemplating the feeling rather than the object which has excited it" (216–17). The examples he offers are the work of his friend Virginia Woolf and of Walter Pater.

Pater repeatedly figures in Eliot's essays as the bad example, as the perverted son of Matthew Arnold's doctrine of culture – in short, as the nadir of effete aestheticism. According to Eliot, "'Art for art's sake' is the offspring of Arnold's Culture; and we can hardly venture to say that it is even a perversion of Arnold's doctrine, considering how very vague and ambiguous that doctrine is" (*SE* 439). Pater's error – including his "flirtation with the liturgy," thereby rendering its solemnities "sensuous" (*SE* 441) – is similar to Donne's mistake. Moreover, Pater's "perversion" of Arnoldian doctrine is closely linked to the notion of inversion, as we will see in the next section. "Eliot's trashing of Pater," according to Richard Poirier, was in part due to Eliot's distaste for fluidity in general, as opposed to cut-and-dried analytic distinctions: "the spectre of tides, of things being made to flow into one another, was especially disturbing to Eliot."[19] Eliot's letters confirm his disgust at feminine fluids – a topic that I take up in the following chapter on Eliot's early poetry. In an unpublished letter to Conrad Aiken (4 January 1926), responding to Aiken's congratulations on the publication of *Poems 1920–1925*, Eliot sent "a page torn out of the *Midwives Gazette*," underlining the words "*blood, mucous, and shreds of mucous*" and "purulent *offensive discharge*."[20] Eliot's borrowings from Pater and his repression of that debt have been amply documented by Poirier and Perry Meisel, while Louis Menand has shown the continuity between Pater's writings and *The Waste Land*.[21]

The virulence of Eliot's disavowal of Pater may also have had to do with his revulsion at the effeteness and homosexuality linked to the latter. Eliot's association of Pater with homosexual perversion is evident in the drafts of *The Waste Land* where Fresca, sitting in her bath, reads Pater along with the openly gay John Addington Symonds and the closeted Vernon Lee (the pseudonym of Violet Paget): "Fresca was baptised in a soapy sea / Of Symonds – Walter Pater – Vernon Lee" (*F* 41). Although Pater did not consider himself homosexual, the same-sex eroticism of his aesthetic doctrine was apparent to many of his readers, contrary to Richard Jenkyns's claim, and was the subject of controversy at the time.[22] The perversion whose seed lay in Arnold's insistently moral writings and which came to flower in Pater, a perversion that combines effeminacy with emotional, even sensuous self-indulgence, is never named by Eliot. Indeed, he did not have to, for Pater, together with Plato, Swinburne, Walt Whitman, and Oscar Wilde, was one of the touchstones of the love that famously dared not speak its name in England in the early twentieth century, a love that was quickly becoming synonymous with the term "perversion." The slippery slope that Eliot deplored from Arnold's "sweetness and light" to Paterian Hellenism, aesthetic decadence, and, finally, sexual perversion was central to contemporary debates concerning the supposed effeminacy of art and what Eliot called the "monopolisation of literature by women."[23] Given the

challenge to male artists by a "philistine" industrial economy, by feminist political demands, and by the late Victorian cult of manliness in the
service of the empire, Eliot's disavowal of Pater is less a sign of his personal refusal to acknowledge his sources than a historical symptom of
Anglo-American cultural anxiety concerning heterosexual masculinity
and the uneasy proximity of the artist to the newly designated "homosexual."

The straight man to Pater and his kind is Aristotle. Unlike Plato, the
icon of Victorian Hellenism and the inspiration for Pater's erotic aesthetic, Aristotle represents a virile, rationalist Greek ideal for Eliot. He
appears in Eliot's early essays as the "perfect critic" whose attention is
not diverted from poetry to the poet. "Aristotle had none of these impure
desires to satisfy; in whatever sphere of interest, he looked solely and
steadfastly at the object" (*SW* 11). Aristotle's analytical method possesses
an ethical value for Eliot as a stepping-stone to ascetic purity. "The end
of the enjoyment of poetry is a pure contemplation from which all the
accidents of personal emotion are removed; thus we aim to see the
object as it really is" and, through "a labour of the intelligence, . . . to
attain that stage of vision *amor intellectualis Dei*" (*SW* 14–15). Aristotle
occupies a position similar to that which Eliot will give to Dante and
Virgil, as a transcendent, "classic" figure, remote from modern concerns, whose literary worth and moral virtue are uncontested. The
conjunction of literary, religious, and sexual values in Eliot's critical
appraisals is even more apparent when we turn to his attack on the type
of mistake that I call inversion.

### INVERSION

Eliot sharply criticizes the practice of poets and critics who, in his judgment, elevate the image over the idea, the sound of words over their
sense, or language in general over the objects to which it refers. Such
reversals of the normal order of language have historically been linked
to a host of political, social, sexual, and moral inversions. Eliot did not
view a topsy-turvy world as a carnivalesque fantasy but as a twisted
nightmare, much as Francis Bacon saw the overthrow of natural or instituted hierarchies: "For . . . women to govern men, sons the fathers, slaves
freemen, are . . . total violations and perversions of the laws of nature
and nations."[24] Although Bacon uses the term "perversion," I prefer
"inversion" as a designation for the linguistic disorder that Eliot diagnoses in order to retain its association with a specific form of sexual

deviation: the inversion of (hetero)sexual desire and gender identity in the body of the invert. By the turn of the century, "inversion" had become the standard sexological term for what was sometimes called homosexuality,[25] while it continued to suggest an insidious, general social and ethical corruption.

Eliot does not employ the word "inversion" in his criticism, yet it is an apt heading for the type of error that he frequently denounced that turns upside down literary, social, and sexual norms. The linguistic inversions that he reproaches are not only structurally parallel to the inversion of moral values, but these two maladies stand in a mutual cause-effect relation in Eliot's text and hence are indissolubly fused. Moral decadence gives rise to decadent writing, and vice versa. The authors whom Eliot censures – Swinburne, Pater, Seneca, Donne, Poe, and Valéry – are the aesthetic equivalent of the sinners execrated by St. Paul, who

worshipped and served the creature more than the Creator . . . For this cause God gave them up unto vile affections: for even their women did change the natural use into that which is against nature: And likewise also the men, leaving the natural use of the woman, burned in their lust one toward another; . . . and receiving in themselves that recompense of their error which was meet. (Rom. 1:25–27; KJV)

Although Eliot does not charge these writers with sexual inversion, the taint of this vice colors his critique of those who abandon the "natural use" of words. The predictable orthodoxy of Eliot's judgments renders all the more surprising his relatively straightforward and sympathetic remarks concerning Alfred Tennyson's love for Arthur Hallam as expressed in *In Memoriam*. Far from condemning the poem, Eliot's sensitive reading of it suggests that, as in the case of the idealized, "personal kinship" between a younger and an older poet, Eliot could envision nonphobically certain passionate male same-sex relations as long as they were literary and not physical. However, Eliot denounces the subversion of literary value by those whose concomitant moral contamination is often signified by the hint of homosexuality.

Swinburne is Eliot's touchstone for linguistic inversion with its attendant ethical degeneracy.[26] In "Swinburne as Poet" (1920), Eliot attacks the "morbidity of . . . language" in his poetry, in contrast to "language in a healthy state [which] presents the object" as it really is. The poet's error stems from his unhealthy interest in words themselves, apart from their reference to objects or to a definite meaning. "In the verse of Swinburne . . . the object has ceased to exist, . . . the meaning is merely the hallucination of meaning, [and] . . . language, uprooted, has adapted itself to an independent life of atmospheric nourishment" (*SE* 327). In the dreamy hothouse of Swinburne's poetry, words are torn from their natural soil and yet are "very much alive" with a "singular life of [their] own," as though fed by their own decadent impulses. Indeed, Swinburne's poetry is so artificial that it is worse than a "sham"; "It would only be so if you could produce or suggest something that it pretends to be and is not. The world of Swinburne does not depend upon some other world which it simulates" (*SE* 327) but, abandoning mimetic responsibility, exists in a narcissistic, autoerotic realm of its own.

Eliot suggests the impure desires that lay at the root of Swinburne's malady when he says that "it is, in fact, the word that gives him the thrill, not the object. When you take to pieces any verse of Swinburne, you find always that the object was not there – only the word" (*SE* 326). Swinburne's "thrill" at the sounds of words, and his consequent transposition of the proper relation between sound and sense, is similar to the "emotional kick" that, Eliot claims, Arnold unwittingly counseled his readers to get out of Christianity "without the bother of believing it," a sensuous self-indulgence that led eventually to "*Marius the Epicurean*, and finally *De Profundis*" (*SE* 434–35). The allusions to Pater and Wilde plainly insinuate the sexual inversion to which the inversion of word and object leads, an insinuation that is reinforced later in the "Arnold and Pater" essay when Eliot again drops Wilde's name as well as mentioning in passing the "perverse" moralizing of André Gide (*SE* 438–39).[27] The nexus of Eliot's references to narcissistic aestheticism and homosexuality is Wilde, famous for his paradoxical reversals and, especially, for his punishment; Wilde thus serves as a warning to those charmed by sounds and surface appearances.

Eliot's critique of the interlocking errors of linguistic and sexual inversion is closely related to what I have termed perversion in the previous section. Both kinds of erring are energized by homophobia, and both presuppose the common belief that same-sex desire is narcissistic or autoerotic. It is useful to distinguish between them, however, in order to show the diverse ramifications of Eliot's sexual anxieties as well as to explore the particular operations of his understanding of error in its various forms.

Eliot's concern with inversion in the linguistic and moral senses seems to have peaked in 1926–27, at the time of his conversion to Anglicanism. In two essays from this period, "Seneca in Elizabethan Translation" and the Clark Lectures, published in *The Varieties of Metaphysical Poetry*, Eliot finds that writers to whom he is sympathetic – Seneca and Donne – are guilty of Swinburne's error. However, his criticism of them is mitigated by his acknowledgement of the corruption of their cultures. Unlike the union of "thought and feeling" in Greek drama, "in the plays of Seneca . . . the word has no further reality behind it," and "the centre of value is shifted from what the personage says to the way in which he says it. Very often the value comes near to being mere smartness" (*SE* 68). Although "the ethic of Seneca is a matter of postures," Eliot excuses him, for "many of the faults of Seneca which appear 'decadent' are, after all, merely Roman" (*SE* 72, 70). Donne is given a similar historical justification for his poetic practice, living as he did in an intellectually "chaotic" age. Juxtaposed to Dante's poetry, in which the "interest . . . lies in the idea or the feeling to be conveyed," so that "the image makes this idea or feeling more intelligible," Donne's poetry suffers from an inversion of poetic values. "In Donne, the interest . . . may be in the ingenuity of conveying the idea by that particular image; or the image itself may be more difficult than the idea" (*V* 120). While Dante's images are "serviceable," Donne's are merely "ornamental" (*V* 121). Throughout his career, Eliot consistently praised Dante for respecting the proper hierarchy of literary value, asserting in "To Criticize the Critic" (1961) that "Dante seems to me to teach that the poet should be the servant of his language, rather than the master of it. This sense of responsibility is one of the marks of the *classical* poet" (*CC* 133; emphasis Eliot's). By contrast, "Donne's method is frequently to proceed from the greater to the less, from the central to the peripheral" (*V* 126), privileging the cleverness of his language over the thoughts to which they should refer, going so far as to "violate . . . the order of nature" (*V* 269).

Edgar Allan Poe, a much less sympathetic figure in Eliot's eyes, fell prey to similar tendencies. In "From Poe to Valéry" (1948), Eliot traces the origins of Symbolism in Poe's poetic practice. Citing Poe's use of "immemorial" in "Ulalume," Eliot asserts that "in his choice of the word which has the right *sound*, Poe is by no means careful that it should have also the right *sense*" (*CC* 31; emphasis Eliot's). Although he disclaims any "psychological or pathological explanation," Eliot attributes Poe's "irresponsibility towards the meaning of words" to his immaturity, damning him with the famous phrase that he had "the intellect of a highly gifted young person before puberty," fascinated like a "pre-adolescent" by cheap mental "delights" (*CC* 32, 35). Poe's reversal of the natural hierarchy of language was to have disastrous consequences for the French poets whom he influenced, including Charles Baudelaire and Paul

Valéry. According to Eliot, with Valéry came "a change of attitude toward the subject matter"; turning upside down the proper order of poetry, Valéry "ceased to believe in *ends* and was only interested in *processes*," especially in his self-conscious use of language in composition (*CC* 39–40; emphasis Eliot's). The ethical, even sexual implications of this inversion of poetic value are evident in Eliot's wry aside that "*la poésie pure*, that kind of purity came easily to Poe" (*CC* 40). Grover Smith is quite wide of the mark in his claim that Eliot here "appears in harmony with the poetic philosophy and practice" of Poe's Symbolist successors.[28] Indeed, Poe's "arrested development" and Valéry's narcissism hint none too vaguely at certain sexual, especially autoerotic, vices.

A very different perspective on the eroticism of language and on relations between men is evident in Eliot's essay on *In Memoriam* (1936). He praises Tennyson for having had "the finest ear of any English poet since Milton" (*SE* 328), yet Tennyson, far from inverting sound and sense, is the examplar of traditional poetic values. Likewise, Eliot does not interpret his sexually charged friendship with Hallam as an index of literary perversion. Eliot's examination of the emotional dynamics of Tennyson's poetry is particularly interesting and unusual in his critical prose. Furthermore, his essay is worthy of attention in light of the reductive approach of many critics to Eliot's relation to Tennyson. Since Harold Bloom charged that "Eliot's true and always unnamed precursor was . . . an uneasy composite of Whitman and Tennyson," it has become routine to cite the latter as an example of Eliot's alleged deceitfulness regarding his sources.[29] Although Eliot famously commented that Tennyson had "a large dull brain like a farmhouse clock,"[30] his view of Tennyson is more generous and nuanced than is commonly believed. Eliot's essay on Tennyson is remarkably sensitive to the complexity of love between men prior to its medicalization as homosexuality. Reading *Maud* and *In Memoriam*, Eliot haltingly suggests Tennyson's emotional or sexual inversion, but he protects Tennyson from the pathological implications of his own analysis. Defending him against the accusation of insipidity, Eliot says,

I do not believe for a moment that Tennyson was a man of mild feelings or weak passions. There is no evidence in his poetry that he knew the experience of violent passion for a woman; but there is plenty of evidence of emotional intensity and violence – but of emotion so deeply suppressed, even from himself, as to tend rather towards the blackest melancholia than towards dramatic action. And it is emotion which . . . attained no ultimate clear purgation. (*SE* 332)

In *Maud*, Tennyson's "profound and tumultuous" feelings "never arrive at expression" because of what Eliot initially calls "a fundamental error of form" (*SE* 332–33). Yet this formal error turns out to be Tennyson's refusal to take up a sexual position in the poem, either as the masculine subject or as the feminine object. "In *Maud*, Tennyson neither identifies himself with the lover, nor identifies the lover with himself" (*SE* 333). Tennyson's emotional distance in the poem, Eliot implies, stems from his reluctance to assume normatively heterosexual roles.

When Tennyson does arrive at "full expression" in *In Memoriam*, he does so by affirming his love for another man, Arthur Hallam. Allowing that he "get[s] a very different impression from *In Memoriam* from that which Tennyson's contemporaries seem to have got," namely, an affirmation of Christian faith, Eliot frankly admits that he reads the poem as an expression of Tennyson's love for the creature, a love greater than that for the Creator.

> Tennyson . . . is naturally, in lamenting his friend, teased by the hope of immortality and reunion beyond death. Yet the renewal craved for seems at best but a continuance, or a substitute for the joys of friendship upon earth . . . His concern is for the loss of man rather than for the gain of God. (*SE* 334)

Far from criticizing Tennyson for inverting spiritual, not to mention sexual, values, Eliot urges his reader to look "innocently at the surface" of *In Memoriam* and thus "to come to the depths, to the abyss of sorrow" (*SE* 337). This surface which calls for a credulous, sympathetic attitude on the part of its reader cannot be Tennyson's theology, which Eliot describes as conventional, but is probably what Eliot wanted to think of as Tennyson's "innocent" love for Hallam.

Eliot's tender treatment of *In Memoriam*'s erotic theme, which even in Tennyson's day was seen as troubling,[31] gains strength in light of his sardonic comments about Tennyson's overtly heterosexual poems, such as "The Two Voices," concerning "the perpetuation of love by offspring" (*SE* 287). Eliot's cynicism toward the "Tennysonian happy marriage, . . . which is one sort of bankruptcy" (*V* 114), is directed against the epithalamium that serves as the epilogue to *In Memoriam*, written to commemorate the marriage of Tennyson's sister Cecilia and Edmund Lushington.[32] Although he is critical of Tennyson's celebrations of heterosexual love, Eliot calls his text of errant, inverted passion "great poetry," with "honest," albeit despairing, feelings.[33]

Eliot's biting criticism of the inversion of literary, moral, and, by implication, sexual norms in Swinburne, Pater, Donne, and Poe – in sharp contrast to his compassionate attitude toward Tennyson's poem of male friendship – situates him equivocally on what Eve Kosofsky Sedgwick calls the male "homosocial continuum," that is, the spectrum of bonds between men that, for at least the past two centuries in Anglo-American culture, has been structured and fractured by homophobia.[34] In one sense, Eliot is an exemplary case of "male homosexual panic," Sedgwick's term for the horrified response of heterosexually identified men to the fact that many cherished and intense kinds of male friendship and affiliation are "not readily distinguishable from the most repro-bated bonds."[35] Far from an aberration, such panic is the "normal condition" of properly socialized men. Eliot's abjection of writers such as Pater as well as his disavowal of their influence on him thus served to virilize and normalize Eliot in the face of the potentially contaminating effects of his male affiliations. Gregory Jay suggests that Eliot's confessed "aversion" to Walt Whitman and his suppression of Whitman's influ-ence, both on his own work and on contemporary poetry in general, is homophobically motivated.[36] However, Eliot's reading of *In Memoriam* calls for a more nuanced analysis of the tension in his work between, in Sedgwick's words, "the *pre*scription of the most intimate male bonding and the *pro*scription of (the remarkably cognate) 'homosexuality.'"[37] Writing at a crucial historical moment in the definition of homosexual-ity and heterosexuality, Eliot often veered into a frightened, violent denial of homosexuality, but he also embraced what he saw as non-pathological forms of male love.

In view of Eliot's antipathy toward sexual inversion, it is surprising to find that in his critical prose he frequently describes in fervent tones a kind of youthful literary passion, what he calls the young poet's "daemonic possession" by an older male poet (*UPUC* 26). The juve-nile poet's inclination is homosocial, even homoerotic, yet it is for Eliot the powerful engine of inspiration. The zeal to write originates in a yearning toward imitative identification with the elder poet, and, even, in the desire for possessive appropriation, to take hold of and overcome him. The forces from which poetry springs, according to Eliot, are thus intimately related to the sexual inversion that he con-demns.

The only passion sanctioned – indeed, highly praised – by Eliot is this special sort of homoerotic ardor by a budding poet for an older, usually dead poet whom he esteems. Eliot's early essays describe a boy who develops a "passionate admiration for some one writer."[38] Such a "love" is "the first step in [his] education," even if the object of his adolescent infatuation is later discarded. Eliot compares the professional maturation undergone by the ephebe through his relation to the senior poet with the personal transformation undergone by a young lover in his first amorous affair. "There is a close analogy between the sort of experience which develops a man and the sort of experience that develops a writer," Eliot writes in "Reflections on Contemporary Poetry" (1919), for "similar types of experience form the nourishment of both."[39] This emotional experience is

a feeling of profound kinship, or rather of a peculiar personal intimacy, with another, probably a dead author. It may overcome us suddenly, on a first or after a long acquaintance; it is certainly a crisis; and when a young writer is seized with his first passion of this sort he may be changed, metamorphosed almost, within a few weeks even . . . The imperative intimacy arouses for the first time a real, an unshakable confidence. That you possess this secret knowledge, this intimacy, with the dead man, . . . who can penetrate at once the thick and dusty circumlocutions about his reputation, can call yourself alone his friend; it is something more than *encouragement* to you. It is a cause of development, like personal relations in life. Like personal intimacies in life, it may and probably will pass, but it will be ineffaceable . . . We may not be great lovers; but if we had a genuine affair with a real poet of any degree we have acquired a monitor to avert us when we are not in love. (39; emphasis Eliot's)

The frankness of Eliot's description of the "crisis" of the young lover-poet, "seized" by his "imperative intimacy" with the "dead man" about whom he has "secret knowledge" – indeed, whose reputation he can "penetrate" so as to "possess" him as his own special "friend" – more than suggests the homoeroticism, and perhaps even the necrophilism, that binds the younger poet with his dead poetic beloved.

In contrast to Harold Bloom's notion of the ephebe's struggle to come into his own by killing off his paternal precursors, Eliot envisions his relation to his immediate source of inspiration as a positive, even amorous filiation. Henry James's relationship to Hawthorne is an exemplary instance of the "personal kinship" between a younger and older writer similar to Hellenic male relations between ephebe and teacher.[40] Eliot doubts "the genuineness of the love of poetry of any reader who did not have one or more of these personal affections for the work of some poet of no great historical importance" (*OPP* 37). Indeed, it is a poet about whom Eliot admits that he has written nothing at all who seems to have had the greatest impact upon him as a young writer. Late in his career, Eliot acknowledged that it was from Jules Laforgue and the minor

Elizabethan and Jacobean dramatists that "I, in my poetic formation, had learned my lessons; it was by them . . . that my imagination had been stimulated," having "read them with passionate delight" during a "period in which the stirrings of desire to write verse were becoming insistent" (CC 18). Eliot's descriptions of his adolescent reading pleasures, like Proust's, are tinged with autoeroticism, recalling the association, drawn by Freud and incessantly reiterated in psychoanalytic and popular literature, between narcissism and homosexuality.[41] His enraptured accounts of his early reading experiences suggest that these formative pleasures, like those of his own "Saint Narcissus," who "wished he had been a young girl / Caught in the woods by a drunken old man" and whose "flesh was in love with the penetrant arrows" (F 93), were charged with homoerotic desire.

The crucial issue for our purposes is not to come to an accurate reckoning of the influences upon Eliot nor to identify his first poetic love but to understand the nature of such a literary love and Eliot's conception of it in terms of his hostility to perverse emotions and to homosexuality in general. For Eliot's harsh criticism of interest in the personality of the poet and his denunciation of the reader's or poet's indulgence in personal feelings contrast sharply to his ardent recollection of his possession of and by the beloved poets of his youth. In "Religion and Literature" (1935), he urges sympathetically that

everyone, I believe, who is at all sensible to the seductions of poetry, can remember some moment in youth when he or she was completely carried away by the work of one poet . . . What happens is a kind of inundation, of invasion of the undeveloped personality by the stronger personality of the poet. (SE 394)

Eliot thus fondly recalls the literary seductions of his youth, but in this essay his memory serves an argument for the protection of youthful readers from the pernicious effects of seduction by the wrong sort of poet.

What seems to happen in Eliot's essays is a shift from the youthful poet's active desire for the older poet, whose secrets he penetrates through his devoted enthusiasm, to a passive sense of the youthful poet's dangerous enchantment or ravishment by the older poet. The tables have begun to turn by the 1929 "Dante" essay, where Eliot writes that "the experience of a poem is . . . very much like our intenser experience of other human beings. There is a first, or an early moment which is unique, of shock and surprise, even of terror . . .; a moment which can never be forgotten, but which is never repeated integrally" (SE 250).

Such a terrifying moment of surrender – Eliot's famous "bewildering minute" that he liked to quote from Cyril Tourneur's *Revenger's Tragedy* – implies a desire all the more exciting and frightening for its perverse eroticism. In a 1935 letter to Stephen Spender that echoes his published remarks, Eliot says that "You don't really criticize any author to whom you have never surrendered yourself. . . . Even just the bewildering minute counts; you have to give yourself up" (*SP* 13). Giving himself up to another male poet was a perilous risk for Eliot, although as he became canonized himself he could look back on his adolescence and view with judicious distance a period when

the poem, or the poetry of a single poet, invades the youthful consciousness and assumes complete possession for a time . . . Much as in our youthful experiences of love, we do not so much see the person as infer the existence of some outside object which sets in motion these new and delightful feelings in which we are absorbed . . . It is not deliberate choice of a poet to mimic, but writing under a kind of daemonic possession by one poet. (*UPUC* 25–26)

Eliot's enigmatic reference to the poet's "daemonic possession" has raised questions concerning the nature of what Eliot elsewhere calls the poet's "unknown, dark *psychic material* – we might say, the octopus or angel with which the poet struggles" (*OPP* 110; emphasis Eliot's).

Rather than speculate on some dim secret harbored by Eliot, we may read his accounts of his adolescent literary passions in terms of the structure of male relations in his critical work. Inversions of the proper order of language and literature – including the privileging of sound over sense, of image over idea, of signs over their referents, and of poetic processes over their ends – issue from a moral waywardness that in turn produces, in Eliot's view, the inversion of the proper order of nature, that is, unnatural sexuality. Although Eliot never explicitly mentions homosexuality or sodomy in his published essays, unlike his letters,[42] his reprobation of literary inversions is energized by his phobic rejection of male same-sex desire. The fact that this disavowal coexists side-by-side with his enthusiastic affirmation of the infatuations that stimulated him as a young poet attests to the dangerous potency that the unnamed desire possessed for Eliot, a desire that draws its strength from its disavowal. Eliot's critical writings bear witness both to the violent split between male friendship and sexual passion as well as to their subterranean confluence. In short, the deviant desire that Eliot denies is also the force that animates his writing. Similarly, Eliot censures violations of the boundaries that determine the order of literature and criticizes practices that relativize literary value and adulterate the social order, yet in these cases, as with perversion and inversion, such errors are constitutive of the very order that they transgress.

### IMPURE MINGLING

At the conclusion of his 1921 essay on John Dryden, Eliot throws up his hands and asks, "What is man to decide what poetry is?" (*SE* 315). Far from a rhetorical question, the decision regarding what poetry is and what it is not – or should not be – is a major dilemma in Eliot's critical writings. The problem first presented itself to him as a matter of maintaining the purity of poetry and criticism. Hence, in *The Sacred Wood*, he enjoined the "pure contemplation of poetry from which all the accidents of personal emotion are removed" (*SW* 14–15) and censured the "impure" mixture of philosophy and poetry (*SW* 160–61). Although he later modified his views and claimed that "pure literature is a chimera . . .; admit the vestige of an idea and it is already transformed,"[43] drawing the line between poetry and nonpoetry was a persistent concern throughout his career.

As a consequence, Eliot often thought of literary error as a matter of impure mingling. Such impurity arises on the formal level, in the mixture of literary genres and the confusion of the conventions proper to specific genres; on the epistemological level, in the confusion between thought and feeling; and on the discursive level, in the confusion of poetry with theology, philosophy, psychology, or sociology. In each case, Eliot sought an ideal of homogeneity, just as in *After Strange Gods* he wished for a society with a racially "homogeneous" population free of "adulterate" elements (20). Impure mingling on these levels is closely related to what Eliot believed was the perverse turning away from the object of poetry for the sake of "impure desires" inasmuch as such diversions introduce external interests into what should be an immaculately disinterested realm. While many of Eliot's specific complaints against discursive interminglings appear motived by his wish to protect his own poetry from damaging psychobiographical interpretations, the larger aim of his arguments against formal, epistemological, and discursive impurities is to demarcate a self-justifying field of literary value uncontaminated by "swarms of inarticulate feelings" and free from profane interests, beliefs or desires, except insofar as the latter were themselves, in Eliot's eyes, likewise "pure." In short, literary and sexual, social, political and religious purity are mutually reinforcing concepts, underwritten by a rhetoric of chastity.

Eliot's attempts to define the proper field of poetry are an exercise in circumscription. Literary purity calls for clear boundaries; the error of impure mingling is hence a boundary violation. Like dirt, defined by anthropologists as "matter out of place," error is a contravention of ordered relations. According to Mary Douglas, "where there is dirt there is system. Dirt is the by-product of a systematic ordering and classification of matter," and so "ideas about separating, purifying, [and] demarcating . . . transgressions" expose the structural relations among apparently discrete cultural prohibitions.[44] In a similar fashion, Eliot's criticism of literary impurities is consistent with his injunctions concerning social and sexual values. Just as his disapproval of the inversion of linguistic and literary norms depends upon his rejection of the homoerotic desires that unwittingly energize his poetry, so Eliot's critique of literary impurity ends up admitting – this time openly but in a highly qualified way – that such impurities are a necessary, interior condition of poetry.

Eliot's insistence upon establishing boundaries for poetry follows from his cartographic sense of literary history. In *The Use of Poetry and the Use of Criticism* (1933), Eliot describes the field of literature as a "landscape" drawn in perspective. "Armed with a powerful glass," the critic "will be able to sweep the distance and gain an acquaintance with minute objects in the landscape . . . ; he will be able to gauge nicely the position and proportion of the objects surrounding us, in the whole of the vast panorama" (*UPUC* 100–101). In a word, the body of Western literature for Eliot is a map; similarly, in *Notes toward the Definition of Culture* (1948), whose epigraph is a definition of "definition" as "the setting of bounds: limitation" (*OED*), culture is figured typographically. In the latter text, Eliot recommends that "the great majority of human beings should go on living in the place in which they were born" (52), just as in the former he tries to settle the proper place of literary works. The stress that Eliot lays upon the literally geographic stability of culture in *Notes*, along with his wish for an ethnically and religiously unmixed society without "freethinking," mobile Jews (*ASG* 20), is thoroughly in keeping with his critical sanctions against promiscuous literary minglings.

The anti-Semitic, neoagrarian values expressed in Eliot's social writings and poetry have justly come under attack, most recently and vigorously by Anthony Julius, who persuasively argues that "anti-Semitism did not disfigure Eliot's work, it animated it."[45] Julius specifies in painstaking detail Eliot's "exploitation" of anti-Semitic conventions, both in his early poetry (notably "Gerontion" and "Burbank") and in his social commentary, insisting that Eliot's racist beliefs cannot be cordoned off from his artistic creations. Against the grain of the New Critical doctrine that defined Eliot's poetic oeuvre, Julius's claim that the poet's "anti-Semitic discourse is an inseparable part of his greater literary undertaking" (29) would, paradoxically, find a sympathetic audience in Eliot himself, who argued that "I cannot see that poetry can ever be separated from . . . belief."[46] Eliot's assessment of impure mingling as an intractable error draws our attention to the tangled, "tentacular roots" of his own thought, lost to sight in Eliot's elevation to the role of "the bishop of modern poetry" in the 1950s.[47] Moreover, as we see in the following chapter, Eliot's early poetry is not, as some critics would have it, a radical exception in an otherwise conservative oeuvre, for the "ambivalence" that Jay finds in the early poetry "between a nostalgia for origins and a drive for revolutionary fragmentation" is present throughout Eliot's literary criticism.[48]

Within the literary field, Eliot sought to demarcate the proper borderlines among literary forms. Early on, he argued for the "inner necessity" of the difference between prose and poetry, and claimed that blurring the distinction in the prose poem is an evasion of the technical demands of each medium.[49] In subsequent essays, he judges Renaissance playwrights according to their conformity to generic requirements, including the exigencies of versification. Eliot everywhere stresses the need to accept the restrictions of art and criticizes Elizabethan dramatists for violating their own rules. In "Four Elizabethan Dramatists" (1924), for instance, he claims that it was "strictly an error" by Shakespeare to introduce into the same play, *Macbeth*, different kinds of ghosts (*SE* 116).

More broadly, error arises from sacrificing aesthetic requirements for the sake of realism. "The weakness of Elizabethan drama," according to Eliot, is "its attempt at realism" and its "lack of conventions" (*SE* 112). He continually attacks sociological and psychological realism; at its best, art aims for universal truths, not particular representations or emotional stimulation. Harnessing art to social or emotive ends is an "impurity" that, in the case of the Elizabethans, sprang from their "unwillingness to accept any limitation" (*SE* 116). So Eliot's task as a critic was not only to reform current critical practices, censuring critics such as Havelock Ellis who would psychologize literature (*SE* 202), but also to correct the Elizabethans themselves, ordering the canon of Elizabethan drama according to what he believed was its internal aesthetic logic, a logic that dramatists of the period nonetheless often disobeyed. Moreover, the formal impurities of Elizabethan drama suggest its sexual licentiousness and unbridled passion.

Eliot's essays of the 1920s are to a large degree concerned with the relation between cognition and sensibility.[50] For instance, he inveighs against the impure mingling of thought and feeling in the work of William Blake, who suffered from a "confusion of thought, emotion, and vision" (*SE* 322). By contrast, it is a mistake to fault Ben Jonson for failing to plumb the abyss of the human psyche. In his intellectually complex plays, "unconscious does not respond to unconscious; no swarms of inarticulate feelings are aroused" (*SE* 148). Eliot allows that the works of his contemporaries "have a depth" that Jonson's lacks, but such profundity is dangerous, for "their words have often a network of tentacular roots reaching down to the deepest terrors and desires" (*SE* 155). Eliot's allusion to the "obscure" emotions explored by Elizabethan writers hints vaguely at unspeakable desires. "Elizabethan morality . . . did not suppress; its dark corners are haunted by the ghost of Mary Fitton and perhaps greater. It is a subject which has not been sufficiently investigated" (*SE* 214). But Eliot does not peer into those dark corners inhabited by Mary Fitton, the "dark lady" of Shakespeare's sonnets, nor does he pry into the even murkier topic of the bard's scandalous love for the "fair youth." Far from specifying the powerful desires unleashed by Elizabethan drama, Eliot prefers to idealize their "very high development of the senses," claiming that their sensuality was fused with language into an aesthetic union that is now lost to us. "With the end of Chapman, Middleton, Webster, Tourneur, [and] Donne, we end a period when the intellect was immediately at the tips of the senses. Sensation became word and word was sensation" (*SE* 209–10). His praise of the Elizabethans' sensuality echoes the incarnation of the Word made Flesh, rendering their prelapsarian, carnal sensibility sacred and impossibly distant, as though the Elizabethan period embodied an imaginary ideal which we moderns can never achieve.

A corollary of the epistemological error of confusing thought and feeling is a distinction Eliot repeatedly draws in his later essays between the intellectual explanation of a poem and an intuitive understanding of it. "The chief use of the 'meaning' of a poem," he asserts, "may be . . . to keep [the reader's] mind diverted and quiet, while the poem does its work upon him: much as the imaginary burglar is always provided with a bit of nice meat for the house-dog"; however, "the more seasoned reader, he who has reached, in these matters, a state of greater *purity*, does not bother about understanding" (*UPUC* 144; emphasis Eliot's).

Here, Eliot's notion of "understanding" refers to the reduction of a poem to its paraphrasable, rational content or to its sources. Eliot is thus thrown back into the previously despised camp of "art-for-art's-sake," which, he says, "contained this true impulse behind it," that it recognized "the error of the poet's trying to do" the work of the prose writer (*UPUC* 145). Hence, while in his earlier essays Eliot had argued for the cognitive value of poetry, prizing "thought" over "emotion" and derogating poetry and poets who indulge their own or their readers' emotions, in his subsequent essays he resorts to a more or less antirationalist theory of poetry. Yet in both cases he claims to be defending the "purity" of poetry.

The rhetorical structure of Eliot's critical project of distinguishing truth from error depends upon the distinction between a pure interior and an impure exterior, a division guarded by critics. But because they are apt to wander, Eliot warns critics against trespassing this limit by introducing nonpoetic discourses: "[T]here is a philosophic borderline, which you must not transgress too far or too often, if you . . . are not prepared to present yourself as a philosopher, metaphysician, sociologist, or psychologist instead" (*UPUC* 56–57). In this passage – a typical and straightforward example of Eliot's rhetorical practice of drawing a distinction that relies for its efficacy upon the terms it thereby differentiates – Eliot also separates two, opposing critical tendencies, claiming that correct criticism lies in the middle. Yet the indeterminacy of this critical mean demonstrates the difficulty that Eliot faced in delimiting exclusive boundaries.

Criticism of poetry moves between two extremes. On the one hand the critic may busy himself so much with the implications of a poem . . . – implications moral, social, religious, or other – that the poetry becomes hardly more than a text for a discourse . . . Or if you stick too closely to the "poetry" . . . you will tend to evacuate it of all significance. (*UPUC* 56)

Confronted with the problem of specifying the proper place for criticism, Eliot concludes by citing that exemplar of "critical integrity," Samuel Johnson. "Within his limitations, he is one of the great critics; and he is a great critic because he keeps within his limitations. When you know what they are, you know where you are" (*UPUC* 57). Eliot's openly tautological praise of Johnson is tantamount to an admission that the guardians of literature must be those who are within the fold, who never need to question where they are because they are already there.

The third type of "impure mingling" that was for Eliot the most troubling dilemma in defining the proper boundaries of poetry is what he called the confusion between poetry and belief. This problem understandably became acute about the time of his religious conversion. In "The Idea of a Literary Review" (1926), Eliot faces "the impossibility of defining the frontiers, or limiting the context of 'literature.' Even the *purest* literature is alimented from non-literary sources, and has non-literary consequences."[51] In his subsequent writings Eliot repeatedly addresses the problem of the infiltration of strictly non-poetic beliefs into the poetic realm. For Eliot, this meant the acceptance of error – the impure mingling of discursive fields – in the service of a higher truth, namely, his Christian belief. However, he continued to assert the purity of poetry against the intrusion of all other discourses.

Eliot's most sustained discussion of the conflict between poetry and religious belief is his 1929 "Dante" essay. "The question of what Dante 'believed'" is one that the reader "cannot afford to *ignore*," although he insists that "there is a difference . . . between philosophical *belief* and poetic *assent*" (*SE* 257; emphasis Eliot's). He maintains that confusing poetry qua poetry and poetry as the literal statement of a philosophic or religious position is "impure" and that, as a reader, "you are not called upon to believe what Dante believed, . . . but you are called upon . . . to understand it" (*SE* 258). At this stage, Eliot continues to make a distinction between "what Dante believes as a poet and what he believes as a man" and to argue that poetry calls for a "suspension of belief" (*SE* 258–59). However, he confesses that he "cannot, in practice, wholly separate [his] poetic appreciation from [his] personal beliefs," indeed, "that 'literary appreciation' is an abstraction, and pure poetry a phantom, and that both in creation and enjoyment much always enters which is . . . irrelevant" (*SE* 271).

Eliot's admission of the necessarily impure nature of literary judgment becomes a recurrent motif in his subsequent criticism. However, his acceptance of "irrelevant," contingent factors in literary appreciation is highly circumscribed. "Literary criticism should be completed by criticism from a definite ethical and theological standpoint," Eliot maintains in "Religion and Literature" (1935), for "the 'greatness' of literature cannot be determined solely by literary standards" (*SE* 388). The separation of "our literary from our religious judgements . . . is not, and never can be, complete" (*SE* 392). A full assessment, he implies, is one that includes a religious, especially Christian, point of view. Christianity, or at least Eliot's version thereof, is a necessary supplement to the criticism of poetry, an essential irrelevancy or intrinsic externality that is vital to its integrity.

In his late essay, "To Criticize the Critic" (1961), Eliot again admits that "it is impossible to fence off *literary* criticism from criticism on other grounds, and that moral, religious and social judgments cannot be wholly excluded" (*CC* 25; emphasis Eliot's). Yet he maintains the standard of an *almost* pure literary judgment, impugns the ethics of aesthetes, and claims the relative purity of poet-critics such as himself. "That . . . literary merit can be estimated in complete isolation is the illusion of those who believe that literary merit alone can justify the publication of a book which could otherwise be condemned on moral grounds," Eliot claims, going on to assert that, "in so far as literary criticism is purely literary, I believe that the criticism of artists writing about their own art . . . carries more authority" (*CC* 25–26). Recouping the ground he has just conceded, Eliot reminds the reader that he has "directed [his] attention on [his] literary criticism *qua* literary," and has not introduced his "religious, social, political, or moral beliefs" (*CC* 26).

Unlike the perverse deviations and inverted desires that appear more or less unwittingly within his essays, the mingling of religious and literary criteria of judgment is a prominent theme in Eliot's later writings. Despite the qualifications with which he hedges about his admission of religious belief as an essential, adulterate factor or a necessary error in literary criticism, Eliot's justification for such a concession is grounds for the inclusion of other impure criteria that he placed beyond the pale. These impurities include philosophical, sociological, and psychological criticism, as well as those so errant in his eyes as to be beneath overt condemnation, such as criticism based upon the analysis of homosexual desire. Although a homosexual interpretation of literary texts was too low for Eliot's explicit condemnation in his published prose, it was not below his notice or his public censure. His successful threat of legal action in 1952 to suppress John Peter's remarkable reading of same-sex desire in *The Waste Land* – a reading in which the word "homosexual" does not appear – makes abundantly clear that norms of sexual purity are at stake in Eliot's injunctions against the supposed contamination of the poetic realm.[52]

Perversely, Eliot's admission of the necessity for strictly nonaesthetic, religious standards of judgment opens the door for their opposite, that is, for literary judgments based upon the critique of the religious values in which he believed. Having admitted this contingency, Eliot cannot get the wayward cat back into the bag. The return of the impurities that

Eliot wishes to cast out of literary discourse, as a kind of required supplement to what should be an integral whole, parallels the return of relativizing forces within what he saw as the true project of literary criticism: to conserve and confirm the absolute nature of literary value.

## DISSEMINATION

"[T]he struggle of our time [is] to concentrate, not to dissipate," Eliot enjoins in *After Strange Gods* (53). By "concentration" Eliot means the conservation of what he calls "our tradition." Hence, to concentrate is "to renew our association with traditional wisdom; [and] to re-establish a vital connexion between the individual and the race" (53). The forces of modernity, by contrast, have dissipated traditional Western values. In literary terms, this has meant "giv[ing] rein to [the writer's] 'individuality'" (35), making each man his own moral authority, thus leading to the decay of or, as in the case of D. H. Lawrence, the utter "absence of any moral or social sense" at all (39).

Eliot chose not to reissue *After Strange Gods* and, according to Christopher Ricks, may have regretted the racism of the vision he drew therein of a "homogeneous" society unified by shared customs, a common religious faith, and "the blood kinship of 'the same people living in the same place'" (18), for which the presence of "any large number of free-thinking Jews [is] undesirable" (20).[53] Nevertheless, *After Strange Gods* makes explicit the opposition in Eliot's work between what he saw as the forces of conservation and dispersal, or between concentration and dissipation. This opposition shapes the rhetoric of much of Eliot's critical prose throughout his career and determines error as dissemination in several senses, ranging from the dispersion of the Western literary-cultural tradition to moral dissipation to the fragmentation of a writer's oeuvre or of an individual text. These criteria of error participate in the logic of errancy as aberrant movement or wandering and are linked to the systematic opposition in Eliot's critical prose between figures for stasis versus flux. In short, error as dissemination in Eliot's criticism presumes a spermatic economy threatened by the dispersion of phallic authority.

Eliot typically uses the terms "dispersion" and "dissipation" to describe the movement away from an authoritative center. For instance, he calls heresy a "centrifugal impulse," leading to Julius's observation that "the tension between the centripetal and the centrifugal is critical to Eliot's work."[54] However, I have chosen dissemination – a word that rarely occurs in his writings – as an overarching figure to designate the diffusion of literary unity on the levels of the text, the oeuvre, and literature as a whole as well as the relativization of moral and literary values. All of these ways of erring underscore the sexual implications of Eliot's demand for the conservation of social and literary energies, as well as his wish, more broadly, to contain the errant effects of writing – what he once termed "the natural sin of language."[55]

In his earliest literary criticism Eliot praises unity, both the formal unity of a particular work and the collective unity of a writer's oeuvre. Hence, according to Eliot in his 1919 essay on Christopher Marlowe, Shakespeare's "vices of style" are worse than Marlowe's because the former's consist of "a tortured perverse ingenuity of images which dissipates instead of concentrating the imagination" (SE 119). Elsewhere, however, Eliot argues that the body of Shakespeare's work is unified by his personality; "the whole of Shakespeare's work is *one* poem," and everything he wrote is "unified by one significant, consistent, and developing personality" (SE 203; emphasis Eliot's). Eliot is not interested in an individual author's psychological constitution but rather in the role that the author, considered as a structural abstraction, plays in anchoring the text to a coherent set of intentions. Shakespeare is simply an authorizing signature, a term for what Michel Foucault has called the "author function" in the works under his name, a designation for the mind that is presumed to have formed the text and to whom the meanings discovered therein can be attributed.[56] Those whom Eliot ranks at the bottom of the hierarchy of Elizabethan dramatists fail because they lack a consistent vision of life that organizes and animates their oeuvres. Eliot's criticism of John Ford and Philip Massinger is aimed at the lack of a cogent design and, by implication, the lack of the sense of a designer standing behind and authorizing their work as a whole.

On a larger scale, dissemination can infect an entire literary period or genre. Considered as a whole, the body of Elizabethan drama, according to Eliot, tended toward dissipation because of "its lack of conventions." In "Four Elizabethan Dramatists" (1924), Eliot criticizes the "general attitude toward life of the Elizabethans [as] one of anarchism, of dissolution, of decay," a moral errancy in keeping with "their artistic greediness, their desire for every sort of effect together, their unwillingness to accept any limitation and abide by it" (SE 116). The Elizabethans' rejection of formal boundaries for their plays had lasting, pernicious effects on English drama, especially its degeneration into realism.

The great vice of English drama from Kyd to Galsworthy has been that its aim of realism was unlimited . . . [S]ince Kyd . . . there has been no form to arrest . . . the flow of spirit at any particular point before it expands and ends its course in the desert of exact likeness to the reality which is perceived by the most commonplace mind. (*SE* 111)

In short, Eliot argues that the failure to observe formal aesthetic rules has led to the expense of English drama in a waste of shame, that is, in vulgar realism. Unrestrained by external authority, the English dramatist "expands" and spends his "flow," thus ending up in the sterile "desert" of modern drama. The degradation of realist drama is in part the result of what Eliot called, in "The Function of Criticism," "listening to the inner voice," the common possessors of which "ride ten in a compartment to a football match at Swansea" (*SE* 27).

In modern times, perhaps the greatest threat to literature, in Eliot's view, is the relativizing effect of the proliferation of discourses, which erodes belief in the inherent value of literature. Concomitantly, the rise of national or provincial literatures undermines what Eliot saw as the universality of great literature, dispersing the literary field into multiple, heterogeneous, local entities. In his essays from the 1940s and 1950s, collected in *On Poetry and Poets*, Eliot is increasingly preoccupied with the relation between literary discourse and society, particularly within a Western world whose cultural, racial, and epistemological fragmentation deprives poetry of its supposed former capacity for general significance. The modern lack of homogeneity dissipates literary criticism into ancillary pursuits, such as source-hunting or psychobiography, and condemns modern poets to a narrow, limited role.

In his critique of the dissemination of literary value, Eliot's rhetoric relies upon a series of oppositions between the universal and the local, between center and periphery, stasis and flux, solidity and errant wandering, inside and outside, and so forth, all of which are aimed at circumscribing the realm of absolute literary value, free from empirical or historical contingencies. Yet the former is purchased at the price of positing the truly great, unquestionably "classic" text as an inert, transcendental ideal, while the latter takes on a perverse sort of vigor and fecundity, effectively displacing the center from which Eliot tries to exclude it. Like the "true world" in Nietzsche's "History of an Error," Eliot's "true literature" fades into an unattainable, unknowable idea that, even within his own defense of it, loses its power to console or obligate.[57] Eliot's later essays thus assume an elegiac tone, mourning the death of true literature, yet such a literature exists only as a retrospective construction; it lives, so to speak, as a corpse. Hence, Eliot's attempts to define such a literature become involved in regresses, retreating ever farther back into the remote origins of Western literature in search of a stable ideal, and become entangled in the double bind of, on the one hand, the need to specify what true literature is and, on the other hand, the absolute unspecifiability of universally great literature. For every argument that justifies a text as true literature also returns it to the realm of particular, contingent, and disseminating values.

In "The Social Function of Poetry" (1945), Eliot argues that, despite the particular purposes of certain poetic genres, the function of poetry in general is its "value for the people" as a whole. This public aim underlies Eliot's distinction between the "eccentric or mad" poet who "may have feelings that are unique but which cannot be shared" and the "genuine poet" who "discovers new variations of sensibility which can be appropriated by others" (*OPP* 9). The former's perverse preoccupation with his private interests prevents him from serving his greater obligation to the poetic tradition.

A fascinating text for an analysis of textual dissemination is "What Is a Classic?" an essay that, like *After Strange Gods*, affirms cultural homogeneity as the necessary foundation for the classic poet and defends the value of the classic text as a transcendent standard of taste opposing the centrifugal forces of modernity. Yet, apparently against himself, Eliot also argues that the absence of a classic in English is "fortunate" for English poets because the literary possibilities of the language have not been "exhausted" by it. Like humanity's fortunate fall from Edenic grace, the imperfection of English literature leaves open a "future" for the literary potential of the language, and the English poet's lack of a classic predecessor gives him room to exercise his lesser talents. The premises of "What Is a Classic?" comprise Eliot's socioliterary creed: the classic text issues from a "mature society" with a "mature language," whose poets have achieved a "common style" and share with their readers a "community of taste" (*OPP* 56–57). English literature as a whole falls short of such criteria, and even the Elizabethan period was not classic, in Eliot's view, because of its "immaturity," by which he means its lack of "order and stability, of equilibrium and harmony"; instead, it manifested "extremes of individual style" (*OPP* 57). In short, the nonclassic age is given to perverse eccentricities, impure stylistic minglings, and a general dissipation of its poetic energies.

While Eliot praises Dante in passing as "the European classic," his aim in this essay is to establish Virgil as the classic poet, not just as an exemplar of classicism, but as the *only* classic, indeed, as a transcendental ideal of "the classic." Although he lists Virgil's qualifications as the classic poet, including his "maturity of mind," his historical consciousness, and his "finer sense of proportion" (*OPP* 62), and although he grounds Virgil's status in the "classic age" from which he sprang, Eliot's elevation of him is based neither on Virgil's individual qualities as a poet nor on the literary properties of the *Aeneid*, but rather on the supposed necessity for an ideal norm or, in Eliot's idiom, for "the classic." The star to guide our modern wandering bark, "Virgil" is a proper name for what Kant called a "regulative principle."[58] In Eliot's words, "the value of Virgil to us . . . is in providing us with a criterion" (*OPP* 71). At bottom, it does not matter much to Eliot what Virgil did right that every other poet has, in one way or another, done wrong, but that Virgil stands as a marker of absolute and unquestionable literary value. Indeed, his value is precisely that he serves as the sign of *pure* value, not as an instance of any *particular* literary values. Moreover, the presumed fact that successive poets have fallen short of Virgil's mark and that modern languages are incapable of achieving the classic recursively and tautologically confirms Eliot's belief in the transcendental nature of that ideal. "No modern language can hope to produce a classic," Eliot asserts, and the failure of other poets' aspirations confirms his faith that "our classic, the classic of all Europe, is Virgil" (*OPP* 73).

The unapologetic Eurocentrism of Eliot's claims and his unabashed use of the first person plural, assuming that "we" Europeans share his tastes as well as his perceived need for a classic ideal and, further, that "we" thereby tacitly accept his authority, may be so offensive to late twentieth-century readers that the self-subverting aspect of his argument goes unnoticed. Much of Virgil's virtue, for Eliot, lies in his remoteness from English literature. Such distance not only places Virgil beyond comparison with modern poets but also protects the latter from being destroyed by him, as were Virgil's successors. Indeed, Eliot argues, Virgil had a fatal influence on subsequent Latin writers. "Every great work of poetry tends to make impossible the production of equally great works of the same kind," and Virgil, as a "great classic poet, . . . exhaust[ed] not a form only, but the language of his time" (*OPP* 66). In a word, Virgil killed off the literary potential of Latin, leaving it, as it were, dead before its time. Yet the death of the Latin language is precisely what enables it to serve as the vehicle for Virgil as the twentieth-century European literary ideal. The classic standard must come from the dead, from the tomb. To approach the classic, according to Eliot, "it is necessary to go to the two dead languages [Latin and Greek]: it is important that they are dead, because through their death we have come into our inheritance" (*OPP* 70). Furthermore, the deadness of Latin is linked to its other strengths – its homogeneity and prized "common style" – whereas English "tends to variety rather than perfection," and "offers wide scope for legitimate divergencies of style" (*OPP* 68–69). As a heterogeneous, living language, English is condemned to errancy; it cannot achieve Latin's "universality" and "comprehensiveness" (*OPP* 69). The death of Latin both ensures Virgil's canonization as "the standard of the classic" and permits the vagrant freedom of English. "We may be glad that [English] has never completely realized itself in the work of one classic poet; but . . . the classic criterion is of vital importance to us" – important in so far as it is an unrealizable ideal by which "to judge our individual poets" (*OPP* 67). In a word, the demise of Latin enshrines it as the eternal ground of literary value and opens the space of error for English poets, at once authorizing their work as derivative and licensing their failures as an inevitable necessity.

Strictly speaking, Eliot's argument for Virgil as the normative poetic ideal is circular: Virgil is our classic because he is dead, and because he is dead, he is our classic. Or, to put it another way, Virgil is the standard of literary value because he is inherently valuable and, because his value is beyond question, he is the sign or mark of intrinsic literary value. In short, Virgil needs no defense because he *is* the defense of the indisputable value of poetry. "Virgil" is thus, for Eliot, not simply the name of a particular poet but the *citation* of absolute literary value.

Far from being simply a flaw in Eliot's argument, his tautological affirmation of Virgil is its very foundation. Such question-begging, according to Nietzsche, is indispensable to the belief in any absolute truth, for

it is only by means of forgetfulness that man can ever reach the point of fancying himself to possess a "truth" . . . If he will not be satisfied with truth in the form of tautology, that is to say, if he will not be content with empty husks, then he will always exchange truths for illusions.[59]

Eliot's willingness to accept the illusion of Virgil's absolute value thus permits him, according to Nietzsche's logic, to escape the unpleasant prospect of exchanging that "truth" for the recognition that it is only an illusion. Eliot's error is thus quite useful, for, again in Nietzsche's words, "there can be neither society nor culture without untruth . . . Everything which is good and beautiful depends upon illusion: truth kills – it even kills itself (insofar as it realizes that error is its foundation)."[60] Yet Eliot's question begging, however enabling it may be for his belief in absolute literary value under the sign of Virgil, nonetheless has a disseminating effect insofar as it raises the unintended implication that Virgil may be merely one poet among others.

Among the questions that Eliot's essay suggests is, Why Virgil? Why is Homer not the classic ideal, for instance, and why is not the equally dead ancient Greek the language of the classic? For Virgil to stand as "the classic of all Europe," he must be sui generis. Eliot anticipates these questions and argues that "it is through Rome that our parentage in Greece must be traced" (*OPP* 73). His wish to erect a literary norm that possesses "gravity" and imperial power is better served by the *Aeneid* than by the *Odyssey*. Moreover, his ideal of a "common measure of excellence . . . in literature" (*OPP* 73) is best fulfilled by Latin. Eliot was consistently drawn to Latin as a means of escaping what he saw as the provinciality of a particular culture or a national literature. The catholicity of Latin acts as an ideal stay against the babel of modern languages and the proliferation of modern literatures.

In "What Is a Classic?" Eliot praises the *Divine Comedy* as "the classic in a modern European language" (*OPP* 61). Earlier, in the 1929 essay on Dante, he claimed that the latter is "the most *universal* of poets in the modern languages" (*SE* 238; emphasis Eliot's) for three reasons. Unlike the "local self-consciousness" of English, Dante's Italian sprang from "universal Latin" (*SE* 240); moreover, "the culture of Dante was not of one European country but of Europe," which in his time was "united" and in which Dante stood at the "centre" (*SE* 240, 242). Finally, Dante's allegorical method "was common and commonly understood throughout Europe" (*SE* 242), embodying a Christian theology to which Eliot was openly sympathetic. Why, then, does he elevate Virgil and not Dante to the privileged position of "the classic of all Europe"? The answer to the question is not just that Virgil is older and remoter than Dante and that his *Aeneid* is the founding text of an empire; indeed, Eliot's choice has less to do with Virgil's qualifications than with the regressiveness of any attempt to locate a pure origin. The need to specify an absolute, unique source of literary value leads Eliot farther back into the historical depths of Western literature, beyond Dante, to a moment before what he saw as the fall into dispersion of multiple tongues and literatures.

Perhaps another reason for Eliot's preference for Virgil as the dead father of Western literature is the fact of his secure interment, as opposed to Homer's partial resurrection in Joyce's *Ulysses*. In "The

Three Provincialities" (1922), Eliot praises Joyce in terms similar to those with which he later praises Virgil: Joyce has delivered a "death blow" to Irish literature as a local entity by taking "what is racial and national and transmut[ing] it into something of international value," indeed, of "absolute European significance."[61] Joyce has killed off traditional Irish literature – a good thing as far as Eliot is concerned – but he has also killed off certain literary potentialities for Eliot. In one of his "London Letters" to the *Dial* in 1922, Eliot implies that *Ulysses* has nearly destroyed the novel and is certainly an example of what "the intelligent literary aspirant . . . will . . . avoid attempting." For "great works of art do in some way mark . . . an epoch, but less often by the new things which they make possible, than by the old things which they put to an end" – in this case, "the old narrative method." Eliot adds that he "should be sorry to see this [old] type of novel disappear."[62] Moreover, it is possible to read Eliot's essay, "*Ulysses*, Order and Myth," not as a ringing endorsement of Joyce's work but as an appropriation of the "mythic method" for himself, even as an oblique way of distancing himself from Joyce.[63] Eliot's praise of Joyce as an international rather than an Irish writer, and, later, as a Christian writer (*ASG* 52), drafts Joyce into the service of Eliot's vision of a continuous literary tradition.

Eliot typically equates the provincial with the errant. To read a literary text in terms of its social or historical contexts is, in his view, to relativize its literary worth. He attributes such a relativization to a "distortion of values . . . which springs . . . from applying standards acquired within a limited area to the whole of human existence; which confounds the contingent with the essential, the ephemeral with the permanent" (*OPP* 72). Evidently undisturbed by the implication of his own argument that the historical and regional variations of English are the source of its vitality, Eliot maintains his belief in the absolute nature of literary value by claiming to sever it completely from every empirical contingency – which, as Barbara Herrnstein Smith points out, means from everything.[64] His attempt to ground literary value by anchoring it in a transcendental ideal or a truly classic text demands that the classic be uncontaminated by particularities, and hence that sharp boundaries be drawn between this central ideal and all peripheral, vernacular concerns. Yet the maintenance of such an ideal requires the suppression of the particular, local, and even personal interests that elicit such an ideal in the first place. In Eliot's case, his interest in maintaining a homogeneous English literary culture, bound by ties of custom and "blood kinship" and legitimated by an authoritative tradition, directly served his own magisterial power as a poet and critic. Far from acknowledging his stake in the literary and cultural norms advanced by his writings, Eliot's work camouflages it in the guise of universal truths. In this sense, *After Strange Gods*, far from being an embarrassing anomaly in Eliot's corpus, is his quintessential work insofar as it is his most explicit statement of the idea of a proper literary community, governed by orthodox literary and social values.

Much of Eliot's later critical writings strikingly resemble recent arguments in the United States and Great Britain concerning the alleged debasement of literary and cultural values by multiculturalist and post-structuralist critics. The "culture wars" among academic scholars, fueled by Alan Bloom's *The Closing of the American Mind*, as well as popular enthusiasm for films based upon novels by Jane Austen, Henry James, and other canonical writers, demonstrate the renewed appeal of Eliot's defense of a shared cultural tradition. Arguing for the contemporary relevance – and the bivalence – of Eliot's critical views, Bernard Sharratt predicts that Eliot is "ripe" for reappropriation by nationalists and pan-Europeanists alike in our post-postmodern age.[65] That an American born in St. Louis would become this century's most prominent advocate of the idea of a unified European culture is, perhaps, one of history's errant, "cunning passages." Eliot's American origin is often, and mistakenly, understood as implicitly undermining his literary program. C. S. Lewis's complaint that "Eliot stole upon us, a foreigner," to foist the modernism of "denationalized Irishmen and Americans" upon Englishmen, finds its counterpart in those who, like Eric Sigg, refer to his use of American ragtime tunes in his poetry or, like Ronald Bush, cite Eliot's "Emersonian" ideas as antidotes to charges of his snobbery or Eurocentrism.[66] Rather than discrediting his cultural and literary values, Eliot's mixed, even impure personal history – neither a true Midwesterner nor Yankee, transplanted to a foreign country – lends force, if not credence, to his strictures on the errancy of the local.

Eliot's national roots have also been taken as evidence that his thought is indebted or at least congenial to American pragmatism. In his doctoral dissertation, Eliot argued that meaning arises through consensus within a "community," leading to Richard Schusterman's claim that this "practical idealism" is the basis for Eliot's theory of tradition and, later, of a "pluralistic" ideal of culture as a "productive tension" between unity and diversity.[67] However, Schusterman's otherwise cogent analysis of Eliot's philosophical ideas relies upon an untenable split between his religious beliefs and his secular thought; as Schusterman admits, the "pragmatism" of the latter is based upon a notion of "intellectual virtue" or intelligence informed by moral principles (44–45). The racial exclusivity of Eliot's cultural ideal, his calls for obedience to orthodox authority, and his wish for a unified Europe on the order of Maurras's l'Action Française cannot be separated from his ethical high-mindedness. Likewise, Frank Kermode's argument that Eliot admired the idea rather than the reality of empire speciously assumes that the former has no historical or political implications.[68]

Although Eliot believed that "the tradition" was threatened from without by the disseminating effects of proliferating local literatures (what are now termed "special interests"), "What Is a Classic?" demonstrates the errancy at work within the very assertion of a central, absolute literary ideal. Not only must such an ideal be vacuous in order to serve as such, but that ideal's sacred fatality transfers literary energies into the debased, exterior realm, so that his essay inadvertently celebrates the demise of the classic. Apparently against his intentions, Eliot effectively endorses the dissemination of literary value throughout peripheral, vernacular literatures whose vigor stems from their freedom from the dead hand of the classic. Eliot's elevation of Virgil permits a reverse reading in which the absence of a Virgil from English literature has given rise to a host of lively bastards and barbarians.

Eliot's authority as the guardian of the literary values of high modernism is so firmly entrenched that it is all the more worthwhile to notice the ways in which both his criticism and poetry stray from the literary, social, and sexual norms that they are designed to enforce. Eliot's interest for readers at the end of the twentieth century may lie in the manner in which his texts are faithless to the tradition and the values that they explicitly endorse.

# CHAPTER 2

# The end of poetry for ladies: T. S. Eliot's early poetry

There's no man in the world
More bound to's mother.

Shakespeare, Coriolanus

Some dissatisfaction
With myself, I suspect, very deep within myself
Has impelled me all my life to find justification
Not so much to the world – first of all to myself.
What is this self inside us, this silent observer,
Severe and speechless critic, who can terrorise us
And urge us on to futile activity,
And in the end, judge us still more severely
For the errors into which his own reproaches drove us?

Eliot, The Elder Statesman

"T S Eliot ends [the] idea of poetry for ladies," James Joyce wrote in one of his notebooks from the early 1920s.[1] Joyce's private assessment of Eliot's poetry is in keeping with the publicly stated aims of many writers of the period. It is, moreover, in agreement with the generally accepted judgment of Anglo-American high modernism as marking the demise of an increasingly enfeebled Victorian and Georgian poetic tradition.

The pronouncements of such influential figures as Ezra Pound, T. E. Hulme, and Wyndham Lewis make clear that one of the chief aims of the modernist movement, as they defined it, was the restoration of virility to poetry. Despite the variety among and the shifts within the views of individual writers, the rhetoric of modernist polemics often endorsed implicitly masculine aesthetic values.[2] Pound praised "hard" poetry, "as much like granite as it could possibly be," as opposed to "soft" poetry with "mushy technique" and "emotional slither."[3] Hulme's celebrated essay, "Romanticism and Classicism," derided the Romantics' "moaning and whining" and the "dampness" of their poetry in favor of

55

the "dry hardness" of the classical poem. Elsewhere, he complains of "imitative poetry" in which "women whimper and whine of you and I alas, and roses, roses all the way. It becomes the expression of sentimentality rather than of virile thought."[4] Following in their footsteps, Eliot's early criticism extols the qualities of "intense frigidity," "aridity," and "hardness" in poetry as opposed to the "vague" prettiness of Georgian verse.[5] In short, the modernist movement, according to Sandra Gilbert and Susan Gubar, constituted a revolt by male writers against what they saw as the effeminate influence of women writers as well as the prominence of women in the literary marketplace as publishers and patrons.[6]

Making a break with "poetry for ladies," Eliot's poetry also sought to forge a link with a set of poetic forefathers. Carol Christ argues that the literary realm had become "increasingly feminized in the eighteenth and nineteenth centuries,"[7] so that Eliot's attempt to define himself as a male poet meant challenging not only a feminized literary culture but also the "powerful female presence" of Eliot's mother, herself a poet. According to Christ, Eliot "associates the poetic effects of the nineteenth century" with the women whom his poems variously desert, betray, or murder. By contrast, he "cast[s] safely distant" the male "voices of the literary tradition, with whom he wishes unabashedly to identify himself."[8] For Eliot, the task of becoming a poet entailed establishing an authorizing filiation with a series of masculine predecessors, a paternal identification whose intensity Christ underplays.

Through the citations in his poetry, Eliot constructed a self-validating genealogy for himself; by placing himself among the dead, he also made a place for himself among the living. Eliot's internal genealogy – fabricated through the related practices of allusion, citation, and quotation – is a tradition of fathers, and Eliot's position as heir to it depends upon the exclusive authority of masculine literary relations. This exclusivity has been largely preserved in the criticism on modernism; until recently, theories and histories of modernism have focused on male writers, and much of the best current work on Eliot remains preoccupied with his relations to, for instance, Milton, Arnold, Whitman, and Browning. While these are important precursor figures for Eliot, the gender dynamics of Eliot's relations to them have been insufficiently explored. With some exceptions, feminist critics have bypassed the group of Eliot, Pound, and their fellows in favor of women writers of the period.[9] Indeed, for many readers Eliot has become virtually a synecdoche for white male high modernism and its attendant evils.

Eliot's strategy of self-validation was enormously successful – too successful. His achievement in constructing a canonizing genealogy effectively stifled critical investigation of its internal errancy, particularly into the ways that it is troubled by feminine and homosexual alterity. As readers we remain his heirs insofar as, believing in his success, we fail to inquire into the interlocking exclusion of women and of same-sex desire in his work. Yet recent critiques of Eliot's anti-Semitism and his political ideology give hope that it is now possible to examine the divisions within his work. Eliot's strategy of self-legitimation is premised upon the authority of the citation or allusion to establish a proper lineage – in short, to authorize Eliot by asserting his fidelity to his literary ancestors. Yet the citation simultaneously implies theft or misappropriation and, hence, the possibility that the author is a faithless usurper. Not only are citations and allusions inherently duplicitous while apparently dutiful; in Eliot's texts they are also leaky vessels through which emerge, unwittingly, indications of gender and sexual anxiety.

This chapter addresses Eliot's relation to paternal and maternal literary authority, beginning with an analysis of his citational practice, then moving to a discussion of the female figures in his early poems. In the first part, "The Paternal Citation," I argue that Eliot's citations, despite their claim of filiation, performatively construct the heritage to which they adhere. Because citationality in general is the site of the dissemination of signs, Eliot's citations are situated in a series of intertextual networks rather than located as marks of discrete, prior influences. However, to understand Eliot intertextually requires that we also read his insistence upon the relay of literary authority from father to son, so that influence and intertexuality are not mutually exclusive interpretive models. Finally, Eliot's citational practice enacts an erotics of domination and submission in relation to paternal authority. The proliferation of quotations, allusions, and other references in his early poems attests to Eliot's concern that he is unworthy of and cannot achieve the ideal represented by the literary tradition. In a word, the structure of literary relations established by his citational practice is masochistic.

Eliot's early poetry tells a different story, what I call "the maternal intertext." In these poems, powerful, dangerous women dominate male speakers, who in turn try to escape from or kill them. While equally masochistic, the representations of sexual violence in "Hysteria," "Whispers of Immortality," and "Ode" record not only female aggression but also sadistic fantasies of revenge by their male victims and, hence, the ultimate triumph of the father. Eliot's resolution of the problem of maternal authority is highly orthodox. In his personal life, he eventually underwent the sort of spiritual discipline suggested by his early "saint" poems and became, like St. Narcissus, "a dancer to God." However, his faithfulness to patriarchal traditions, in both his poetry and his life, was possible only through the violent abjection of the most powerful single influence upon his work – his mother, Charlotte Stearns Eliot, together with her substitutes, including Vivien Eliot, the other woman who made him suffer. Charlotte Stearns Eliot is the unacknowledged precursor whom all of his early poems, in one way or another, silently cite.

As we saw in the previous chapter, the norms that Eliot asserted in his literary criticism are based upon the rejection of certain errant practices and desires which often return within his own criticism – indeed, which are constitutive of those norms themselves. A similar movement occurs in his early poetry, for Eliot's citations *gesture toward* filiation but stray from any authorizing origin. To take the most obvious example, the perpetual enigma of *The Waste Land* is that its citations, as re-cited in Eliot's notes, refer to its supposed origin in medieval grail legends, and yet no grail appears in the poem, and the best critical efforts have been unable to fit the poem into the form of its declared predecessor. Instead, as Michael Levenson comments, the allusions in *The Waste Land* continually shift their frames of reference, so that the poem as a whole represents Eliot's "inventive" and unfinished "effort to obtain a tradition."[10] Taking Levenson's claim a step farther, I argue that the citations in Eliot's early poetry are engaged in perpetual errancy. His citations have unintended, disseminating effects, first, by virtue of the necessary vagrancy of all citations, which depend upon the contingencies of interpretation in order to be read *as* citations, and, second, by virtue of the circular production of an internal genealogy within his poems through their citations. Like the perverse egotism that Eliot denounces in his criticism, this act of autopoesis renders Eliot the "father" of the fathers to whom his poems refer and defer.

The most interesting form of erring in Eliot's poetry, though, is evident in its sexual dynamics. Similar to the inversion of textual and sexual order that Eliot decries in his criticism yet which serves as a powerful engine of his own writing, Eliot's citations announce his allegiance to a host of literary fathers with whom he identifies and to whose authority he submits. The poet's "continual surrender of himself," as Eliot writes in "Tradition and the Individual Talent," is a surrender to "something which is more valuable" – the literary patrilineage (*SE* 17). The son's submission to his literary fathers enacts a scenario that Freud describes as "moral masochism," in which Eliot's profuse citations represent gestures of love and reparation toward the figure of the father whose power is internalized as an ego-ideal. Yet the authority that Eliot cannot admit in his prose but only reveal in his poetry is that of the mother. Eliot's early poems are driven by what one could call an inversion of sexual and textual authority, in which maternal domination elicits the son's resentful sadism, manifest in the figures of overpowering women, impotent men, and the latter's acts of violence, real or imagined, toward the former. Finally, this sort of sadomasochism, the seamy underside of Eliot's citational testimony to the paternal literary tradition, is common to many modernist texts. Gilbert and Gubar note that, alongside images of "female potency," "images of impotence recur with unnerving frequency in the most canonical male modernist novels and poems," citing as examples Ford's *The Good Soldier*, Lawrence's *Lady Chatterley's Lover*, and Hemingway's *The Sun Also Rises*.[11] However, Eliot's sadomasochism contrasts sharply with Joyce's representation of feminine authority, which openly revels in the pleasures of masochism. Moreover, his abjection of female alterity differs dramatically from Proust's Albertine, whose enigmatic otherness incites the interpretive efforts of the narrator of *Remembrance of Things Past*.

I have chosen to focus on Eliot's early poetry because the intertwined issues of gender and sexual authority are closer to the surface and less resolved there than in his later work, where the sexual dynamic has hardened and Eliot's citational practice changes, reflecting his status as an internationally renowned critic no longer anxious to establish his literary lineage. Eliot's conversion to Anglicanism and his assumption of British citizenship in 1927 along with his abandonment of his wife a few years later were signal decisions that solidified and clarified the ambivalent tendencies in his previous writing. My other reason is personal. Some years ago, as a graduate student, I read Eliot more or less as others of my time – as the priggish tyrant of the canon whose authority was as oppressive as his politics were offensive. Under the obligation to write about him, I unexpectedly stumbled upon "Ode," a poem that Eliot published in *Ara Vos Prec*, his first book of poetry, and subsequently suppressed. The poem was an embarrassment to Eliot, who confessed in a letter to his brother (15 February 1920) that

I have not sent this [*Ara Vos Prec*] to Mother or told her about it. I thought of cutting out the page on which occurs a poem called "Ode" and sending the book as if there had been an error and an extra page put in. . . . The "Ode" is *not* in the edition that Knopf is publishing, all the others are. And I suppose she will have to see that book.[12] (*L* 363; emphasis Eliot's)

I was immediately fascinated by "Ode," an enigmatic, minor poem that opened up for me an entirely new view of Eliot's oeuvre as the site of inadvertent but telling errors.

In a sense, Eliot considered "Ode" as itself a mistake, omitting it from all later editions. It is the only poem that he published which he never collected, Christopher Ricks observes in his notes to "Ode," included as an appendix to *Inventions of the March Hare*, his recently published edition of Eliot's early poems.[13] Moreover, "Ode" appears in a volume whose title page contains a spelling mistake: *vus* was substituted for *vos*. The printer's lapse was in fact due to Eliot's error; he did not know Provençal and mistakenly transcribed the opening phrase from Arnaut Daniel's speech in the *Purgatorio*, canto 26. However, this speech was a favorite of his that he quoted often and that served as a citational touchstone for him. In his 1929 essay on Dante, he offers the following translation: "And so I pray you, by that Virtue which leads you to the topmost of the stair – be mindful in due time of my pain" (*SE* 256). Eliot's parapraxis may be read not only as his wish to conceal the pain that the poems in *Ara Vos Prec* express, as James Loganbach argues,[14] but also – and I think this more likely – as symptomatic of Eliot's divided relation to literary authority and his repression of his aggressivity in that relation.[15]

Eliot's wish to conceal "Ode" from his mother's eyes by pretending that the printer had made an error is particularly interesting because he was very eager to publish his work in order to justify his choice of a poetic vocation to his parents. In a letter (6 January 1919) to John Quinn in New York, who was trying to persuade Knopf to publish a collection of his essays and poems, Eliot wrote:

You see I settled over here in the face of strong family opposition, on the claim that I found the environment more favourable to the production of literature. This book is all I have to show for my claim – it would go toward making my parents contented with conditions – and towards satisfying them that I have not made a mess of my life, as they are inclined to believe. (*L* 266)

His father's death the next day only increased Eliot's urgency to see his work into print. Writing again to Quinn (26 January 1919), Eliot says that "my father has died, but this does not weaken the need for a book at all – it really reinforces it – my mother is still alive" (*L* 269). *Ara Vos Prec* should thus have been the very thing to prove to his mother and his dead father that he had *not* made a mistake with his life, but he could not show it to her – and I have not found evidence from their letters that she ever saw it – because of "Ode," the abjected text in Eliot's poetic oeuvre. The poem is, therefore, the centerpiece of my discussion of Eliot's early poetry because it condenses a number of revealing errors, ranging from the dense opacity of its allusions to Eliot's slip of the pen, and provides an especially charged point of contact between what I am calling the paternal citation and the maternal intertext in Eliot's work.

## THE PATERNAL CITATION

Eliot is well known for his determined, even insistent, allusiveness, for those "fragments" so famously "shored against [his] ruins" – itself a quotation – and for the tone of nostalgic despair they evoke. Eliot self-consciously invoked and memorialized the literary tradition throughout his early poetry. Indeed, "Tradition and the Individual Talent" could not be more explicit on the necessity for the "mature" poet to pay homage to the literary tradition, to set himself "among the dead," and to hold in his consciousness the "ideal order" comprised by "the whole of the literature of Europe from Homer" (*SE* 14). The authority of these textual monuments legitimates the work of the son who aspires to join the ranks of the fathers; moreover, it is the presence of the past that itself animates his work, for "not only the best, but the most individual parts of his work may be those in which the dead poets, his ancestors, assert their immortality most vigorously" (*SE* 14). The wind from the past breathes life into the otherwise dead letter of the present; likewise, the ideal order of these monuments is not a conceptual abstraction for Eliot but a living patrimony that "compels" the poet's deference. In his essay "The Function of Criticism," whose title cites Matthew Arnold, that father of criticism with whom Eliot had an ambivalent relationship, this deference has become a moral obligation, the duty to eschew the antinomian "inner voice" that urges "doing as one likes" (in Arnold's words), and to obey the higher authority embodied in the literary canon. "There is accordingly something outside of the artist to which he owes allegiance, a devotion to which he must surrender and sacrifice himself" (*SE* 24).

However, it is in the heart of this avowal – in the strategy of allusion – that Eliot's claims to authorizing filiation are threatened. For by setting himself among the dead, Eliot likewise erects a mausoleum, a representation of an originary past within the interior of his texts, in the reflection of their citations. Inasmuch as such a representation is nonidentical to itself, the reflexive relationship between the text and its self-proclaimed sources cannot be a faithful mirror. Specifically, the divergence within the genealogical self-representations of Eliot's early poems between the paternal sources that Eliot credits and the maternal intertexts that energize them produces a consistent distortion, a sort of warping of the citational mirror.[16] Perhaps there is no more faithful yet traitorous guardian of that memorial inscription than the citation, the moment in the text when authority is simultaneously asserted and denied.

Citationality, as I use the term here, is a general practice or operation with various specific modes and local effects which include quotations, allusions, direct references, indirect borrowings, scholarly notes, formal imitations, parodies, pastiches, and similar instances of what J. L. Austin has called "parasitic" uses of language.[17] Austin's derogation of cited language (e.g., in poems and plays), as opposed to "serious" or authentically intended, ordinary language, is the occasion for Jacques Derrida's expansion of the concept of citationality in his critique of Austin. According to Derrida, the instances of literary citations that Austin cites are not anomalies but are "modification[s] of a general citationality – or, rather, a general iterability" that is the necessary condition for the legibility of language. "The possibility of disengagement and of citational graft which belongs to the structure of every mark"[18] precludes anything other than a temporary halt to the duplication of signs, a process that is explicit in the quotation but which inhabits all language. Furthermore, the familiar distinctions between quotations, allusions, intertextual references, scholarly annotations, and so forth tend to obscure the issues of authority and iterability that they share; in order to focus on these issues I therefore group them together under the heading of the citation, reverting to the particular terms when necessary to underscore specific aspects of the larger inquiry. Finally, these seemingly self-evident distinctions themselves become problematic in certain cases that do not fit neatly into any category, particularly when it is difficult to assign any authorial intention to the intertextual resonance of (what might be) an allusion.

Taken in this broad sense, the citations in Eliot's early poetry serve a variety of purposes. By appealing to a readership that shares his literary culture, Eliot's citations reinforce the value of that culture as well as validate the literariness of his own poems. Critics as diverse as A. Walton Litz and Harold Bloom agree that Eliot's allusions function to assert the unity of what he believed to be the literary tradition as well as his own place in it, although Litz attributes this strategy to the cultural chaos born of the First World War, whereas Bloom links it to Eliot's defensive anxiety over his belatedness as an American poet.[19] As an act of identification with the authority of the literary tradition, Eliot's citations, even when ironic or juxtaposed to demotic, extraliterary quotations, attest to his claim to inherit paternal power and thus to become the rightful son of his literary forebears. However, this legitimating claim is undermined by its own, internal errancy in three different ways: through the waywardness of citationality in general; through the circular nature of authorial self-justification in citations; and through the psychosexual dynamics of Eliot's desire for and identification with his literary forefathers.

The traditional understanding of citationality is based upon a literary mnemonics in which a later text recalls its source through the citation. Yet the citation operates paradoxically: it anchors the later text by affirming its lineage from the previous text but, because the contexts it opens are indeterminate, the citation is not the end but the endlessly repeated beginning of reading. Moreover, insofar as linguistic signs in general are intelligible only through their reiteration, they constantly engender new contexts in which they may be read, a movement suggested by the etymological link between "iteration" and *iterare*, meaning to journey as errancy.[20] As a consequence, the citation appears, yet inevitably fails, to ground a text because the foundation to which it points is itself implicated in the textual errancy that the citation is supposed to arrest. If citationality is not a return but a wandering, then misinterpretation is a repetition of the error that befalls a text every time it re-cites (and recites) its origins. Finally, Eliot's canonical anchorage is produced not by the fidelity of his citations but by the ongoing efforts of subsequent critics to restrict the boundaries of intelligibility or the sanctioned contexts in which those citations are read.

As its Latin root indicates, the citation is a "summons" (*OED*), calling the reader to appear before the authorities. By repeating the words of another, the citation recalls a secondary yet prior discourse; it is thus caught in the peculiar logic of the requisite but superseded supplement, a logic that is especially evident in the allusion. Considered among the minor tools of the writer's trade, allusions are often taken to be graceful adornments to the body of the text, which, if they get out of hand and interrupt the reader too often, force her to resort to the lowliest of critical aids: the "reader's guide." The annotators who compile such guides typically disavow any intention to interpret but merely attempt to assist the reader by offering information, claiming that their intervention will only bring the reader that much closer to the text. For example, the annotators of Joyce's densely allusive *Ulysses* find themselves in the awkward position of asserting both the necessity and the ultimate irrelevance of the fruit of their enormous labor, which exceeds *Ulysses* in length.[21] To complicate the embarrassment, Fritz Senn points out that "incorrect" annotations of *Ulysses*, such as erroneous translations and spurious interlingual associations, sometimes provide "better" readings of the text.[22] Ezra Pound's annotator, Peter Brooker, echoes the common sentiment when he modestly claims that his notes are "instructive rather than interpretative," and that his guide is "not intended as a substitute for criticism, but as an assistance towards it," a crutch that the maturing student will eventually throw away. Yet this crutch may itself be disabling, and, hence, Brooker is anxious lest his text "intervene too much between the student and the poems themselves," an intervention that on the previous page he describes as "a necessary assistance."[23]

In the preface to Eliot's *Inventions of the March Hare*, Christopher Ricks finds himself in an equally ticklish position. His valuable annotations are more than twice the length of the text of the poems, including their variants. Ricks vows to "abstain" from interpretive annotations, promising to supply only "information" concerning Eliot's sources and repeatedly denying any wish "to use the notes for exegesis, *critical* elucidation, explication, or judgement." Nevertheless, he admits parenthetically that "interpretation, selection, and judgement are inseparable from annotating" (*I* xix–xxvi; emphasis Ricks's). The best intentions of the annotator cannot save him or her from the contradictions built into the traditional concept of the citation, according to which it and its annotator are supposed to efface themselves. Borrowed from another author, citations and allusions should restore the text to its sources. The allusion hallows the text as a memorial to the past that has fathered it and whose authority it invokes. One who alludes is thus an heir to the past evoked by the citation. According to Susan Stewart, "the gesture of allusion is shaped by a nostalgia for the lost event; the object serves only as a souvenir of our knowing. In allusiveness we seek to follow the trace of the event to its origin, an origin which eludes us."[24]

Walter Benjamin's remark that quotations possess "not the strength to preserve but . . . to destroy"[25] suggests the violence that is also at work in citationality, which involves the tearing of at least two texts: the so-called original as well as the secondary text. The task of literary scholarship is thus a sort of perpetual mending in order to maintain – or manufacture – the seamless continuity of the literary tradition. Yet scholarly source-hunting never escapes the appearance of triviality, and the reader who turns to the annotation for a solution to the problem posed by the citation typically finds not the clarity and assurance of a birth certificate but further enigmas. Instead of domesticating and repairing the text, the annotation or scholarly footnote seems to estrange it. To alter the figure, the allusion or citation is the scene of a crime – indeed, of a patricide – but the reader as well as the author is robbed, at least of the illusion of an intact text. For quotations and allusions erupt within a discourse that pretends to be the discourse of the author, introducing a double voice that loosens the text from its moorings in authorial intention and sends it wandering in a textual regression without a certain terminus. As the supplement of a supplement, the quotation or allusion strays from the text, transgressing its purportedly autonomous and self-enclosed structure, not by referring it to another, more authoritative source but by sending it reverberating through the corridors of language.

The echo of allusions is often thought to take on a peculiar resonance, even a hollowness, in Anglo-American modernism, for which Eliot's early poems, especially *The Waste Land*, are representative examples. Thus, John Hollander argues that *The Waste Land's* "heap of broken images contains . . . entire figures broken off, or away from, their bases and backgrounds," so that the "vast allusive apparatus of *The Waste Land*" seems like a "suppression" rather than a "recognition" of the poem's intertextual echoes.[26] A common theme in the criticism of Eliot's poem is the bivalent character of its citations, at once disruptive and cohesive of the continuity of the literary tradition upon which it draws. For instance, Gregory Jay calls Eliot's allusive method a "bricolage" that "transgress[es] the conventions of poetry" but simultaneously "rebuilds" them.[27] More harshly, Maud Ellmann claims that, through his use of allusions, Eliot covertly affirms the literary tradition that he overtly "vandal[izes]" and "desecrates."[28] The notion that Eliot's citational practice faces in two, opposite directions, whether because of his own mixed or disingenuous motives or because of the complexity and conflicts of his historical moment, is now standard. The limitations of this approach are apparent in the reversibility of the opposed pair of terms, unity versus fragmentation, for the one can always be shown secretly to inhabit the other, leading to the conceptual impasse from which much criticism on Eliot suffers. Moreover, such a notion is in keeping with the long-standing and somewhat naive view that quotations, allusions, and the like operate by playing upon the similarity and dissimilarity between the two contexts involved, the old and the new, the tension between them producing a certain bittersweet charm.[29] In many modernist texts, especially Eliot's, this charm assumes a distinctly elegiac tone stemming from the loss of the original context.

Rather than simply memorializing a prior text, the modern citation might be said to inscribe the withdrawal or loss of its origin. Thus, Stewart argues that, in the allusion, "it is . . . the disappearing *event* which is alluded to, tradition made tantalizing by a desire for the [absent] context."[30] In short, the modernist literary allusion refers back not to a past text but to the *pastness* of that text. For these reasons modernism has come to be regarded not only as the literature of the fragment but also, in Jean-François Lyotard's phrase, as "the literature of regret."[31] If quotations, allusions, and various other forms of citation mark the rupture of the literary tradition as well as melancholic elegies of its loss, and if, as Hannah Arendt claims, "the transmissibility of the past [has] been replaced by its citationality,"[32] then citations, rather than adorning the text, have come to structure it. A minor appurtenance of the text, an accessory of its garb, the citation is the organizing principle of the modernist work. According to Lyotard, modernist art is marked by a "nostalgia for presence" in which the unpresentable can only be alluded to or regretfully quoted in another voice as a retreating presence lost in the veils of signification.[33] Nonetheless, such a departed origin is a retrospective fantasy, Eden constructed through a rear-view mirror, which serves principally to justify the glory of postlapsarian ruins in much the way that New Criticism's valorization of irony buttressed claims for aesthetic value.

The retro appeal of the citation rests upon the illusion that, despite its inevitable failure, it could or at least should have been able to convey its signified. However attenuated its link with the original text, the citation still allegedly carries the shadowy memory of that first presentation, the imprint of the absent author. Yet citations are notoriously apt to betray the best – or worst – intentions of the one who cites. Derrida's account of Plato's effort to suppress the vagrant and parricidal effects of writing thus applies to citationality. Although Plato wanted to exclude writing from "living memory," the former returns to the interior of memory because it is constitutive of that which it also threatens. In Derrida's words, "the outside is already *within* the work of memory. The evil slips in within the relation of memory to itself."[34] Likewise, the citation introduces "the outside" – all the supposedly empirical contingencies that befall literary discourse – into its interior. Moreover, as Proust argues in his essays on Ruskin, reading and writing as acts of remembrance inevitably entail forgetfulness and infidelity. Hence, the errancy of the citation frustrates the reader or writer who would comfort himself with alluding even to the event of disappearance. The text-of-origin never disappeared but only appears, and appears as such, within the aureate haze of its vanishing. In other words, the citation projects an apparitional origin.

The waywardness of citationality in general is closely related to the second type of erring: authorial self-justification through the citation. As we saw in the previous chapter, Eliot's determinations of literary and critical rectitude derive from the practices and desires that he rules out of literary discourse. Likewise, the institution of a self-validating ancestry depends upon nothing short of what Eliot repeatedly condemns – the poet's seizure of power. Eliot's gestures of submission to the literary tradition scarcely conceal the fact that he effectively establishes that tradition and himself as its heir through the citations that purportedly derive their authority from it. While deferring to his literary forefathers and voiding his own texts of perverse egotism, the citations in Eliot's poems performatively constitute these forefathers as such and Eliot as their son. Engendering his own progenitors, Eliot deftly veils his usurpation in elaborate displays of surrender. Indeed, the word "tradition" is etymologically intertwined with "traitor"; they share a common root in the Latin term *tradere*, meaning "to hand over, to hand on, to deliver," and, hence, "to traduce or betray."[35] Traditional authority and its traitorous other also have, as it were, a common future for, inasmuch as the literary tradition is passed on through quotations, allusions, and the like, it is consigned to the inadvertent betrayals of the citation.

If citations functioned ideally in Eliot's texts as a means of autopoesis, mutually defining and affirming Eliot as a poet in terms of a literary tradition that is itself defined and affirmed through those citations, Eliot would be free of actual fathers, having become his own father. This is, of course, not the case. One way to pierce the circular structure of Eliot's citational practice is to look at his relations to the father figures in his life and work, and to examine specific moments of citational vagrancy in his poems. By attending to deviations in the citational chain, we can decouple the interlocking lines of authority that support the patriarchal reading of his poetry. The intertextual inadvertencies of his early poetry are especially evident in their psychosexual dynamics. Eliot's citational practice and his relations to paternal authority are isomorphic; both enact an erotics of domination and submission. As a preface to an analysis of the sexual implications of his citational practice, it may be useful to discuss the concepts of influence and intertextuality.

Eliot's use of citations seems to conform to the traditional notion of literary influence. The numerous quotations, allusions, and echoes in his early poetry serve, in the first place, to accredit him as the knowledge-able possessor of a wide range of mostly canonical texts in the European literary tradition. The *Dial*'s review of *The Waste Land* commended his erudition: "Eliot is almost the only young American who is neither ignorant of nor terrified by the classics," for "he knows them and under-stands their relation to the work which went before and came after them."[36] In a 1918 essay defending the work of Ezra Pound, Eliot asserts that Pound's "erudition" is indispensable to his ability to "bring the past to bear upon the present" and roots him firmly within the European literary tradition: "we may confidently assert that a poet ought to be highly educated," for "a large part of any poet's 'inspiration' must come from reading and from his knowledge of [literary] history." Praising Joyce, "another very learned literary artist [who] uses allusions," Eliot likewise validates his own poetic practice on the grounds that it taps the wellsprings of Western literature.[37]

Yet any poet's extensive use of quotations and allusions runs the risk of appearing as a prop to his infirmities and hence as a sign of his crippling dependence upon his sources of influence. In his 1920 "Massinger" essay, Eliot guards against such implications by arguing for the originality of the right kind of poetic borrowing and for the unity of the poem into which such "thefts" are inserted. "Immature poets imitate; mature poets steal," and "a good poet will usually borrow from authors remote in time, or alien in language, or diverse in interest" (*SE* 206). Eliot's distinction between good and bad borrowing has become a commonplace, recited by Harold Bloom in his differentiation between "strong" and "weak" poets and by Hollander in his distinction between "great" and "minor" writers.[38] Apparently taking his own advice, Eliot borrows from poets who are "diverse" and often "remote in time," yet he took pains to erase his debts to nearer, especially nineteenth-century British and American, writers. Eliot's failure or refusal to acknowledge the latter points again to his use of allusion as a means of constructing a literary genealogy within his own poetry. In this sense, his allusions function metalepically, through the diachronic association of figures such that the earlier text (the source of the allusion) seems an echo of the later text. The trope of metalepsis or transumption has been taken up by Bloom under the heading of "apophrades" or "the return of the dead," and used by John Guillory as "the trope of literary history."[39] In each of these cases, the posterior text reconfigures literary history through its retrospective echoings.

The discrepancy between the influences to which Eliot admitted and those that he overlooked or suppressed has given rise to a minor critical industry concerning his denied affiliation with Romantic and American poetry.[40] His critical prose was, in Graham Hough's words, "a strategy for presenting his poetry," a way of creating "a climate" hospitable to his work and providing him with a properly "English poetic ancestry" – especially important for a young, nervous American exile who, as "Prufrock" attests, was sensitive to social humiliation.[41] Eliot's citational practice is thus productive rather than derivative – not an unprecedented phenomenon. According to Jorge Luis Borges, "every writer *creates* his own precursors,"[42] an observation anticipated by Eliot's argument in "Tradition and the Individual Talent" and later used to considerable profit by Bloom against Eliot.[43] The disparity between Eliot's declared origins and the tacit or suppressed influences on his work encourages investigation of alternative genealogies for Eliot.

My purpose, though, is not to demonstrate Eliot's creation of a particular literary heritage for himself but to examine the psychodynamics of his citational practice. The principal referent of Eliot's citations is to the paternity of the literary tradition; understood as a general operation, his citations point not so much to individual precursors as to literary authority itself. Taken collectively, they aim at claiming this authority for himself, yet their profusion suggests the uncertainty of Eliot's claim. Rather than demonstrating his true filiation or producing a simulacrum thereof, Eliot's citational practice is evidence of his literary orphanhood. Moreover, Eliot's frantic testimony to literary influence is an indication of the intertextuality of his early poetry, including Eliot's lack of complete authorial control over his texts.[44]

One of the effects of Eliot's citational practice is to set his own texts and those to which they refer into an intertextual orbit, what Roland Barthes has called "a multidimensional space in which a variety of writings, none of them original, blend and clash."[45] The "stereographic plurality" of Eliot's early poems pulls them in opposing directions. They may be read, in Barthes's terms, either as "works" or as "texts": on the one hand, as filial productions owned and controlled by Eliot, their author–father, whose allusions are objectively traceable to discrete sources, or, on the other hand, as a network of signifiers "woven entirely with citations, references, echoes, [and] cultural languages" that "can be read without the guarantee of its father."[46]

The concept of intertextuality usefully directs attention to the broader cultural presuppositions that impose norms upon literary interpretation. In Eliot's case, these norms have tacitly imposed a heterosexist, masculinist norm upon the reading of his oeuvre. Beyond the specific sources of the literary references in Eliot's texts are what Barthes calls the "anonymous, untraceable, and yet *already read*" citations that constitute his work as an exemplar of literary modernism.[47] Moreover, readers of Eliot's texts are situated by them within this "already read," presumed to share a certain discursive field and hence to grasp the intertexts that render Eliot's text intelligible within the framework of that field.[48] In other words, Eliot's texts presuppose sets of prior texts or pre-texts as well as conventions of reading them – indeed, norms of literariness – which his work both sustains and upon which it relies for its legibility and value.[49] Although sometimes charged with flattening texts into a neutral tissue of citations, the concept of intertextuality enables an analysis of the crossing and clash of intertexts as well as an exploration of the psychodynamics of and within texts – what Jonathan Culler calls the "textual unconscious."[50] In Julia Kristeva's formulation of the concept, drawn from Mikhail Bakhtin, intertextuality refers to "an intersection of textual surfaces" or "a dialogue among several writings," such that "any text is constructed as a mosaic of quotations; any text is the absorption and transformation of another."[51] This textual process is ideologically productive, for what she calls the "ideologeme" is the point of contact between a text and all the other texts that it integrates or refers to, thus coordinating the text's historical and social dimensions on a variety of levels.[52]

Within the general heading of intertextuality, the application of Lacan's notion of transference to the scene of reading is of greater value for my purposes. As Shoshana Felman and Barbara Johnson have argued, the act of reading is always to some extent transferential, for to read a text is not simply to be situated within it by its presuppositions but also to take an active role within it, typically through identification.[53] Because the interpretation of a text repeats on the level of reading the psychodynamics internal to it, the inside/outside boundaries of the text cannot be strictly maintained; moreover, the psychosexual issues played out in the text are reiterated and inflected by the critics who confront it. Such a model of intertextuality provides a way of understanding the usual response of critics, who are customarily male, to the pathos of male heterosexuality, the structure of male sadomasochism, and the scenes of male victimization at the hands of rapacious females represented in Eliot's early poetry. In short, these poems involve their readers in a nexus of gender and sexual identifications and desires.

Eliot's early poetry is a site of conflict between the centripetal and centrifugal forces of citationality, between his claims to authority through those citations and their inadvertently disseminating effects, and, finally, between the conceptual models of influence and intertextuality. In one sense, theories of intertextuality offer more useful paradigms with which to interpret Eliot's profuse citationality. Instead of assuming that the numerous quotations and allusions in Eliot's poems are indications of influence and, hence, that quotations are property owned by an author, taken over by another, and discovered by the critic, Eliot's literary references are, in Barthes's phrase, "a tissue of quotations" within the broader realm of endlessly transferable citations.[54] However, to read Eliot intertextually also requires that we come to terms with his identification with and desire for the father. Contrary to Bloom's model of "the anxiety of influence," it requires us to understand rather than to dismiss Eliot's insistence upon the relay or influx of paternal authority through the citation as well as the ways in which that authority has been passed on, in turn, by his critics. In this sense, the interpretive paradigms of influence and intertextuality need to be read across rather than against each other.

A word of caution is due here. "The paternal citation," as I am using the phrase, does not refer simply to relations of influence, nor does "the maternal intertext" juxtapose the model of intertextual relations against that of influence. Eliot's paternal relations, mediated textually through citations, are generated by and manifest desires and felt obligations that may be psychoanalytically described as masochistic, although Eliot characterized them in the Christian idiom of morality, guilt, and spiritual discipline. This religio-sexual dynamic appears in a somewhat different version in the gender relations depicted in his early poems. I use the term "maternal intertext" as the general heading for these representations because Eliot's relation to female authority, including the power of female sexuality, is not mediated through citations but is portrayed in various, often occluded ways within his poems. Moreover, these poems point back to Eliot's relationship with his mother and his wife, whose roles in Eliot's poetry are crucial yet obscure. Reading the suppressed intertexts of Eliot's early poetry allows us to explore decisive personal and cultural (the "already read") forces at play in Eliot's text, specifically, the nexus of gynophobic and homoerotic energies that coincides ambivalently with his revealed intentions.

Along with the waywardness of citations in general and their specific use as a means of authorial self-justification in Eliot's poetry, the third way in which Eliot's citational practice is errant concerns the same-sex and, in particular, the father–son relations that his citations enact. Sandra Gilbert and Susan Gubar noted several years ago that models of authorship and the transmission of literary authority take for granted that authors and the relations among them are exclusively masculine. This is certainly true in Eliot's case. Not only do his citations refer virtually without exception to male writers, but the readership that these citations assume and help to constitute is also presumptively masculine. While this situation is not unprecedented, it does suggest that what Maud Ellmann has called Eliot's "compulsion to citation"[55] is rooted in the homosocial relations instituted and confirmed by those citations. Although seemingly marking the smooth transfer of the poetic mantle from father to son, citations are instead the site of what were for Eliot disturbing desires and frustrated identifications. These desires and identifications took the shape of an erotics of same-sex domination and submission that is enacted in Eliot's citational practice, thematized in the religious forms of discipline to which he subscribed, and represented in scenes of sadomasochism in his early poetry. Moreover, Eliot's desire for and identification with male authority partially accounts for the violent abjection of women so evident in his work up to and including *The Waste Land*. Eliot's citational practice and his displaced representation of female literary and sexual power are "erring" insofar as they stray from his stated intentions as well as from their reinstatement in the canons of literary criticism.

Literary relations between men are usually figured in terms of money rather than sexuality.[56] In the traditional model of influence, literary borrowings are the sign of indebtedness, although it may be turned to profit and the allusiveness of a text thereby accounted among its riches. By such reckoning, *The Waste Land* possesses, in F. R. Leavis's words, "a wealth of literary borrowings."[57] Its "rich allusiveness" is by now a cliché,[58] to which Peter Middleton gives a sardonic twist with his remark that *The Waste Land* is "a bank statement of [Eliot's] literary investments."[59] The calculation of the gain and loss of citationality is customarily believed to depend upon what the poet who cites does with the borrowed text. In this matter, Eliot's assessment of the act of quoting as a disreputable financial transaction has become, through countless reiterations, a mark of literary value:

Immature poets imitate; mature poets steal; bad poets deface what they take, and good poets make it into something better, or at least something different. The good poet welds this theft into a whole of feeling which is unique . . .; the bad poet throws it into something which has no cohesion. (*SE* 206)

The application of Eliot's judgment to his poetry has been subject to much debate. His own literary borrowings sometimes seem more like those of Donne, who, according to Eliot, "merely picked up, like a magpie, various shining fragments of ideas as they struck his eye, and stuck them about here and there in his verse," which is consequently "a vast jumble of incoherent erudition on which he drew for purely poetic effects" (*SE* 138–39). Whether Eliot's "shining fragments" are better assimilated than those of Donne is of less importance here, though, than his rhetoric of evaluation in which the cited text is a piece of property, if only a tawdry trinket.

The capital upon which literary citations borrow may be considered as a kind of literary semen, the sign as well as the embodiment of authorial potency. If the pen is a metaphorical penis, and if the product of that pen is figuratively semen, then the relation between the original poet and the one who steals, borrows, appropriates, or otherwise makes the former's text his own is engaged with homoerotic desires and conflicts. Moreover, the transmission of literary influence to which the citation attests, even if it also signifies the later poet's resistance to that influence, implies the infusion of phallic power. The word "influence" comes from the medieval Latin term *influentia*, meaning "to flow into," including "the supposed flowing or streaming from the stars or heavens of an etherial fluid acting on the character and destiny of men." In modern English usage, the term retains an echo of the older sense of a kind of astral semen, as "the exercise of personal power by human beings, figured as something of the same nature as astral influence . . . The inflowing immission or infusion (into a person or thing) of any kind of divine, spiritual, moral, immaterial, or secret power or principle" (*OED*). Even as thefts, Eliot's quotations and allusions testify to the paternal power that flows through them, and his pilferage of the European literary tradition bears witness to the seminal force that infuses them. The homoerotic implications of such an infusion between male writers has, however, escaped the notice even of critics, such as Bloom, who are otherwise attentive to the sexual aspects of influence.[60]

Despite Eliot's oft-quoted comments on poetic theft, his usual view of literary relations, both in theory and in practice, is far more benign and openly filial, as stated in "Tradition and the Individual Talent," for instance, and in keeping with the older notion of influence as evident in its etymology. Indeed, this premodern and prepsychoanalytic concept of influence as the relay of authority from the older to the younger poet through the emission of spiritual semen is, in a sense, free of the virulent homophobia that, since the emergence of sexology around the turn of the century, has characterized male bonds, literary or otherwise. Eliot imagined his relations to those poets who inspired him in his youth in explicitly erotic terms, apparently protected from homophobic anxiety because they were idealized. Yet his literary bonds were exclusively with other men, both the paternal authorities he accepted and those whom he rejected or suppressed. His relation to his immediate tutor, Ezra Pound, was, at least in Pound's view, charged with same-sex energies.[61]

The reader of Eliot's early poems is addressed as another man. Eliot's critics – mostly men themselves – have in general responded sympathetically to his solicitation of the reader as "mon semblable, – mon frère," as Eliot quotes from Baudelaire. By contrast, the woman reader finds little place for an identification with Eliot's speakers, for there are few female doubles or subject positions in his poetry. Steve Ellis admits that *The Waste Land* "envisages its readership as primarily male, and . . . where we can posit an addressee it is gendered," for instance, in the evocation of "Phlebas, who was once handsome and tall as you" – an admission that leaves women distinctly unauthorized or "non-implied" readers.[62] Yet their exclusion from Eliot's homosocial poetry unintentionally allows female readers insight into its errant workings. Thus, Christine Froula reads *The Waste Land* as "the product of a *failed* female identification, one that [Eliot] could neither fully live . . . nor abandon."[63] Indeed, one of the larger aims of this study is to make it possible for women (and feminist men) to read Eliot's work with empathetic understanding.

While Eliot's citational practice establishes an orthodox relationship to literary authority, modeled upon the traditional concept of the penetrating effects of the older poet's influence, this practice seems motivated by a psychodynamic that, for Eliot, was distinctly deviant. Far from expressing a secret wish to kill off the true fathers, whom he refuses to cite, and disingenuously claiming foster fathers, Eliot's citations demonstrate his wish to be like his literary forebears, behind which stands his wish to be loved by the father. In other words, contrary to Bloom's model, based upon the positive oedipal complex, I argue for a "negative" oedipal configuration in Eliot's poetry, one in which the father is the object of love. Most critics who read Eliot psychoanalytically adopt

Bloom's premises. For instance, Gregory Jay claims that, in Eliot's "implicitly homoerotic relation to the father-lover-author, poetic narcissism fulfills itself by transference onto the father figure," a move that he mistakenly sees as a "regression."[64] By contrast, Eliot identified himself with his chosen literary patriarchs, internalized them as ideals, and wanted to accede to their ranks, yet he was painfully aware of his failure to achieve this goal. In Ronald Bush's view, he suffered from "a perpetual feeling of unworthiness – a sense of inadequacy attendant on a life of self-examination."[65] In psychoanalytic terms, Eliot was caught in the double bind of masochism, enjoined to live up to the paternal standard but believing himself unable to do so.

According to Freud, the masochist is trapped by the conflicting demands of his conscience or the superego who commands, "You *ought to be* like this (like your father)," and "You *may not be* like this (like your father) – that is, you may not do all that he does; some things are his prerogative."[66] The power of the superego derives from the subject's introjection both of the idealized image of his father and of the symbolic authority of paternity, what Jacques Lacan calls the "Law of the Father." At bottom, though, the cruel demands of the superego are always, Freud argues, "a substitute for a longing for the father."[67] In other words, the strength and even the sadism of the masochist's conscience stem from his having all too successfully incorporated not only the ideal that his father represents – hence, the injunction to "be like" him – but also the crushing weight of the father's power. The result is what Freud calls the "moral masochist's" excessively rigorous conscience as well as an unconscious sense of guilt and need for punishment.[68] Despite his antipathy to psychoanalysis, Eliot eloquently describes the masochist's dilemma. In his last play, *The Elder Statesman*, Eliot puts into the mouth of Lord Claverton, the eponymous statesman, words that could have come out of his own:

> Some dissatisfaction
> With myself, I suspect, very deep within myself
> Has impelled me all my life to find justification
> Not so much to the world – first of all to myself.
> What is this self inside us, this silent observer,
> Severe and speechless critic, who can terrorise us
> And urge us on to futile activity,
> And in the end, judge us still more severely
> For all the errors into which his own reproaches drove us?

> (*CPP* 545)

The psychodynamics of Eliot's citational practice enact a relation to literary authority similar to Eliot's personal relationship to his own father, Henry Ware Eliot, Sr., to his grandfather, William Greenleaf Eliot, and to his familial heritage as a whole. Late in life, in a lecture delivered upon his return to St. Louis, Eliot testified to the burden of paternal authority in his description of his grandfather, who set "the standard of conduct" for the family, even from beyond the grave. The family's "moral judgments," according to Eliot, "were taken as if, like Moses, he had brought down the tables of the Law, any deviation from which would be sinful" (*CC* 44). Eliot's father was equally rigorous, disapproving of his son's marriage and poetic vocation and believing on his deathbed that Tom had ruined his life.[69] More broadly, Eliot's relation to the paternal literary tradition is patterned upon his relation to his family tradition. Eliot's outspoken rejection of his grandfather's Emersonian Unitarianism constituted a throwback to his Puritan New England forefathers. Similarly, his adoption of English citizenship, his conversion to the Anglican church, and his espousal of an openly English ethnocentrism in *After Strange Gods* are expressions of a paternal identification reaching beyond his actual father.

These gestures of identification were accompanied by an enthusiasm for political order and religious asceticism. Eliot's well-known public assertion that he was a "classicist in literature, [a] royalist in politics, and [an] anglo-catholic in religion" has its corollary in his private, devotional life.[70] According to Lyndall Gordon, "all of his adult life he had been haunted by a sense of guilt – most frequently . . . sexual guilt," which found "relief" upon his conversion by his adoption of a program of spiritual discipline, as though he were eager to be punished.[71] The erotics of this religious experience of domination and submission were evident as early as 1914, when Eliot was preoccupied with studying the lives of saints and wrote "The Love Song of Saint Sebastian" and "The Death of Saint Narcissus" in which he associates asceticism and sensuality, devotion and punishment. "I am one whom this sense of the void tends to drive towards asceticism or sensuality," he wrote privately to Paul Elmer More, while in a 1928 essay he aligns these twin impulses, commenting that the eroticism of Richard Crashaw's religious devotion was "partly a substitute for human passion."[72] Both his personal life and his poetic work are strongly marked by identificatory desire for the father's love and approval; tormented by his sense of failure and guilt, Eliot found satisfaction as a Christian through pain and self-denial, and, as a poet, through citational gestures of reparation and penitential humility.

The other face of masochism is sadism. Throughout his early poetry Eliot typically depicts women as threatening figures who torment and castrate men. The female-dominated literary salon of "The Love Song of J. Alfred Prufrock," for instance, was modeled after that of Adeleine Moffat, a Boston grande dame, which Eliot attended.[73] In psychoanalytic terms, the powerful females who populate these poems and who dominated his early personal life play the part of the phallic mother. Endowed with the virility and power of the father, Eliot's women are the ones who, figuratively speaking, administer the beatings suffered by his masochistic heroes. According to Freud, the prototypical male masochistic fantasy is one of being beaten by the mother, yet behind this fantasy is another, displaced fantasy in which the son is beaten by the father. The mother is simply a stand-in for the father, meant to screen the son from the ultimate wish expressed by the fantasy: that the son is loved by the father.[74] The beating-fantasy, in Freud's view, originates in the son's homosexual desire for the father.

The displacements and aggressions at work in sadomasochism are evident in "The Love Song of Saint Sebastian" (*I* 78), which opens with a scene of flagellation:

> I would flog myself until I bled,
> And after hour on hour of prayer
> And torture and delight
> Until my blood should ring the lamp
> And glisten in the light;
> I should arise your neophyte
>
> (lines 4–9)

The climax of the speaker's devotion to the woman is her strangulation: "I should love you the more because I had mangled you." That the veiled target of his "love" is, in fact, masculine is implied by the homoerotic subtext of the poem, of which Eliot was aware. Enclosing the poem in a letter to Aiken, he wrote, "I have studied S. Sebastians – why would anyone paint a beautiful youth and stick him full of pins (or arrows) unless he felt a little as the hero of my verse? Only there's nothing homosexual about this" (*L* 58). Although no arrows appear in this poem, there are plenty in its companion piece, "The Death of Saint Narcissus," where the male speaker images himself as a "young girl" raped by "a drunken old man." The sexual climax of the concluding lines confirms the link, in Eliot's work, between masochism and homosexual desire:

Because his flesh was in love with the burning arrows
He danced on the hot sand
Until the arrows came.                                    (lines 33–36)

If the object of love in "Saint Narcissus" is male, the object of aggression in almost all of Eliot's poetry is female, the mother having assumed, as it were, paternal authority. Indeed, in his "saint" poems Eliot followed the example of his mother, who was fond of writing about the devotional passion of saints and martyrs.[75]

It is thus unsurprising that the representations of female domination in Eliot's early poetry quickly reverse into fantasies of sadistic revenge. His poems up to and including *The Waste Land* resentfully record maternal triumph at the expense of the son. Eliot tried to resolve the problem of female authority by splitting women into venerated, Beatrice-like figures or degraded bitches and slatterns. His religious asceticism transformed the powerful woman into "Ash Wednesday's" remote "Lady of silences," whose "three white leopards" have "fed to satiety / On my legs my heart my liver." When these blanched bones later speak affirmatively, in *Four Quartets*, the dominating woman is eliminated completely.

What I have described as the paternal citation therefore intersects with the powerful but abjected other of Eliot's early poems – the maternal intertext. Eliot's citational strategy, although subject to the errancy of citations in general, effectively produces his status as a poet through textual gestures of filiation – acts of homage and reparation toward paternal authority. His poems thus enact an erotics of domination and submission between father and son, or between the poetic forefathers and the young poet who would be their heir. Yet disrupting this imaginary communion is the female figure who also mediates it, the spectral woman who troubles so many of Eliot's early poems yet whom they can never finally kill off – the maternal intertext.

## THE MATERNAL INTERTEXT

Eliot's early poetry represents an attack on female authority both personally, as an assault upon the power wielded by his mother and subsequently represented by women in general, and historically, as an assault upon female social, sexual, and literary potency. Maternal authority looms large in his early work, manifested in the depictions of powerful older women in "Portrait of a Lady" and *The Waste Land*, in the degraded but dynamic figure of Grishkin in "Whispers of Immortality," in allusions to *Coriolanus*, and, finally, in Lady Monchensey, the deadly and dying matriarch of *The Family Reunion*. Eliot's early work participates in the reaction of early twentieth-century male modernist writers against what they viewed as the feminization of Victorian literary culture as well as against the incursions of the feminist New Woman. To complicate matters, Eliot's assault on maternal authority is ambivalently combined with an elevated, idealized love for the mother.

Because Eliot saw his poetry as part of a masculine tradition and himself as its heir, female literary authority was a debilitating threat. The maternal intertexts in his work reveal Eliot's inability to overcome female power or to acknowledge it except negatively, through fantasies of revenge, murder, and other forms of abjection. Feminine literary and sexual energies are invariably an errant other in Eliot's oeuvre, excluded from his prose writings but everywhere apparent in his early poetry. Eliot wanted to establish exclusively masculine lines of authority from father to son, but in his poems and plays he wrote incessantly of dead or incapacitated fathers and of phallic women whose power he could neither master nor admit. In this sense, Eliot's poetry is itself erring, straying from his apparent intentions and attesting to a power that he disavowed.

The crucial figure in Eliot's early poetic and personal life was his mother, Charlotte Stearns Eliot, who in many respects assumed the mantle of paternal authority in her family. She revered and wrote a biography of her father-in-law, William Greenleaf Eliot, dedicating it to her children "Lest They Forget,"[76] thus carrying on the family's patriarchal tradition. By contrast, Eliot's father was a distant figure in his son's life and was deaf at the time of his birth.[77] The infirmity of Henry Ware Eliot, Sr., isolated him from his son and contributed to his eclipse by maternal authority; he is the prototype of the dead, absent, or incapacitated father who appears frequently in Eliot's work. By all accounts, Charlotte Stearns Eliot played the dominant role in the childhood of her youngest son. She was the author of religious poetry and a historical verse drama, *Savonarola*, which Eliot later published and which bears some parallels to his own work. Moreover, she projected her literary ambitions onto her son. In a letter to Eliot written when he went to college (3 April 1910), she remarks that "I hope in your literary work you will receive early the recognition I strove for but failed" (*L* 13). Mrs. Eliot was not known for her failures, though, and was a prominent member of the literary salons and clubs that her son satirized in "Prufrock" and that he disparaged in a letter to Pound complaining of "the feminization of modern society" (*L* 96).

Charlotte Eliot was preoccupied with upholding the family's English heritage. For instance, in a letter to Bertrand Russell, she mentions that she "is glad all of our ancestors are English with a French ancestry far back on one line," and she sent Russell a copy of her biography of the family patriarch. Perhaps wishing to impress Russell further with the family's legitimacy, she writes that she is "sending Tom a copy of a letter written by his Great-great-grandfather in 1811, giving an account of his grandfather . . . who was born about 1676 – in the county of Devon, England – Christopher Pearse" (L 138–39). Her gesture is strikingly reminiscent of her son's habit of quoting literary authorities. Mrs. Eliot's correspondence with Russell has the tone of a father-to-father chat concerning Tom's well-being.[78]

It appears that Mrs. Eliot not only recorded and upheld the family's patriarchal legacy but also assumed the role of the father in relation to her son. In Lacanian terms, her maternal control was invested with symbolic paternal authority, or the Law of the Father. The effects of the phallicization of the mother are far-reaching in Eliot's texts and an understanding of them provides biographical depth to the radical dichotomy between, on the one hand, Eliot's identification with an exclusively masculine literary authority and, on the other hand, his poetic and dramatic depictions of powerful and dangerous women. While Lyndall Gordon claims that Eliot "accepted his mother's domination in good humour" and Peter Ackroyd stresses that Eliot "was genuinely devoted to his mother," his love for his mother coexisted with thinly veiled hostility toward female power.[79]

In a 1931 review of John Middleton Murry's psychobiography of D. H. Lawrence, Eliot notes that Lawrence suffered from "a 'mother complex.'" Although Eliot does not explain what he means by the phrase, he argues that Lawrence's way of dealing with the problem is "a sign of the times," against which he inveighs.[80] In his view, the proper way of coping with a such a complex is through "Christian discipline and asceticism" (774). Murry's book touched a sensitive nerve in Eliot; it gave him "the creeps" and left him "shudder[ing]" at the prospect of what future critics might do to him (769). Yet Eliot subsequently advised his students that Lawrence's *Phantasia of the Unconscious*, which explores the destructive effects of an idealized love of the mother upon her son, demonstrates insight into "mother love."[81]

Eliot's response to Lawrence, whom in this review and elsewhere he calls "a very sick soul" (772; *ASG* 66), reveals the complexity and centrality of his relationship to his mother and of the mother–son bond as it figures in his early poetry. The love for the mother produces a divergence in Eliot's representations of women into virgins and whores, into exalted images of divine women whose apotheosis is Dante's Beatrice, and into depraved, carnal women whose nadir is Fresca in the drafts of *The Waste Land*. Such a split in a man's understanding of women, according to Freud, typically issues in psychical impotence, for such a man can only love a woman for whom he has no desire, and he can only desire one whom he cannot love.[82] Yet Eliot's admission of his sense of "the sexual act as evil" (*SE* 429) gave religious justification and a certain masochistic pleasure to the thought of the baseness of his desires. Moreover, his belief in the sinfulness of sexual relations sanctioned sadistic violence against women, for, in Sweeney's words from "Fragment of an Agon," "Any man has to, needs to, wants to / Once in a lifetime, do a girl in." This dehiscence between elevated and degraded women at once veils and exposes the aggression toward maternal authority that underlies it.

The misogyny of Eliot's early poems, far from being an unfortunate exception or a vulgar flaw, was productive and enabling for him. As Anthony Julius has argued concerning his anti-Semitism, Eliot's animus against women was a motivating force in his writing. Donald Hall puts the matter in starkly personal terms, "Eliot married Vivien in order to be impotent, to suffer, and to write poems."[83] Not merely a transcription of his tortured private life, Eliot's poetic representations of strong women triumphing over male victims, who retaliate through dreams of revenge or withdraw into protective and resentful asceticism, served as an empowering and artistically fructive fantasy. In brief, the feminine "other" that his poems continually abject are interior to their imaginative structure. More broadly, as Eliot acknowledged in his review of Murry's book on Lawrence, the problem of female power lies at the core of modernist literature. Eliot was not alone in recording fatal mothers and dead or incapacitated fathers as well as in being uneasy that, even as he authorized himself by affiliating with literary fathers, he was somehow unmanned by his "feminine" position.

Regarding Baudelaire's "vituperations of the female," Eliot remarked in his 1930 essay on the French writer that

[h]e has arrived at the perception that a woman must be to some extent a symbol; he did not arrive at the point of harmonizing his experience with his ideal needs. The complement, and the correction to the *Journaux Intimes*, so far as they deal with the relations of man and woman, is the *Vita Nuova*, and the *Divine Comedy*. (*SE* 430)

Yet Eliot could just as easily have been speaking of his own experience and of the representation of women in his work, for his early poems are pervaded by an obsession with supposed female corruption and with the women's bodies as sites of entrapment and pollution. These traditional figures of female depravity are subsequently exchanged for the opposed trope of the virginal Lady in "Ash Wednesday," a figure that Eliot no doubt thought a "complement" and "correction" to his earlier, misogynistic representations. However, this later, beatific figure of the feminine remains a supplementary inscription within a discourse motivated by a fear and loathing of women, for "the lady up there" is simply the reverse of "the lady down there," as Eliot juxtaposed the idealized and reviled representations of women in Italian Renaissance literature (*V* 115).

Three poems from the 1910s, "Hysteria," "Whispers of Immortality," and "Ode," manifest these fears of female carnality and sexual appetency especially clearly. Among the most neglected poems in Eliot's corpus, "Hysteria" and "Ode" are linked by the fact that Eliot chose to substitute the former for the latter in the 1920 American edition of *Poems*. The better known but narrowly interpreted "Whispers of Immortality" elaborates the motifs articulated in the other poems, responding to the threat of female sexuality by envisioning women's bodies as reified objects and sexual desire as necrophilic.

## "HYSTERIA"

The prose poem "Hysteria" (1915) represents a man confronted by a laughing woman who feels as though he is being engorged or sucked in by her laughter: "As she laughed I was aware of becoming involved in her laughter and being part of it." Neither is the alarmed man sharing her laughter nor is he its object; rather, her laughter is inexplicable, apparently unmotivated, and disturbingly uncontrollable, whose effect is to overpower or "inhale" him. The poem's title announces what is evident in its first few lines: the woman is hysterical. Thus, the text initially contrasts a mad woman and a sane man, who is silently horrified by her behavior, which violates social decorum and implies both her insanity and carnality. The scene sketched out in "Hysteria" closely resembles the many social occasions in which Eliot was embarrassed and infuriated by Vivien's loud, vulgar displays of emotion in public. John Mayer observes that "the situation seems a synecdoche for the course of the marriage" between them, and that Eliot responded to his wife's public outbursts by a "determined . . . suppression of Vivien's personality. Eliot gained control, but at an increasing psychic cost to Vivien. Photographs of her taken over the course of the marriage offer painful witness to the literal *consumption* of her self."[84] Vivien's physical diminution points to a reversal of power between female and male, or, in the tropology of "Hysteria," between consumer and consumed.

The menace of the woman's body is clear at the end of the first sentence when her laughter causes her to bare her teeth, described in an odd conjunction of military and sidereal metaphors as "accidental stars with a talent for squad-drill." The *vagina dentata* revealed by her laughter is the terrifying center of the poem. Her brutal mouth devours the male speaker: "I was drawn in by short gasps, inhaled at each momentary recovery, lost finally in the dark caverns of her throat, bruised by the ripple of unseen muscles." Unmistakably identified with the womb, the woman's mouth is a "dark cavern" with teeth that, like the Medusa's head, possesses the power to castrate. The link between the mouth and the uterus is overdetermined by the poem's title, "hysteria" deriving from the Greek word for womb, *hystera*.

A number of critics have noticed that the speaker of the poem, while describing the woman's hysteria, unwittingly exposes his own. His dread of the woman's flesh, his sense of fragmentation, and his calculating attempt to subdue her lead Grover Smith to the blunt conclusion that "[i]t is he, not the lady, who is hysterical."[85] The woman's consuming gullet in fact discloses the man's terror of becoming "involved" in her body; in short, he fears dissolution by his engulfment in feminine flesh. According to Tony Pinkney, the speaker's fixation on her mouth and breasts recalls the infant's primitive, "oral relation to the breast," a stage in which he believes himself to be one with the mother.[86] In his Kleinian reading, Eliot's "Hysteria" is an ambivalent fantasy of fusion with the maternal body for whom the laughing, powerful woman is a substitute.

Despite the usefulness of Pinkney's interpretation, it does not fully explain the speaker's sense of the aggressive, deadly force of the woman's laughter. Her laughter is a sign of her sexual agency or, in Eliot's understanding if not his terminology, of her phallicism. She is thus like the priapic Mr. Apollinax, whose laughter is also an indication of his potency. Modeled upon Bertrand Russell with whom Vivien had a brief affair during 1915, shortly after her marriage to Eliot, Mr. Apollinax is a lecherous, Sweeney-like figure of virility. Moreover, his "submarine and profound" laughter resonates in "Ode," where "subterrene laughter" mocks the male speaker who suffers from sexual and poetic impotence. These three poems elaborate a pattern that runs throughout Eliot's early poetry in which phallic types (both male and female) are juxtaposed to Prufrockian characters who are the shy, resentful, and somewhat effeminate victims of the former. Characteristically, the speaker in "Mr. Apollinax" thinks of "the worried bodies of drowned men" and vindictively entertains the fantasy of "the head of Mr. Apollinax rolling under a chair." His imaginary decapitation would, so to speak, cut this professor down to size (Russell was a visiting professor at Harvard in 1914, when Eliot was his pupil), and it returns us to the intertwined figures of the Medusa's head, the castrating *vagina dentata*, and hysteria.

What makes "Hysteria" especially important for the present study is that the engulfing mouth of the laughing woman serves as a weapon; her oral aggressivity is the mark of her overwhelming sexual energy. In keeping with Eliot's poem, Jacques Lacan luridly describes the female mouth as "the primitive . . . abyss . . . from which all life emerges, this gulf . . . in which everything is swallowed up, no less the image of death in which everything comes to its end."[87] The reversal of feminine interiority versus masculine exteriority effected by "Hysteria," in which the womb becomes a symbolic phallus, is repeated in other early poems, including "Whispers of Immortality" and "Ode." In all of these cases, the penetrated becomes the penetrator, and the eviscerated becomes the eviscerater. These poems also recount the often ineffectual vengeance of their male protagonists upon the women who dominate them. The story of Eliot's career and that of many men in his generation of modernists may be understood as a confrontation with female sexual agency, for masculine authority seemed to have become as enfeebled and effeminate as the old waiter of "Hysteria."

At the moment when the speaker of the poem feels as though he is about to be swallowed by the laughing woman, an "elderly waiter" intervenes, attempting to appease her by "hurriedly spreading" a tablecloth and inviting the couple to "take their tea in the garden." Like the frightened speaker who tries to control the situation by asserting social conventions, the old waiter is pathetic; his hands tremble, and his insistent, repeated request – "if the lady and gentleman wish to take their tea in the garden, if the lady and gentleman wish to take their tea in the garden" – expresses the speaker's own desperation and sense of helplessness. The waiter's stutter resembles the symptom of one of Freud's hysterical patients, Frau Emmy von N., and linguistic disorders were, he thought, a sign of hysteria.[88] Moreover, the elaborate and obsessive description of physical details in this scene ("a pink and white checked cloth over the rusty green iron table") confirms the speaker's anxiety. In the final sentence, he resolves to regain his self-possession by sheer force of will: "I decided that if the shaking of her breasts could be stopped, some of the fragments of the afternoon might be collected, and I concentrated my attention with careful subtlety to this end." He counters the sexual threat posed by the woman through mental self-control in much the way that Eliot coped with his "hysterical" wife, Vivien.

Considered by doctors to be "the most confusing, mysterious and rebellious of diseases,"[89] hysteria was epidemic among middle- and upper-class women in the late nineteenth and early twentieth centuries. Its symptoms included unpredictable fits of screaming, laughing, crying, and a host of other behaviors. Moreover, female hysterics – and they were virtually all female – were thought to be malingerers, "'petty tyrants' with a 'taste for power.'"[90] Freud called hysteria a "powerful weapon" used by spiteful and underhanded women to "get their way."[91] Lacking a clear somatic cause, hysteria was symbolically linked to female physiology as a disease of the uterus – the "wandering womb" idea from Plato's *Timaeus* – while the variability of its symptoms comprises the contradictions inherent in the nature of women.[92] While hysteria was believed to result from the frail female constitution, it was nonetheless suspected to have its sources in a potentially voracious sexual appetite. Eliot's poem attests to the fear, expressed by contemporary clinicians, that women were "veritable sexual powderkegs" and hysterical fits a symptom of their latent lust.[93]

The date of the composition of "Hysteria" suggests that the poem bears a close connection to Eliot's disturbance at his wife's emotional instability, evident shortly after their marriage in June 1915. Vivien Eliot was described by friends as "vivacious" and gay, while Russell said she displayed "impulses of cruelty from time to time."[94] According to Peter Ackroyd, her diary entries show her "subject to worry and depression but with sudden changes of mood that would release in her exuberant and unexplained high spirits."[95] Vivien's erratic moods may have been caused by hormonal imbalances associated with an irregular and excessive menstrual cycle that today would be diagnosed as menorrhagia or dysmenorrhea, yet her doctors were puzzled by her symptoms, vaguely labelling them hysterical "nervous disorders."[96]

A more likely cause of Vivien's behavior is attributable to her consumption of ether, a toxic substance that produces a range of symptoms from which Vivien suffered, including digestive trouble, insomnia,

premature aging, nervous prostration, brooding melancholy, and outbursts of hysterical behavior or laughter.[97] There is ample evidence that
she drank ether. Aldous Huxley claimed that she was an "ether addict,"
Virginia Woolf and Edith Sitwell remarked on her smelling of ether,
while, more charitably, Cyril Connolly noted that "[s]he wrote some
charming, light-hearted pieces for the *Criterion* (as Sibylla – see *The Waste
Land* epigraph) but became destructive and self-destructive, then took to
ether . . . and finally went mad."[98] Anthony Fathman points out that
Eliot's biographers have "garbled their accounts of [her] ether symptoms so as to suppress the evidence of drinking,"[99] perhaps in order to
retain the pathological image of Vivien as having, in Gordon's words, a
"hysterical nature."[100] Biographers agree that the Eliots had a "disastrous" honeymoon during which both were sick and nervous.[101] The
sexual failure of the Eliots' marriage may have been due to what
Ackroyd calls Eliot's "fastidiousness" and what Gordon allows as his
"inhibition, distrust of women, and a certain physical queasiness"
regarding women's bodies.[102]

   The general tendency amongst Eliot's critics is to portray him as the
long-suffering victim of a crazy wife. Ronald Bush introduces her by
calling her Eliot's "problem," while Richard Ellmann offers a colorful
description of Vivien as a witch: "Eliot remained . . . under her spell,
beset and possessed by her intricacies for fifteen years and more."[103]
Gordon is more evenhanded, noting that, although "one feels invited to
dismiss her as a burden Eliot painstaking upheld," Vivien no doubt
found Eliot rather hard to take as well, yet she "left no one to speak for
her."[104] Indeed, Gordon is willing to ask not only what was wrong with
Vivien but what was wrong with Tom. However, in the face of the evidence she supplies, she inexplicably claims that "the women closest to
Eliot in no way shaped his judgement of their sex," and that "Eliot's view
of women had much more to do with traditional and literary prejudices
than with the reality of his marriage."[105] On the contrary, Eliot's early
poetry bears unmistakable traces of the pain and confusion of his personal experience as well as of prevalent cultural conventions concerning
women. The figure of the hysterical woman that appears in his poetry,
with her capricious moods and ominous, "dark caverns," is the product
of the historical pathologization of the female body, a discourse that
Eliot reproduced and recited in both his life and work.

   Eliot's early poems typically focus upon the effects of female hysteria
on men who are subjected to mysterious or violent female behavior
rather than on the hysterical woman herself. In some cases, the male

speaker is presented as the victim of female hysteria, as in the scene with the neurasthenic woman in part 2 of *The Waste Land*, believed to be modeled upon Vivien. In others, such as "Sweeney Erect," a more robust man is capable of withstanding these female assaults. The brutish Sweeney ignores the epileptic fit of the woman with whom he has just had sex, who "[c]urves backward, clutching at her sides" in an *arc-en-cercle*; "hysteria / Might easily be misunderstood," observe the "ladies of the corridor," who are concerned for the reputation of the whorehouse. Eliot's portraits of hysterical women coincide with the threat posed by female sexual aggression. In "Sweeney among the Nightingales," "the man with heavy eyes" escapes the whores with their "murderous paws" because he is sufficiently worldly to understand their "gambit." Burbank in "Burbank with a Baedeker: Bleistein with a Cigar" is less wary and falls prey to "Princess Volupine," the "phthisic" Cleopatra of a decaying Venice. The beautiful sirens in the excised portion of part 4 of *The Waste Land*, "Death by Water," like "Belladonna, the Lady of the Rocks" in the first section of the poem, lure the sailors to their death with "[a] song that charmed" and "frightened" (*F* 67).

In keeping with literary conventions, feminine power in Eliot's early poems is often figured as an engulfment by women who preside over interior spaces. For instance, the young man who wanders the streets in "Rhapsody on a Windy Night" is enticed by a prostitute lounging in a doorway, who wears a knowing and inviting smile as he passes by. The image of the doorway that "opens on her like a grin" is suggestive of the many doors, windows, and rooms into which men are lured at their peril, which they enter only reluctantly but from which they inevitably withdraw, as in "Sweeney among the Nightingales." These rooms are indicatively feminine spaces, represented as stifling enclosures like the opulent and decadent room described in the "Cleopatra" passage in part 2 of *The Waste Land*, originally entitled "In the Cage." They are often sites of a potentially deadly seduction, as in "Portrait of a Lady," in which the male speaker escapes the woman's room, whose "atmosphere" is like "Juliet's tomb," to seek a masculine outdoors, to "take the air" and smoke tobacco. Those well-known rooms in "Prufrock" from which "the women come and go" are claustrophobic torture chambers where female "eyes . . . fix you in a formulated phrase," and where the speaker is "formulated, sprawling on a pin, / . . . pinned and wriggling on the wall."

In poem after poem up to the mid-1920s, male subjects appear as victims of female hysteria and sexual aggression. However, a simple inventory of the frequency and consistency of these figures misses the internal contradictions and tensions within the structure of these texts that render them unstable. "Whispers of Immortality" offers a useful example of such internal conflicts.

## "WHISPERS OF IMMORTALITY"

Often considered little more than an exercise in technical virtuosity – a view to which Eliot's comments on his study of Théophile Gautier's poetry have lent support – "Whispers of Immortality" (1918) is important as a statement of the erotic implications of Eliot's affiliation with a set of dead literary fathers and his abjection of the all-too-animated Grishkin. Although formally at opposite poles, "Hysteria" and "Whispers of Immortality" share a similar gender dynamic for, in both poems, Eliot's male speakers try to escape from sexually dangerous women. In the later poem, this escape entails a pathetic resort to the "dry ribs" of a desiccated masculine tradition. His gesture is characteristic of much of his early poetry and points to the sense of embattlement and even defeat at the hands of women that permeates the work of so many of his contemporaries, such as Ford Madox Ford, Ernest Hemingway, and D. H. Lawrence, whose texts are likewise littered with male victims of strong women.

Because "Whispers of Immortality" discusses Webster and Donne, it is typically interpreted in terms of Eliot's praise of them in "The Metaphysical Poets" (1921). However, the paternal citation in this poem is to fathers who are themselves "possessed by death" – morbid in life and, now dead, powerless to save the modern poet – while the poem is compelled by what I have been calling the maternal intertext – female sexual energies embodied by the debased Grishkin. It is thus an errant text, straying from the authority of Webster, Donne, and their company to a troubled preoccupation with female potency which the unnamed "we" of the poem tries to evade. The tortuous logic of the poem turns upon a series of oppositions between intellect and sensuality, bone and flesh, that are tacitly gendered as masculine and feminine. In short, the poem tells a tale of paternal literary authority supplanted by vigorous, carnal, modern women.

"Whispers of Immortality" begins by invoking John Webster, a man obsessed by the morbidity beneath the garb of flesh.

> Webster was much possessed by death
> And saw the skull beneath the skin;

And breastless creatures under ground
Leaned backward with a lipless grin.

(lines 1–4)

These lines closely recall the opening scene of Cyril Tourneur's *Revenger's Tragedy*, in which Vendice, the avenging hero, enters with a skull in his hand and pronounces against a "marrowless age" that has "stuff[ed] the hollow bones with damned desire" (i.i.5–6). This corrupt age has been duped by sensual pleasures; by contrast, the skull, from which the flesh has dropped away, is a symbol of purity and honesty, of the ability to see through appearances to the truth, like "that eternal eye / That sees through flesh and all" (i.iii.73–74). The moral spinelessness that Vendice denounces is the result of female wiles, especially the use of cosmetics as a mask, which the men in the play have effeminately adopted. Near the climax, Vendice again holds up the skull and proclaims, "Here might a scornful and ambitious woman / Look through and through herself. See, ladies, with false forms / You deceive men, but cannot deceive worms" (iii.iv.97–99). His speech contains one of Eliot's favorite citations of erotic desire: "Are lordships sold to maintain ladyships, / For the poor benefit of a bewildering minute?" (iii.v.75–76).

The following lines of "Whispers" also strip away the flesh from the female body – specifically, the breasts and the lips. The smiling skull gives the lie to feminine seductions but, as in *The Revenger's Tragedy*, the recumbent corpse possesses a certain grotesque attraction. The next stanza makes explicit its necrophilic charm:

Daffodil bulbs instead of balls
Stared from the sockets of the eyes!
He knew that thought clings round dead limbs
Tightening its lusts and luxuries.     (lines 5–8)

The startling image of the daffodil bulbs evokes the well-known Jacobean vision of death in life. However, viewing this image in conjunction with the subsequent description of Grishkin's "friendly bust" as a "pneumatic" inflatable device, what is most striking about the replacement of the eyeball with daffodil bulbs is its fetishization of body parts. As the condensation of erotic desire upon a particular bodily part and the displacement of desire onto that part, fetishism is enacted and parodied by the images of "daffodil bulbs" and "pneumatic" breasts.[106] Eliot implies that erotic desire is a fetishization of or a necrophilic clinging to "dead limbs." Ironically, lust is *more* luxurious when it fixes itself upon an insensate bodily object.

If the first two stanzas of the poem are a simple denunciation of the lusts of the flesh, the third and fourth go farther, suggesting that the lusts of the flesh are as nothing compared to the lusts of the mind; the mind is superior to the body in its capacity for sexual temptation and gratification.

> Donne, I suppose, was such another
> Who found no substitute for sense,
> To seize and clutch and penetrate;
> Expert beyond experience,
>
> He knew the anguish of the marrow
> The ague of the skeleton;
> No contact possible to flesh
> Allayed the fever of the bone.
>
> (lines 9–16)

Just as the mind "tightens its lusts" by clinging fetishistically to "dead limbs," so no actual bodily "contact" can "substitute for sense" in seizing, clutching, and penetrating. The erotic imagination exceeds any possible erotic experience, figured as an act of aggression. Finally, "[n]o contact possible to flesh" can bring comparable satisfaction because sexual desire is at bottom a "fever of the bone," a primordial "anguish" and not simply the effect of occasional physical temptations. Likewise, the fulfillment of desire in erotic possession can only be achieved on the level of "sense," in sexual fantasy.

These two stanzas have received considerable attention from critics largely because of Eliot's essays on Donne and Webster, especially his assertion that in their work "there is a direct sensuous apprehension of thought, or a re-creation of thought into feeling," after which a "dissociation of sensibility set in" (*SE* 286, 288). The long-standing habit of reading "Whispers of Immortality" through the lens of "The Metaphysical Poets" follows from F. O. Matthiessen, yet it slights the second half of the poem.[107] On the contrary, "Whispers of Immortality" contradicts the notion that thought and the sense may be unified by presenting Webster and Donne as ones for whom sensory experience was nothing more than clutching at "dead limbs." The second half of the poem, with its presentation of the sensual Grishkin in contrast to the "dry ribs" of metaphysics, offers arid intellectual comfort, not the happy unification of sensibility. Attentive to these problems, Grover Smith argues that the poem is an "argument for the inadequacy of any embrace" and, even if Webster and Donne had achieved a unity of mind and body, such a unity is long gone and is now known only intellectually.[108] Either way, the poem fails as an apologia for the metaphysical sensibility.

Much of the confusion in the interpretation of "Whispers of Immortality" is due to the ambiguity of the word "sense." The dominant reading of the poem rests upon taking the term as a reference to *sensory* experience, not to *consciousness* or *mind*. To interpret "sense" as sensory experience in line 10 commits one to the paradox that Donne "found no substitute" for bodily perception but that he also found inadequate any "contact possible to flesh."[109] Taking "sense" as mind or consciousness avoids this contradiction and provides a coherent reading of both sections of the poem as well as the division between them.

In the first four stanzas, the two sets of images that emerge most prominently are those of bone and dead flesh. The flesh is mortified in the necrophilic consciousness and the attractions of the body are heightened by objectifying the erotic act, a "contact" not "possible to flesh" because the sources of desire are rooted in the "bone." The opposition between bone and flesh sets up a dichotomy between inner and outer layers, between corporal superfice and skeletal primordiality. Webster's vision, Eliot asserts, pierced the veil of skin with its delusive appearances to the truth of the skull beneath. The terms of this opposition are gendered, for sensuous, erotic flesh is female – soft and deceptively beautiful, suggesting carnal fertility and depravity – while the dead bones, however fevered and anguished, possess masculine firmness, honesty, and austere purity. Stripped of the corruptible flesh, the bones hold the promise that they shall one day live again.

The second section of the poem shifts to a description of Grishkin, a loose foreign woman who wears mascara and invites sexual pleasures:

> Grishkin is nice: her Russian eye
> Is underlined for emphasis;
> Uncorseted, her friendly bust
> Gives promise of pneumatic bliss.
> (lines 17–20)

Grishkin's grotesquely exaggerated, mechanically inflated breasts are chiastically aligned with the "lipless grin" of the "breastless creatures" in the first stanza. Deader than the dead bones that give the lie to her promised "bliss," Grishkin's friendliness is a thin veil for the dangers that lurk in her smile, evident in her comparison to a jaguar in the next stanzas:

> The couched Brazilian jaguar
> Compels the scampering marmoset

> With subtle effluence of cat;
> Grishkin has a maisonette;
>
> The sleek Brazilian jaguar
> Does not in its arboreal gloom
> Distil so rank a feline smell
> As Grishkin in a drawing-room.
>                                   (lines 21–28)

The introduction of the jaguar poses an initial contrast between the animal and the woman, reducing Grishkin's civilized and feminine maisonette to banality. The jaguar possesses a rich and potent natural eroticism against which Grishkin, like the typist in *The Waste Land*, has only the tawdry props of modern sexuality. However, the seventh stanza reverses the opposition between animal and woman for, according to Pinkney, "the 'sleekness' of the jaguar now seems to belong with the clean lines and angles of the modern maisonette . . . , while in her 'rankness' Grishkin has expropriated Nature of its most coarse and luxuriant energies."[110] Confined to an apartment or drawing room, Grishkin makes a foul jungle of these domestic spaces. The reversal of the nature/culture opposition parallels that between male and female, so that Grishkin's perverse bestiality also signifies her unnatural virility. With her feline stench, she is a more dangerous predator than the jaguar, which, in the first edition of the poem, Eliot identified with the masculine pronoun but which he later neutered. In the sexual economy of cats in his oeuvre – from the ominous, catlike "yellow fog" of "Prufrock" to the whimsical portraits in *Old Possum's Book of Practical Cats* – they are typically male but also, as in "Whispers of Immortality," gender transitive.[111]

Grishkin and the jaguar share a "feline smell."[112] Eliot repeatedly evokes the odor of "female smells in shuttered rooms," including the "smells of dust and eau de Cologne" ("Rhapsody"), to suggest the pestilential atmosphere of these female spaces, an odor that attracts and distracts the male speaker of "Prufrock": "Is it perfume from a dress / That makes me so digress?" A parallel passage from *The Waste Land* describes a woman's room permeated by "her strange synthetic perfumes," a scent that "troubled, confused, / And drowned the sense in odours" (lines 84–89). These feminine effluvia are a tamer version of the noxious fumes emitted by Fresca in a suppressed section of *The Waste Land*. A cheap, "can-can salonnière," Fresca is a "sly domestic puss puss cat" whose perfumes are "cunning" weapons in her social "manoeuvers": "Odours, confected by the artful French / Disguise the good old hearty female stench" (*F* 23, 27). Like Fresca, the jaguar "Compels" its prey, the marmoset (a South American monkey), with its odiferous emanations, a "subtle effluence of cat." Yet the Russian Grishkin is far more dangerous than the Brazilian animal as she stalks her victim – a human version of the monkey – fairly reeking of predatory lust.

At bottom, "Whispers of Immortality" claims for the male cat a purity that it denies to the woman. Grishkin not only proves more powerful than the jaguar but seems better able to "seize and clutch and penetrate" than the modern-day heir of Webster and Donne. Moreover, her virility aligns her with the fetishism that Eliot attributes to those poets. If the fetish is, as Freud argues, a substitute for the fantasized maternal penis or, more broadly, for the little boy's belief in maternal power,[113] Grishkin condenses the debased figure of the whore and the mighty figure of the mother in Eliot's texts. In short, she is a site of the maternal intertext in Eliot's early poetry: a moment in which female potency – at once abjected and elevated – threatens to overwhelm the cited authority of literary and philosphical fathers.

The final stanza juxtaposes Grishkin's lascivious "charm" to the austere "dry bones":

> And even the Abstract Entities
> Circumambulate her charm;
> But our lot crawls between dry ribs
> To keep our metaphysics warm.
>
> (lines 29–32)

Grishkin is expanded to embody the fatal success of feminine attractions around which "even the Abstract Entities / Circumambulate" in worship. As opposed to those who adore female beauty, "our lot," says Eliot, self-pityingly, is to crawl "between dry ribs." Despite their mortal anguish, parched bones are preferable to rank flesh, for only the former carry the promise, albeit only rustlings or "whispers," of "immortality." These concluding images return to the motif developed in the first section of the poem. Its two sections reflect and invert the other: whereas the first strip away the flesh from the bone by exposing the necrophilia of carnal desire, the last accumulate increasingly repulsive images that climax in the perverse triumph of female seductiveness, capable of luring even the "Abstract Entities" of philosophers to celebrate women's fatal power.

The seven manuscript versions of "Whispers of Immortality" support as well as add some further dimensions to this reading of the poem. In one draft, Eliot writes that "I think John Donne was such another / With passions chiselled out of stone," who "toothed the sweetness of the bone."[114] Praising the flinty hardness of Donne's desires, Eliot draws a further contrast to the "[u]ncorseted" looseness of Grishkin's soft bosom. The firmness of male eroticism is far more attractive to Eliot than the dangerously "friendly bust" of the woman. Moreover, his discarded variants introduce a male speaker who comments on his sexual inexperience or incapacity. Unlike Donne, Eliot writes in the penultimate draft of the poem, "To seize and clutch and penetrate: / This passes my experience." The final lines of the same version stress the speaker's individual plight: "But I must crawl between dry ribs / To keep my metaphysics warm."

Beyond suggesting the personal implications of the poem for Eliot, these drafts also draw attention to the nostalgic homosociality that underwrites them. For Eliot, the austere, even morbid eroticism of Donne, Webster, and their company represented an escape from female flesh; likewise, their poetry offered an refuge from a feminized modern aesthetic. Hence, his wish to "crawl between dry ribs" expressed a longing to crawl into the bony embrace of those metaphysical poets. The ever alert Ezra Pound seized upon this implication of Eliot's poem, and his first comment on its penultimate draft was "SODOMY!" Pound put his finger on the homoerotic impulse of the portrayal of male sexuality in "Whispers of Immortality" and, especially, on Eliot's identification with a lost paternal authority. This underread poem thus serves as a significant point of conjunction among the various forces at work in Eliot's early poetry: his desire for and wish to be like his literary forebears, his sense of the loss of the father and his love for him, and his ambivalent relation to female authority, including his violent abjection of and intense devotion to maternal power.

Despite his disgust at the Grishkin figure and the female flesh she so heartily embodies, Eliot returns to it time and again in his early work; he, too, "[c]ircumambulate[s] her charm." Eliot's fascination with this trope is the obverse of the murderous insistence of his texts upon "doing in the girl." As Maud Ellmann remarks of *The Waste Land*, "enthralled by the femininity that it reviles,"[115] Eliot's early poetry is shaped and twisted by textual strategies of displacement and denial, by reiterated depictions of women as hysterical, bestial, or rapacious. The elaboration and coherence of the female images of "dark caverns," rotten flesh, and "feline smells" in Eliot's poems through the 1910s and 1920s testify to the desperate measures to which he resorted and render all the more compelling his comment in the Baudelaire essay on the necessity of "harmonising" one's "experience" with one's "needs," for "such suffering as Baudelaire's implies the possibility of a positive state of beatitude" (*SE* 423). Written after his conversion, Eliot's 1930 essay is a major statement of his effort to come to terms with his sense of the depravity of sexual desires and of female carnality. Recognizing the "reality of Sin" for him meant the chance for "a New Life; and the possibility of damnation is so immense a relief in a world of electoral reform, plebiscites, sex reform and dress reform, that damnation itself is an immediate form of salvation . . . from the ennui of modern life" (*SE* 427). Like many of his contemporaries, feminist and working-class upheavals drove him to the consolation offered by authoritarian ideologies; in Eliot's case, submission to religious authority carried the sexual charge elicited by masochistic devotion.

Eliot's adherence to Anglican orthodoxy and his praise of Baudelaire's execrations of women are linked by the pleasure Eliot found in the sensation of his own sinfulness. Baudelaire's belief in feminine corruption provided an alternative to the sexologists' notion of sexual health and to what Eliot saw as the mechanism of sexual relations in the modern world, represented by Grishkin's "pneumatic" bosom and the typist's "automatic hand" in *The Waste Land*. Although Baudelaire had "an imperfect, vague, romantic conception of Good," he was "able to understand that the sexual act as evil is more dignified, less boring, than the natural, 'life-giving,' cheery automatism of the modern world. For Baudelaire, sexual operation is at least something not analogous to Kruschen Salts" (*SE* 429). A proprietary aperient marketed in England in the 1920s and 1930s, Kruschen Salts claimed to provide a feeling of vigorous health (*OED*). By contrast, Baudelaire grasped the terrors of sexuality and was "man enough for damnation," understanding that there is "a gap between human love and divine love"; "hence his insistence upon the evil of love, hence his constant vituperations of the female. In this there is no need to pry for psychopathological causes" (*SE* 429–30). Protecting himself from the interrogations of psychologists, Eliot justifies his self-incriminating sense of sexual depravity, suggesting that he, too, is "man enough for damnation." Baudelaire thus provided a cover against the incursions of modern female power, to which Eliot added a "complement": the split between Baudelaire's degraded whores and Dante's angelic Beatrice. This divergence seemed to negotiate the deadlock between the primitive "ague of the skeleton" and Grishkin's modern, "pneumatic bliss." A quite different way is represented in "Ode."

## "ODE"

"Ode" is a poem that critics love to hate. Smith calls it "Eliot's nadir; mediocre as some of his quatrain poems are, they are all better than this."[116] Those who dislike Eliot point to the poem as being especially awful and credit him with having "sensibly never reprinted" it.[117] Those who are sympathetic to Eliot and who bother commenting on the poem typically describe it, in Stephen Spender's words, as "arid, dead almost"[118] or, as Mayer puts it, "Eliot's most tortuously opaque poem."[119] Yet the poem's very badness suggests its relevance to an inquiry into the errancy of Eliot's poetry. Moreover, the embarrassing aspects of the poem, such as its dense allusiveness and its indelicate reference to "blood upon the bed," place it squarely within our investigation of the paternal citation and the maternal intertext of Eliot's early work. In a word, "Ode" is a significant document of the conflict between Eliot's identificatory desire for affiliation with his literary fathers and the disruption of that affiliation by female sexual energies.

"Ode" announces itself anonymously and generically as a lyric poem. A draft version of the poem, published in *Inventions of the March Hare*, bears no epigraph but carries a date, "on Independence Day, July 4th, 1918." According to Edmund Wilson, this date was tacked on to mislead the reader; he was "positive" that the poem alludes to Eliot's wedding night, 26 June 1915.[120] For a poem whose citations are notoriously difficult to track, it is remarkable that even its title is compromised in its citational reference. "Ode" arouses further questions by virtue of the silence in which it has been shrouded. Appearing in *Ara Vos Prec* (1920), "Ode" was deleted from the Knopf edition of *Poems* a few months later, where it was replaced by "Hysteria," and never published again. As we know from his letter to his brother, Eliot tried to prevent his mother from reading the poem and likely succeeded in doing so. Both the origin and the disappearance of the poem are thus lost in rumor. T. S. Matthews passes along the gossip: "Edmund Wilson said that when Eliot was asked why he omitted 'Ode' from all future collections, he replied, 'An oversight'; obviously untrue, said Wilson."[121] "Hysteria," substituted for "Ode," is thematically parallel to its predecessor, both poems representing a devouring, rapacious woman and a horrified male victim.

The *Ara Vos Prec* edition possesses an epigraph from Shakespeare's *Coriolanus*, which it misquotes and mispunctuates: "To you particularly, and to all the Volscians / Great hurt and mischief" (IV.v.67–68). If the title offers no clue to this enigmatic poem, the epigraph, another thresh-

old to the text, ought to, for one of the functions of epigraphs is to epit-
omize the sense of the poem as a whole. Like the inscriptions on monuments and coins, epigraphs declare the text's lineage, for the epigraph's
power to frame or orient the interpretation of the text is the result of its
claim to reinscribe the intentions of the poem's "first" author. However,
the misleading and erroneous epigraph of "Ode" does neither; as a
deviant quotation, it is symptomatic of the errancy of citationality in the
poem as a whole. This errancy may be attributable to the maternal
authority of which the epigraph is a displaced and concealed expression.
An examination of this relatively minor moment in "Ode" thus sheds
light on Eliot's citational practice in general.

On the face of it, the epigraph sounds like a curse upon the Volscians,
but, tracing it back to *Coriolanus*, one finds that these words are uttered
as a confession by Coriolanus to the Volscian commander as he turns
traitor to Rome and allies himself with his former enemies. Attempting
to assimilate Coriolanus's statement to "Ode," Matthews argues that the
epigraph is Eliot's oblique "acknowledgment of guilt" at having con-
tracted a poor marriage.[122] Yet Eliot quotes Coriolanus's statement in a
way that lends it a very different, even opposite, significance as an
accusation rather than an admission. The explanation for this reversal
lies in those passages of *Coriolanus* that Eliot does not cite yet which constitute "Ode's" maternal intertext concerning the eponymous hero's
relationship with his mother, Volumnia. This virile woman, like Lady
Monchensey in *The Family Reunion*, exercises devastating control over her
son; indeed, Coriolanus dies because he succumbs to her authority.
Volumnia frequently instructs her son and twice alludes to their almost
incestuous relationship (III.ii.64–65; I.iii.2–3). Long a preoccupation with
Eliot, *Coriolanus* is the subject of his unfinished "Coriolan," which contains a lengthy apostrophe by the son to his mother. Confronted by a
rebellious mob demanding his resignation, Eliot's Coriolanus yearns to
be united with his mother, "hidden" from the violence of the populace:
"Mother / May we not be some time, almost now, together" (*CPP* 88).
Eliot's version is a sentimental rendering of Shakespeare's account of
Coriolanus's love for Volumnia, which, taken with his sympathy for "a
broken Coriolanus" in *The Waste Land*, suggests that "Ode" be read in
terms of his sense of the compelling fatality of mother love.

If the poem describes Eliot's marriage to Vivien, the epigraph's
apparent curse is a displaced accusation against the demanding woman
whom he felt he had betrayed by wedding Vivien – Charlotte Eliot, who
disapproved of her son's marriage. The epigraph condenses Eliot's

resentment and guilt toward his mother, energies that in the poem are directed into violence against the bride. Eliot's reversal of the original significance of the quotation expresses yet obfuscates his sense of having turned traitor to both his mother and his wife, cloaking his intentions in an allusion that refers to the relation between Coriolanus and the Volscian commander, Aufidius, to whom the former's words are addressed. Eliot's epigraph conforms to his model of citationality by establishing a link between literary fathers and sons, covertly citing the maternal authority that he cannot openly acknowledge. Finally, concealed within the duplicitous folds of the citation is the love between Coriolanus and Aufidius. In the scene from Shakespeare's play, after Coriolanus announces his betrayal, Aufidius recalls their comradely affection and his love for Coriolanus: "that I see thee here, / . . . more dances my rapt heart / Than when I first my wedded mistress saw / Bestride my threshold" (iv.v.116–19). Coriolanus's fall stems not only from his submission to the effeminizing influence of his mother but from his faithlessness to Aufidius.[123] This homoerotic undercurrent is a subtext of "Ode" and a number of Eliot's early poems, running against the grain of their designated paternal citations.

"Ode" is broken into three sections, beginning with the words "Tired," "Tortured," and "Tortuous" respectively. The poem is highly elliptical, its clearest narrative passage being the middle section in which a young husband discovers "blood upon the bed." The persona of the poem is an exhausted poet/bridegroom, victimized by his succuba/bride, "indignant" and "resentful" at his conjugal disappointment.

The first section introduces this "[m]isunderstood" and "retired" poet or "profess[or] of the calamus," a surrogate for the author of the text, one to whom the Muses no longer speak.

> Tired.
> Subterrene laughter synchronous
> With silence from the sacred wood
> And bubbling of the uninspired
> Mephitic river.
>            Misunderstood
> The accents of the now retired
> Profession of the calamus.
>
>         (lines 1–7)

The "silence from the sacred wood" recalls the title of Eliot's first collection of essays, also published in 1920, as well as the ancient grove of the Muses.[124] Like Mr. Apollinax's "submarine" laughter which evokes "the worried bodies of drowned men," and like the laughter of the woman in "Hysteria" whose brutal mouth engulfs the male speaker, the "Subterrene laughter" of "Ode" springs from a watery grave. A common image in Eliot's early poetry where it is often linked to female seduction, "death by water" attributes a fatal, castrating power to this supposedly life-giving, uterine element. Indeed, what is striking about Eliot's otherwise conventional use of sexual figures is his phallicization of the female body, especially the mouth/womb. Like the Thames in *The Waste Land*, the "Mephitic river" in "Ode" is polluted, breeding noxious odors with a perverse fecundity that mocks the sterility of the poet.

In the poem as a whole, the representation of women diverges between, on the one hand, the bride on whose body the calamus is supposed to write and which should serve as the vessel for its seed and, on the other hand, the deadly succuba who poisons the seed, rendering the calamus impotent. This divergence within the poem's gynophobic tropology, which extends through a series of intertextual allusions, generates enormous tension in the citational structure of the text. Moreover, the split in the representation of the female object of the poem parallels a split in its authorial male subject.

The "profession of the calamus" signals the position of what Neil Hertz, following Paul de Man, calls the "author surrogate" in the text.[125] According to de Man, any text written under a signature and understood under that name possesses a "specular structure" in which "the author *of* the text" and "the author *in* the text" are engaged in a process of tropological substitution. The "autobiographical moment" in a text takes place "between the two subjects involved in the process of reading in which they determine each other by mutual reflexive substitution."[126] "Ode" is therefore an autobiographical text, not only in terms of the resemblance between its scene of nuptial horror and Eliot's personal experience on what Bertrand Russell called his "pseudo-honeymoon" with Vivien,[127] but also in terms of the relation within it between Eliot as its author and Eliot as the reader of himself as its author. The introduction of the "profession of the calamus" serves as one of several specular moments in the text. The male subject who writes and reads himself in "Ode" bemoans his poetic enervation yet also announces his claim to seminal authority and to a place within the literary patrilineage. The author surrogate of "Ode" is in the hapless predicament of the writer in Plato's *Phaedrus*, whose "pen [*kalamos*] . . . sow[s] words" that, cut off from the author's supervision, drift "all over the place" and "cry out for the assistance of their parent."[128] Even as he complains of being "Misunderstood," Eliot's penman asserts his true profession, the reference to the "calamus" alluding to the classical origin and prestige of that vocation.

Plato is not the only father cited here, though, for the other mighty wielder of the calamus to which "Ode" apparently alludes is Walt Whitman, whose name is conspicuously absent from Eliot's prose except in his disavowals of Whitman, and whose reinstatement as one of Eliot's important precursors has been the burden of much recent criticism. "Ode" seems to cite the author of the "Calamus" poems not once but twice; Whitman's "O Hymen, O Hymenee!" from "Children of Adam" appears unexpectedly in the second stanza. The absence of any apparent textual relation between "Ode" and either the "Calamus" poems or "O Hymen, O Hymenee!" has frustrated the attempt to attribute them as sources of Eliot's text. Critics searching in vain for a link between "Ode" and Whitman sometimes conclude, like Cleo McNeally Kearns, that Eliot "misread" Whitman on account his homophobia.[129] By contrast, Mayer and James E. Miller, Jr., claim that the reference to Whitman is Eliot's concealed expression of regret at the loss of a prior homosexual attachment, which has been replaced by a tortured marriage bed.[130] Neither reading is convincing, although the latter is supported by the previous allusion to the friendship between Coriolanus and Aufidius.

The question of the elusive or illusory presence of Whitman in "Ode" can only be answered by considering it within the context of Eliot's citational practice in general. As we have seen, Eliot writes himself by writing – and writing off – the father, preoccupied as he was with affirming his legitimate place among the patriarchs of the European literary canon. The disputed reference to Whitman demonstrates the internal errancy of citations, which both recall an absent source or father and desire his death. For not only does the "pen . . . sow words" that stray beyond the author's intentions, as Plato puts it, but, even worse, those vagrant words do perfectly well without their father's authorization. The equivocal site of fidelity and patricide, the citation is irreducible to either. What is at issue, finally, is neither Eliot's identification with Greek literature nor his disavowal of American poetry but the indeterminacy of citations as marks of paternity. "Calamus" and "Io Hymen, Hymenae" are *no more or less* indications of Eliot's anxiety toward an American precursor than they are of his true affiliation with Plato or Catullus.

Similarly tortuous is the citational structure of the second section, in which the specular play between the author in and of "Ode" turns upon the troubled and divided figure of woman. What is perhaps most curious about this nuptial poem is that the bride never directly appears and is represented only metonymically by the "blood upon the bed." This striking image marks a decisive break in the poem.

> Tortured.
> When the bridegroom smoothed his hair
> There was blood upon the bed.
> Morning was already late.
> Children singing in the orchard
> (Io Hymen, Hymenae)
> Succuba eviscerate. (lines 8–14)

"Io Hymen, Hymenae," its parenthetical status underscoring the irony of Eliot's antiepithalamium, appears in a poem by Catullus, "Collis o Helliconii" (no. 61), celebrating the marriage of Manlius Torquatus to Vinia Aurunculeia. The latter is hedged about with reservations that Eliot echoes; its tenth stanza cries out, "Where else can the lover, / tortured, turn? / what greater god among men? / Hymenaeus Hymen Io! / Io! Hymen Hymenaeus."[131] The image of the "Children singing in the orchard" recalls Catullus's description of Vinia, "lovely as a flower-laden myrtle," "each branch . . . tipped with blossom." As a source, however, Catullus's poem sheds little interpretive light on "Ode"; if anything, the preceeding poem, "Collis o Helliconii," with its figure of the "screaming vulva" of a "She-cat," is closer tropologically and tonally to "Ode."

The obliquity of this allusion – if one could call it that – enacts the duplicity of the fictive or proleptic allusion in the preceding line, "Children singing in the orchard." The evocativeness of the line makes it sound like a quotation, and maybe it is. Shakespeare's *Coriolanus* "heard the children's voices" (III.i.31), and, in *The Waste Land*, Eliot quotes Verlaine's line, "Et O ces voix d'enfants, chantant dans la coupole!"[132] Years later, Eliot writes of "Children's voices in the orchard" ("New Hampshire"); we hear again "the hidden laughter / Of children in the foliage" in "Burnt Norton" and, again, "The voice of . . . / . . . children in the apple-tree" in "Little Gidding." Clearly, there are far too many origins, and echoes, of this questionable citation. Its excessiveness implies that, instead of alluding to a source, the line is a metacitation.

"Children singing in the orchard" is the *performance* of citationality. It meets what Stewart calls the "'happiness conditions' for the speech act [of allusion], . . . but the referent does not exist" or is irrelevant.[133] Rather, Eliot is alluding to himself alluding, inscribing not an original intention but a simulacrum thereof. The failure of his "true" allusions to function as interpretive glosses and the effectiveness of his so-called spurious allusions in evoking the sense of a tradition have been a long-standing issue regarding the notes to *The Waste Land*. Yet the validity of Eliot's citations depends not upon their factual authenticity but upon the mirage they offer of a background for the text.[134] Indeed, Eliot plays possum not only in the Notes but in his citations in general, which pretend to provide instruction to the reader on how a poem is to be inter-preted. By miming the genealogical self-representation that they purport to institute, citations deflect the specular structure of that representation onto the process of reading. In other words, the belief that the meaning of the text is a reflection of its origins is parodied in "Ode," so that the reader of the poem, far from being clued in by its citations to the poem's essential meaning, is thrown back upon the vagaries of interpretation. Just as the allusion offers the masquerade of depth, of a source outside the text that could govern its reading, the opacity and indeterminacy of the poem's relation to this "outside" inhibits such an escape and instead reinscribes the *desire* for it at the very location in the text – the certifying citation – where it should have been possible. "Children singing in the orchard" is, thus, the mime of memory, an allusion whose authority lies in its nostalgic effect.

Such nostalgia is shattered by the concluding line of the stanza, "Succuba eviscerate." The bride, the blood of her breached virginity still on the bed, is exposed as a seductive demon/whore who has assumed human form in order to eviscerate or disembowel the bridegroom in his sleep. With the introduction of the succuba, the husband's wound is sub-stituted for the wife's "blood upon the bed." His bodily integrity has been breached, while her fecund womb turns out to be a deadly weapon. The feminine and masculine tropes are chiastically reversed so that, no longer a sign of receptive and sensuous, albeit corruptible, flesh, the woman's body is figured as the agent of rapacious violence, while the man's body, sterile and impotent, assumes the masochistic triumph and moral authority of the victim. Finally, the grammatical ambiguity of the phrase, "Succuba eviscerate," allows at least a double reading: the succuba may be the eviscerated or the eviscerator.[135] Although Eliot's early poems typically represent male victims of female predation, this formal equivocation between victim and victimized suggests another twist in the scene sketched out in the stanza – the bridegroom exchanges his masochistic defeat for sadistic revenge.

Neil Hertz describes such a moment of crisis in a text as "the end of the line": "What is repeatedly represented, at the end of the line, is a . . . 'subject' [the surrogate of the author] confronting a split or doubled 'object.'" Under the pressure of the confrontation, this structure breaks down, "giving way to scenarios more or less violent, in which the aggressive reassertion of the subject's stability is bought at some other subject's expense." "Women," Hertz drily notes, "are frequently the victims of choice."[136] Turning against the bride, the bridegroom attributes to her the evil that had crept into his bed and from which he now purifies himself by expelling her, whose sacrifice purchases his integrity. This is a story told over and over in Eliot's early poetry. According to Pinkney, "any Eliotic text . . . wants to . . . do a girl in," because the poems are strategies unconsciously deployed in a pre-oedipal struggle with the mother's body; in Maud Ellmann's idiom, they represent repeated gestures of abjection by a male subject desperate to recover his sense of wholeness.[137] Pinkney's and Ellmann's readings of the psychic combat in Eliot's work explain the reversibility of masochism and sadism in "Ode" as an expression of the (male) subject's primitive desire for and fear of an "oceanic" merging with maternal flesh.

Eliot's early poems thus invite an interpretation of them as oblique citations of a maternal intertext, engaged in combat not with a Bloomian father but with a Kleinian or Kristevan mother.[138] Such a reading of "Ode" also accounts for its replacement by "Hysteria," for the disemboweled/disemboweling succuba and the devouring mouth of the hysteric are similar representations of female phallicism. However, installing the mother instead of the father as the primal precursor displaces but does not fix the slippage of citationality. The choice of authorizing sources for a citation is itself motivated by the ideological concerns of readers. Consequently, I stress the image of the "blood upon the bed" in "Ode" not just to reinterpret an obscure, minor poem but to reorient our understanding of Eliot's poetic oeuvre. Facing up to the errant female sexual energies within his poems, like many other modernist texts, is necessary if we are to continue to read Eliot with something other than hostility or incomprehension.

Eliot's terse phrase, the "blood upon the bed," seems to express a shudder at the sheets polluted by the blood of the woman. She is, in Kristeva's terms, the abject of the text, that which must be cast out in order to protect the subject from being swamped by the other. According to Kristeva, the abject appears at the moment of the subject's earliest effort to escape from the mother's body in order to exist independently, a never fully successful attempt to demarcate corporeal boundaries that is re-enacted in religious rituals of purification. The abject continues to be experienced as horror at the potential collapse of the border between the inside and the outside of the body and, hence, as loathing for urine, blood, sperm, and excrement. Moreover, these despised bodily fluids carry an ambivalent erotic charge, so that "the abjection of these flows from within [may] suddenly become the . . . 'object' of sexual desire – a true 'ab-ject' where man, frightened, crosses over the horrors of maternal bowels."[139]

Kristeva's account of the fear and desire aroused by corporeal fluids is especially apposite given Eliot's well-known disgust at the "purulent offensive discharges" of women's bodies during menstruation or childbirth.[140] In "Ode," the male subject's fascinated terror at the bloody sheets discloses the eroticism of the abject, which in Eliot's poetry sometimes takes the form of necrophilia, what Frank Kermode aptly calls his "mortuary eroticism," evident in Eliot's preoccupation with drowned young men (*SP* 13). Moreover, the image of "the blood upon the bed" draws its special power from its association with menstrual blood. Besides its biographical reference to Vivien's gynecological problems, this image links menstrual blood to the succuba/vampire figure in a way that Eliot would have read in Baudelaire's "Les Metamorphoses vampire."[141] The menstrual mark in "Ode," together with all that it condenses of the fear of female bodily fluids, offers a direct contrast between Eliot's poem and Joyce's celebrated representation of Molly Bloom's discharges in the "Penelope" episode of *Ulysses*. Unlike the latter, "Ode" constitutes the bride as a Medusa-like figure, from the sight of which Eliot turns to the reassuring myth of Perseus and Andromeda.

The last stanza of the poem attempts a reconstitution of the subject by means of a set of allusions to the classical myth.

> Tortuous.
> By arrangement with Perseus
> The fooled resentment of the dragon
> Sailing before the wind at dawn.
> Golden apocalypse. Indignant
> At the cheap extinction of his taking-off.
> Now lies he there
> Tip to tip washed beneath Charles' Wagon.
>
> (lines 15–22)

The shift of locale from the bloody bridal chamber to the distant scene of classical mythology through the recitation of a familiar story is a consoling gesture. Indeed, it is the essence of citationality in the canonical sense, which Eliot recognized in his interpretation of Joyce's systematic citation of Homer in *Ulysses* as "a way of controlling, of ordering, of giving a shape and a significance to the immense panorama of futility and anarchy which is contemporary history" (*SP* 177). However, as many critics have observed, Eliot's theoretical statements neither govern his poetic practice nor are free from their own, internal errancy. In "Ode," the efficacy of the classical allusion is diminished by its doubling for, while the passage owes its authority to Ovid, its disjointed narrative follows Jules Laforgue's burlesque revision of Ovid's tale, thus confusing the tracks of the allusion.

Beyond the double palimpsest of Ovid and Laforgue, Eliot's use of the Perseus and Andromeda myth establishes a series of intertextual links between his poem and the many Victorian renditions of the myth. Works by Robert Browning, D. G. Rossetti, and others largely follow the Ovidian story in which a helpless, naked, and virtuous Andromeda is chained to a rock, about to be devoured by a monster. Perseus, who has just killed the Medusa, saves her by slaying the monster and subsequently weds her. As Adrienne Auslander Munich points out, the representations of the classical myth by Victorian writers and painters are at once rescue fantasies, in which the hero takes possession of the maiden, and rape fantasies, in which the passive, bound virgin is depicted pornographically, yet in which the hero's rapacious desire is redeemed by marriage.[142] More broadly, the Perseus and Andromeda myth functioned for Victorian male writers, in Munich's words, as a "conservative remedy for the disease of the times" – the revolt of women. "The chained woman waiting to be rescued responds to the challenge of a new kind of woman who . . . claim[s] that she can unshackle herself . . . The myth counters feminist aspirations by telling the maiden that she needs the hero, she needs marriage."[143] Eliot's revision of the myth, refracted through Laforgue, attests both to its reactionary political import in Victorian literature as well as to the modern failure of the myth to domesticate women. In short, Eliot remakes it as a tale of male defeat at the hands of woman.

In *Six Moral Tales*, Laforgue frames the myth of Perseus and Andromeda as a story told by a tutor, Monsieur Amyot de l'Epinal, to a princess, presenting the narrative as a deliberate rewriting of the traditional myth in order to teach the girl a "moral lesson."[144] The pedagogical function of Laforgue's story underscores the implicit didacticism of the citation itself. The reader, like the immature princess and, even more, like the bride of "Ode," requires the instruction which Laforgue/de l'Epinal/Eliot supplies by offering an exemplary tale. Moreover, the reading lesson is also a sexual lesson aimed at disciplining the rebellious girl.

A "sulky," "mewling" "coquette," a "savage little adolescent" cared for by her "considerate" and generous dragon, de l'Epinal's Andromeda is also sexually demanding. Although he cannot satisfy her "legitimately famished thighs" because of his bestial form, the dragon patiently tells her the platonic "Truth" about love. She fails to appreciate these lessons, however, and fantasizes about phallic birds who would "draw out the burning core of her little wound." When Perseus appears, the dragon, who knows how the story turns out in Ovid's narrative, counsels Andromeda that Perseus "has come to kill me, and to take you away from me," warning her against making a "poor match." Frightened, Andromeda promises to come to an "arrangement" with Perseus to save the dragon, but quickly sees how "coquettish" and "affected" Perseus is and rejects him. The self-reflexivity of Laforgue's version of the Ovidian myth is foregrounded by Perseus's depiction as "a silly comic opera hero," constantly preening himself and showing off his thaumaturgical tricks. When the Medusa's magic fails to work, Perseus slays the dragon; overcome by grief, Andromeda refuses his necklace of golden coins and clasps the dead monster, swearing her love and acknowledging that "he was . . . an accomplished gentleman, a scholar, and a fertile poet." Her kiss revives the dragon, who is subsequently transformed into a "well-equipped young gentleman" capable of answering to her sexual desires. The story ends happily as they sail away together. De l'Epinal's moral is that "young ladies" should "look at a monster twice" before disdaining him, for "the story shows" that "[h]e may well be worthy to become the happiest of the triangle."[145]

Reversing the positions of Perseus and the dragon – no longer the outcast of the story, the dragon becomes its hero and moral center – Laforgue's narrative might be read as a gloss upon "Ode." Andromeda's remorse at her vicious, demanding behavior and the vindication of the sexually inadequate dragon, who turns out to be a misunderstood poet, implies that Laforgue's tale serves as a revenge fantasy upon the succuba/bride of Eliot's poem. However, the syntactical disruptions in the poem's third stanza obstruct any direct equivalence between these narrative layers and therefore the possibility of drawing a univocal conclusion from the citation.

In Laforgue's story, the princess objects to her tutor's interpretation, referring to the arrangement of the stars in which the constellations of Perseus and Andromeda lie together whereas the stars of the dragon are "like outcasts." According to Ovid's version of Perseus's triumphant, "Golden apocalyse" and the dragon's exile, the latter sits "beneath Charles' Wagon."[146] Although the tutor dismisses her objection by claiming that the configuration of the stars "doesn't prove anything," their competing citations make explicit the exchangeability of the figures of the dragon/Perseus/bridegroom/poet. In accordance with Laforgue's tale, the dragon's "resentment" in "Ode" is "fooled," resulting in the apocalyptic revelation of his true nature and in Perseus's "indignation" at his "cheap extinction," leading to the latter's petulant, nocturnal departure. Taking the place of Ovid's defeated dragon, so easily dispatched by the conquering hero, Laforgue's Perseus is the innocent victim in the citation from *Macbeth* ("The deep damnation of his [Duncan's] taking-off"). Moreover, the victimized bridegroom who "smoothed his hair" is linked both with the sexually and poetically inadequate dragon as well as with Perseus in Laforgue's story, who "looks in the mirror while he rearranges his golden curls." Perseus's coquetry also aligns him with Laforgue's Andromeda and de l'Epinal's immature princess.

The multiple crisscrossings among these texts overdetermine any reading of "Ode" in terms of its citational references. Instead of a genealogy, the citations in Eliot's text offer a series of itineraries without any discernible end. Indeed, the difficulty of tracing any particular citation in "Ode" to its source and the excessiveness of the poem's citationality in general may attest to Eliot's wish to conceal another, personal allusion within the folds of the Ovidian, Laforguean, and Shakespearean references. Shortly after his marriage, Eliot was involved in a sexual triangle with Vivien and Bertrand Russell in which he was the "outcast" member.[147] Their arrangement was probably tacit, although Eliot's humiliation may have found displaced expression in the dragon's "resentment."

If there is a hero or at least an antihero in Eliot's tortuous tale, it is the poor dragon who has tolerated the whims and sexual demands of a coquette whom he cannot satisfy. Inverting the Victorian version of the Perseus and Andromeda myth, "Ode" is a poem about the failure of marriage; in place of Andromeda's erotic bondage and rescue, the poem depicts her dominating the submissive dragon. Eliot thus converts a narrative used to celebrate female domesticity into a complaint against female power and a lament for the impotence of the effeminate Perseus and the pathetic dragon. No longer an antidote to the dangers of assertive women, Eliot's remaking of the classical story represents the catastrophic effects of unshackled female sexual desire – the bondage of men by women.

The final lines of the poem serve as an epigraph that restores its male subject by memorializing him, placing him simultaneously in the stars and underneath the waves. Miller has noticed that the poem concludes "with a body beneath the waters."[148] In the last stanza, the authorial subject of the poem seems to write his own elegy as the voice from beyond the grave or from beneath the watery floor. The conclusion of "Ode" thus succeeds in eliminating its abjected bride but resigns the poem to narcissistic circularity as the drowned corpse of the surrogate gazes back at the living death of the author. The elegiac conclusion restores the specular pair of author and surrogate by means of the figure of prosopopeia in which the speaker addresses or apostrophizes himself as dead. Speaking from beyond the grave, he departs from the world that has misunderstood him and the bride who has tormented him. This transcendence, bought at the price of the subject's death, stabilizes the poem in a suicide fantasy. Yet, obscured by the citational evasions of the text are the veiled figures of Vivien and Charlotte Eliot as well as, beyond them, all the Andromedas that modernist male writers found so threatening.

## THE WASTE LAND

The errancy of paternal citations and the disruptions of maternal inter-texts are everywhere evident in *The Waste Land*, which elaborates the conflicts evident in "Hysteria," "Whispers of Immortality," and "Ode." In the wake of scathing criticism directed against Eliot in the 1970s and 1980s by Harold Bloom, Maud Ellmann, Terry Eagleton and others, the literary pieties that formerly exalted the poem have been abandoned, leaving it a rather tarnished literary icon. *The Waste Land* is now primarily of interest for precisely the errant tendencies that were previously corrected, explained away, or ignored; its fragmentation, obscurity, and anti-Semitic and misogynistic representations appear as symptoms of modern aesthetic and social dilemmas. Attractive to current readers insofar as it resists coherence, the poem has lately been interpreted as a critique of literary and sexual proprieties. Harriet Davidson, for instance, argues that it lacks "respect for tradition," is fascinated with "mutation, degradation, and fragmentation," split between a longing for "'improper' sexual desires" and a wish to be "rid" of them.[149]

In a curious twist of literary history, recent critics of *The Waste Land* have returned to the questions that concerned its initial readers, before its elevation to the status of a classic. Troubled by its disorderliness and its debasement of literary value, John Crowe Ransom complained in 1923 that "Eliot inserts beautiful quotations into ugly contexts," and that his poem is "a considerable affront against aesthetic sensibilities."[150] Trying to recapture this sense of *The Waste Land*'s offensiveness, critics at the end of the century stress its chaotic structure, its multiple voices, and its internal conflicts, which render it an unfinalized, open text. In so doing, however, they continue to beat a dead horse. Since the poem's publication, readers have been obsessed with the issue of its unity versus its fragmentation, torn between its centripetal and centrifugal forces, divided between its assertions of coherence and its dispersal of authority. Noting its "fissured" critical history, Pinkney observes that, "if you choose the terminology of religious transcendence, then *The Waste Land* emerges as a politically conservative poem," but if "you employ a Bakhtinian terminology, then *The Waste Land* is virtually a revolutionary poem, opening the cultured, upper-class salon to the heteroglot 'streets.'" Finally, he admits, "in this poem, heteroglossia and the monologic battle it out to an exhausted standstill."[151]

This tedious debate, which has swamped criticism of *The Waste Land*, is characteristic of many modernist texts. Modernism in general, including the works of Joyce, Proust, Malcolm Lowry, and many others, is marked by a hypertrophy of marginalia, a surplus of internal and external self-annotation that manifests a much-remarked twentieth-century anxiety concerning the integrity and status of the literary work. The encyclopedic excessiveness of Joyce's and Proust's novels foregrounds stylistic play at the expense of narrative cohesion, while the incessant allusiveness of Eliot's poems interrupts their structural unity. To cut through the tiresome antimony of the modernist literary text as a totality or a fragment, and of the values attributed to these terms, requires an examination of how literary value is produced, particularly the ways in which analyses of literary texts are tautological elaborations of cultural values that the texts are believed to embody. Nowhere is this more necessary than with *The Waste Land*.

The chef d'oeuvre of modernism, *The Waste Land* is effectively an inkblot of its readers' understandings of its literary-historical moment. Eagleton sees a deceptive equivocation in the poem, which is both a "wholesale demolition and salvage job" of aesthetics; its disjunctive form "mimes the experience of cultural disintegration," yet its allusions surreptitiously "attempt to construct an ideal order" transcending the collapse that it represents.[152] Similarly, Paul Morrison charges that *The Waste Land* is an anodyne to the "fragmentation it diagnoses," soliciting "the most traditional forms of authority" while depicting their demise.[153] Strictly speaking, Eagleton and Morrison are neither wrong nor right, for *The Waste Land* is sufficiently unstable to support even self-contradictory interpretations such as Eagleton's, which itself deceptively equivocates between praise for its "decentered," "progressive form" and denunciation of its "totalising, mythological forms." Eagleton's and Morrison's real target is the canonical orthodoxy that the poem has come to represent, as read in the context of Eliot's conservative social criticism. However, Eliot's early poetry and critical prose manifest such interior errancy that to judge *The Waste Land* as either "conservative" or "radical" is to miss the crucial point that his works stray from their apparent intentions. Attending to their internal dehiscence may not avoid the critical projection of values onto Eliot's texts, but it may make one less hasty to conclude that they serve a definite political end. Moreover, it allows us to go beyond the exhausted impasse of the unity versus fragmentation debate to a more nuanced consideration of the poem's ideological as well as formal problems.

*The Waste Land* depicts in painful and desperate ways the modern dilemma of masculine heterosexuality. Discussing its historical representation, John Bowen persuasively asserts that the poem compels its readers to face "dying civilizations," its citations serving as an "obituary" of the Austro-Hungarian, Ottoman, Russian and British empires. *The Waste Land*, "like Schliemann's Troy, is a ruin of a ruin, comprising treasures and detritus, glittering jewels and broken potsherds scattered on a plain," its "historical importance" lying in "its willingness to remain a ruin and not seek to become a monument," notwithstanding attempts of critics "to rebuild the city." For this reason, he argues, *The Waste Land* is "the least nostalgic [poem] in the language," and Eliot, "an agent of the secret discontent of his own class."[154] Challenging the traditional, elegiac interpretation of the poem's allusive texture, Bowen's account parallels, in another thematic register, the ruination of paternal authority evident in Eliot's early poetry.

Eliot is an agent of the "secret discontent" of his sex, to rephrase Bowen. The nostalgic yearnings for maternal union or for paternal filiation in his poetry are framed by hardnosed, violent abjections of femininity and homophobic displacements of masculine affection. Like Eliot's other early poems as well as his prose writings, *The Waste Land* records the catastrophic failure of the Law of the Father, not, as Davidson would have it, a "resigned . . . acceptance of the . . . Symbolic" order.[155] Reading Eliot's texts as symptomatic of modern masculine uneasiness, my aim is not to restore their canonical value but to use them as a means of exploring the function – and dysfunction – of their interlocking sexual and literary investments. *The Waste Land's* notoriously profuse and esoteric allusions, like those in "Ode," are a performance of citationality that displays both the iterative constitution of discursive authority and the particular deviations that citational practice takes in Eliot's texts.

From its publication, the notes to *The Waste Land* have lain at the crux of debates over its meaning, disputed as offering a controlling, mythical or "moral programme," according to Ellis, or as so much "junk, litter, [and] debris," in Pinkney's view.[156] The proliferation of allusions, including but not limited to those that Eliot lists in the notes, are blamed for leading readers astray and have confounded efforts to situate the poem in a definitive interpretive context. The surplus of significance produced by the citations generates an economy of excess, virtually an unreserved expenditure of semantic capital, that continually diverts citational chains into fruitfully wasteful avenues or alleyways, rendering the poem a Venice of textual prodigality. Eliot's note on Tiresias, his most explicitly pedagogical one, offers an example of the citational errancy of *The Waste Land* and its sexual pressures.

Eliot instructs the reader that Tiresias "is the most important personage in the poem, uniting all the rest." Many a desperate reader has grasped at this straw and proclaimed Tiresias the "protagonist" whose vision governs the poem,[157] but Calvin Bedient rightly points out that he is a voyeuristic "seer," a peeping Tom peering through the blinds at a seedy sexual skit. Although Bedient unconvincingly maintains that "there is a single presiding consciousness in the poem," it is not Tiresias, who is merely one of the impersonations of what Bedient calls its "poet-protagonist."[158] The sordid scene of seduction that Tiresias watches possesses a crass carnality which, like that of Grishkin, is riveting in its mechanical vulgarity. Eliot's misleading note continues: "Just as the one-eyed merchant, seller of currants, melts into the Phoenician Sailor, . . . so all the women are one woman, and the two sexes meet in Tiresias." Thus endowed with a spurious androgyny and dubious spectatorship, the figure of Tiresias has often obscured the powerful sexual conflicts in the poem. Male and female, far from joining in the poem, diverge and exchange places in violent disjunctions, much like the bride and bridegroom of "Ode." In the rhizomic underworld of *The Waste Land*, Tiresias is linked to that other prophetic fraud, Madame Sosostris, her tarot cards containing a "one-eyed merchant." In short, Tiresias is a trope for the drag-like metamorphoses of masculine women and effeminate men.

"The change of Philomel" in part 2 is one of several moments in the poem in which a presumptively male subject is put in the position of a violated woman. The transformation of the raped Philomela of Ovid's tale into a nightingale parallels the transformation of the "raped" male subject into a mutilated, feminized poet (or author surrogate). The "changed" Philomel is a peculiar gesture of female identification yet does not entail sympathy for women; no mention is made of Procne's violent revenge upon Tereus, nor of Philomela's web.[159] For a man to be feminized in *The Waste Land* simply means that he is figuratively sodomized by a powerful woman, like the bridegroom victimized by the succuba in "Ode."

The scene in which Philomel appears is dominated by a Cleopatra-like lady, enthroned upon a "Chair," her phallic endowment expressed by her glittering "jewels," her "fiery," savage hair, and, especially, "her strange synthetic perfumes" that "drowned the sense in odors." The lady's "enclosed" and enclosing room is, bizarrely, a sea in which the self-pitying male subject comes to grief. The theme of drowning, relentlessly repeated from Eliot's earliest poems through *Four Quartets*, is inextricably bound up with anxieties concerning women and male sexuality. Anthony Julius rightly situates the drowning motif in the context of the murders of women in his poetry, remarking that "Eliot inaugurated his literary career with lines about undrownable women and drowned men; towards its end, he wrote a play [*The Family Reunion*] in which an apparently undrownable woman drowns."[160] The plangency of "Prufrock's" concluding death scene ("Till human voices wake us, and we drown"), like the "Death by Water" section of *The Waste Land*, lends what one is tempted to call a "fatal attraction" to this feminine element. As late as "The Dry Salvages," Eliot elegizes sailors lost "in the sea's lips / Or in the dark throat which will not reject them." That the engulfing gullet of "Hysteria" becomes in the later poem a "strong brown god" indicates the gender-switching that takes place in all of the drowning scenes: as helpless victims of masculine women, the drowned young men are feminized. The "staring forms" that lean from the walls of the lady's room in "A Game of Chess" none too subtly imply who will be her next trophy.

What makes this common male complaint interesting is its potential for unsettling heterosexual norms by opening up homosexual possibilities. These remain tacit, densely coded, and deniable intimations in *The Waste Land* yet are suggestive of the sort of tender affection between men that Eliot recognized in Tennyson's *In Memoriam*. An important subtext for *The Waste Land*, as we know from its original title, is Charles Dickens's *Our Mutual Friend*, in which the topos of drowning plays a prominent role. The deaths of Headstone and Riderhood, who drown while locked in an antagonistic yet strangely amorous embrace, draws attention to the same-sex eroticism of Eliot's drowning scenes. The mutual specularity of the conclusion of "Ode," with the drowned corpse of the bridegroom gazing back at the face of the morbid poet, constructs male same-sex desire as doomed narcissism, what Eliot, in his review of Murry's biography of Lawrence, called "a venture of despair."[161] Submarine associations connect "the drowned Phoenician Sailor, / Those are the pearls that were his eyes. Look!" (lines 47–48) of Madame Sosostris's tarot deck and the eroticism of hyacinths ("I remember / The hyacinth garden. Those are the pearls that were his eyes" [lines 125–26]) with Apollo's dead young lover, Hyacinth. A circuitous chain links Hyacinth in Ovid's *Metamorphoses* to the symbolist literature that informs Eliot's early poetry – the fetishistic image on "hyacinth hair" in Poe, Baudelaire, and Mallarmé, Huysman's occult Hyacinthe in *Là-bas*, and Pater's portrait of Hyacinth, trembling on the verge of explicit homosexuality.[162]

The homoerotic implications of Eliot's hyacinth were first drawn by John Peter who, like Miller and Mayer, finds a biographical source for them in Eliot's youthful friendship with Jean Verdenal.[163] The Verdenal story has often been dismissed as unfounded conjecture or malicious gossip.[164] Textual evidence that "the 'hyacinth girl' appears to be male," according to G. Wilson Knight, or that hyacinths are "allied to the protagonist . . . in his hidden figuration as the hyacinth boy," in Bedient's words, have been met largely with silence.[165] Instead of opening up *The Waste Land* to a more ample reading of the complexity of same-sex desire and cross-gender identification, the multivalent implications of the hyacinth allusion have induced the complaint that dirty-minded critics sully Eliot's reputation and impugn male friendships.[166]

In response to this charge, we might recall Eliot's remark in his note on Tiresias that "the one-eyed merchant, seller of currants, melts into the Phoenician Sailor." The former, a figure in Sosostris's "wicked pack of cards," reappears as "the Smyrna merchant," Mr. Eugenides, "with his pocket full of currants" (lines 209–10) and his homosexual proposition. Taking Eliot at his word, the continuity between the sleazy Eugenides and the handsome, elegized Phlebas attests to the disavowed erotic currant they share. Far from proving that Eliot was secretly homosexual or that the "hyacinth girl" is Verdenal in disguise, these contiguities demonstrate the vagrancy of forbidden desires and identifications which Eliot considered errant and, especially later, tried to distinguish sharply. Indeed, they testify to the force of Eliot's determined, stiff-upper-lip affirmation of heterosexual masculinity.

Most important for a reading of the figure of hyacinth – including its female version as "the hyacinth girl" – is that, together with the trope of drowning, it condenses male delicacy and same-sex passion within the protective veil of death. Just as Headstone and Riderhood embrace under water, and just as Tennyson warmly expresses his love for Hallam when the latter is cold in the grave, so homoeroticism in Eliot's poetry invariably takes the form of necrophilia, not only because it is safer that way but because homosexuality is itself seemingly fatal. In short, *The Waste Land* splits sanctioned homoeroticism from degraded homosexuality, in much the way that women are split between virgins and whores. Critics have continued the job of policing the boundary in order to prevent the Smyrna merchant from corrupting the Phoenician sailor.

Finally, the drowning figure elucidates the relation between misogyny and homoeroticism in Eliot's poetry as well as its manifest attractiveness to him. The sea is simultaneously the site of death (by mother) and a refuge from her. Eliot's treatment of the motif in *The Family Reunion* (1939) is representative of the continued significance of this powerful trope in his later work. In *Four Quartets*, the drowning goes on: "The houses are all gone under the sea" in "East Coker," and the sea "tosses up our losses . . . / And the gear of foreign dead men" in "Dry Salvages." However, *Four Quartets* and Eliot's plays are notably free of the allusions that pervade his early poetry. This profound change in Eliot's citational practice corresponds to the virtually complete absence of disruptive, maternal intertexts in his later texts. Although sustained consideration of that body of work lies beyond the scope of this study, *The Family Reunion* calls for attention insofar as it recapitulates and tries to resolve the central conflict between paternal and maternal authority in his early poetry.

## THE FAMILY REUNION

This ironically titled play represents Eliot's last literary attempt to free himself from his family. Bringing the figure of the mother on stage, Eliot diegetically represents the forces that formerly erupted in the interstices of his poems. Indeed, *The Family Reunion* reverses the configuration of the early poetry by directly addressing previously obscure maternal power and by abandoning appeals to paternal authority through the citation. The play is, as Hugh Kenner observes, a revisionary "rewriting of the long-unfinished *Sweeney Agonistes*": "Throughout *The Waste Land*, in *Sweeney Agonistes* and *The Family Reunion*, Prufrock, disguised as Sweeney and as Harry, drowned this woman over and over."[167] This time he succeeds. The play's cast of characters is familiar: a dead father whom his son can "hardly remember"; a harried son, Harry, who killed his wife by shoving her off the deck of an ocean liner but who isn't sure if he "only dreamt I pushed her"; a domineering mother, Amy, the dowager Lady Monchensey, who controls the paternal estate and "who always wanted too much for my children"; and a trio of "whispering aunts" and two ineffectual uncles.

The striking characteristic of this family is that each of the principals desires the death of at least one of the others. Before his demise, the "diffident" father schemed on how to "get rid" of his wife, having "yielded" too long to her power. Amy is not only happy that her daughter-in-law has drowned but, a cousin speculates, she "had killed her by willing." It is common knowledge in the family that Harry wanted to kill his wife, and one uncle dismisses his confession of murder on the grounds that "it is simply the wish to get rid of her / Makes him believe he did." Most of all, though, Harry wants to kill his mother, which he succeeds in doing at the end of the play by abandoning her. Leaving home, the site of "danger" and "death," Harry frees himself from his mother's suffocating power and, almost magically, causes her to die.

Eliot modelled *The Family Reunion* on Aeschylus's *Orestes*, interwoven with the Christian motif of guilt and atonement. Critics have largely followed Agatha's injunction that the play "is not a story of detection, / Of crime and punishment, but of sin and expiation." Rather than a Greek tragedy or a Christian allegory, *The Family Reunion* resembles the crime fiction of which Eliot was fond – he was especially interested in the murders of women[168] – and seems like an allegory of Eliot's personal life. Moreover, the play dramatizes in an almost comical way the aggressions that energize his earlier poetry. The motivating conflict between Harry and his mother is displaced onto the offstage drowning of his wife, for these female figures are fundamentally exchangeable. Although the wife was merely a "restless shivering painted shadow" (strikingly similar to Vivien), she was nonetheless tenacious. Harry cannot believe he succeeded in pushing her off the deck: "I had always supposed," he confesses, "[t]hat she was unkillable." Downing, his servant, offers the excuse that his wife's mood swings made Harry "depressed," and besides, "She wouldn't leave him alone." Tormented by guilt, Harry is hounded by "ghosts of the drowned," the Eumenides, but obliquely blames his murderous act on his mother, who made all her children feel like "failures." "The rule of conduct" in the family, he says, was "pleasing mother," who "[n]ever punished us, but made us feel guilty." Amy's devouring "voracious[ness]," her sister Agatha implies, lies at the bottom of the bloody business.

Agatha is the most intriguing character in *The Family Reunion*. A powerful, independent woman, like Miss Nancy Ellicott of "Cousin Nancy," a New Englander who "Strode across the hills and broke them," Agatha is shielded from the vengeance typically wreaked upon such women in Eliot's poetry, perhaps because she hates women. Having made a career as headmistress, she describes herself as having spent "thirty years of solitude, / Alone, among women, in a women's college, / Trying not to dislike women." Her virility renders her more of a man than any other character in the play, and she is given the privileged role of the wise truth-teller. It is she who informs Harry about his father and who castigates Amy for her "fury for possession." In effect, Agatha stands in for the father that Harry never had. Finally, she has the last word in the play, instructing the audience on "the pilgrimage / Of expiation" and intoning the benediction.

Eliot was dissatisfied with *The Family Reunion*, divided as he saw it between "the tragedy of the mother and the salvation of the son." Commenting on the play years later, in "Poetry and Drama" (1951), Eliot's sympathies had shifted to the mother, while he now found Harry "an insufferable prig" (*OPP* 90–91). The intervening years evidently tempered the vindictiveness directed against Amy in the play, restoring his maternal allegiance. *The Family Reunion* seems to be an incompletely therapeutic dramatization of Eliot's dysfunctional family or even an indirect confession of guilt for the crime of wanting to kill one's wife. In a letter to Martin Browne, who produced the play, Eliot explained that "the effect of his married life upon Harry was one of such horror as to leave him . . . psychologically partially desexed; . . . it has given him a horror of women as of unclean creatures."[169] However, it would be a mistake simply to conclude, in Downing's words, that Harry – or Eliot – "[s]uffered from what they call a kind of repression," a diagnosis mocked in the play by the introduction of a doctor to figure out what is wrong with Harry. Rather, Eliot's works are eloquently expressive of the discontent of modern men toward prevailing gender and sexual arrangements. *The Family Reunion* frankly confronts the complex sexual identifications and abjections, the maternal yearnings and paternal filiations, even the murderous violence of which the fabric of modern masculinity is woven.

In conclusion, Eliot's work calls for rereadings that locate alternative citations in his texts. Excavating the maternal intertexts hidden within the profusion of Eliot's paternal citations also opens up the possibility of a more generous understanding of the textual circuits of errant desires, including but not limited to those between men. Furthermore, the effacement of the mother in the critical construction of Eliot's oeuvre has gone hand-in-hand with the forgetting of other, defaced figures of women in his texts – their hysterics, whores, and succubae. The trouble with Harry, Eliot remarks, is that he "wants to *forget*."[170] The ceaseless recitation of Eliot's paternal citations by generations of critics, including those openly hostile to him, has locked Eliot's work within an exclusively patriarchal literary tradition that is, moreover, blind to the nuances of masculine identification and love. Rather than pursuing the errancy of his citational practice, Eliot's critics have too often assumed its orthodoxy, thereby confirming or dismissing him as a father-figure of the modernist canon and limiting inquiry into his texts. To loosen his work from its restrictive mooring in the institutionalized discourse of modernism requires the demystification of the citation's pretensions to authority, principally as a vehicle of traditional legitimation. As a precedent, one may cite the betrayals of Eliot's own citational practice, itself a summons to errant, perverse readings.

# CHAPTER 3

# *Text of error, text in error: James Joyce's* Ulysses

How will you pun? You punish me? . . . Tell me I want to. Know.

> Joyce, "Sirens," *Ulysses*

Guesswork it reduced itself to eventually.

> Joyce, "Eumaeus," *Ulysses*

## JOYCEAN ERRANCY

Fritz Senn has remarked that "errors seem to cluster around Joyce."[1] Demonstrating in ample detail that "*Ulysses* is full of errors and faults, lapses, slips, misprints, [and] false analogies,"[2] Senn's account raises larger questions of the significance of error in Joyce's text. While usually treated as an interpretive problem, the profusion of errors in *Ulysses* has, since the Kidd–Gabler controversy, provoked consideration of the nature of textual error, both in the restricted sense of the corruption of the text of *Ulysses* and in the broader sense of its textual instability. Moreover, the indeterminacy of the text of *Ulysses* supports a third view, in which the many errors with which the text is rife give rise to a general discursive errancy. Cut loose from the narrative and linguistic anchors that make possible the distinction between truth and error, or between meaningful, willed purposes and mere mistakes, random accidents, and stochastic arrangements, *Ulysses* has come to be seen by many as a wandering text ungoverned by authorial orderings.

These three conceptualizations of error – interpretive, textual, and discursive – are each fully and directly implicated in *Ulysses* with gender difference and sexual perversion, specifically, with feminine alterity and homosexuality. Rather than simply comprising part of the thematic content of a book whose formal complexity offers special challenges to its readers, the intertwined issues of feminine alterity and homosexual alterity are crucial to and even structurally formative of Joycean errancy at every level. In this chapter, I will begin by briefly discussing the problem of error on the three aforementioned levels. The second section of the chapter is devoted to an examination of the figure of femininity in *Ulysses*, while the third, longer section is focused on homosexuality.

*Ulysses* is an important site of the modern discursive struggle over the meaning of gender and sexuality. These asymmetrical but fundamentally interrelated issues are represented in very different manners in Joyce's text. His far more explicit depiction of female sexuality, in contrast to his muted, oblique portrayal of (almost exclusively male) homosexuality, reflects the epistemology of sexuality in our culture in which women, their bodies, and their desires are the object of incessant male investigation, whereas masculine desire, especially for other men, remains for the most part veiled. My purpose in examining the ways in which error functions in *Ulysses* is thus to inquire into the failures and lapses in the general system of knowledge about sexuality in the book, first by examining what Stephen and Bloom think they know about women. The willful ignorance at the heart of their supposed knowledge of women brings me to the second, larger topic of the understanding of homosexuality in *Ulysses*. Again, the question of error enables us to read the omissions, displacements, and disavowals through which same-sex desire is ambivalently apprehended. Finally, inasmuch as femininity and homosexuality are both deviations from the male heterosexual norm, they are always already "in error," whether openly celebrated as such or despised and concealed.

The peculiar interpretive difficulties posed by the rampant errors in Joyce's "epical forged cheque" (*FW* 181.16) have been extensively explored by critics. Such errors range from local lapses, such as the missing *t* in Bloom's "Plasto's high grade ha" (*U* 4.69–70), which seemingly imitate the textual corruption of *Ulysses*, to, on a larger level, the discontinuous plurality of styles throughout the book. This plethora of styles, according to Karen Lawrence, causes a "breakdown of the novel as a form and the creation of an encyclopedia of narrative choices," none of which serves as an authoritative voice.[3] Likewise, the proliferation of documentary details in *Ulysses* ironically calls into question the validity of documentary evidence, while the excess of Homeric analogies undermines the explanatory power of analogy itself. Given *Ulysses'* radical departure from narrative and literary conventions, it is not surprising that many of Joyce's critics have directed themselves toward at least accounting for, if not fixing, the forms of its straying.

In contrast to Eliot's attempts to ward off error in his critical prose and to suppress the maternal intertext in his poetry, Joyce's textual strategies in *Ulysses* seem to embrace the productive possibilities of error. The many misjudgments and mistakes made by characters in the text, such as the repeated confusion regarding the racehorse "Throwaway" and the digressive vagrancy of the narrative structure of the novel as a whole, far from inhibiting criticism, have fueled the engine of the Joyce scholarly industry. The efforts of many critics have been aimed at reducing the problems raised by these various kinds of error through appeals, for instance, to an "arranger" whose hidden hand, David Hayman supposes, "exercises . . . control over his . . . materials."[4] Hugh Kenner also reckons that "some mind, it is clear, keeps track of the details of this printed cosmos, and lets escape from its scrutiny the fall of no sparrow," and he thus adopts Hayman's "arranger" as a voiceless consciousness behind the text.[5] Although the assumption of some God in the machine has been typical of Joyce criticism,[6] such an omniscient Arranger must be, as Frederic Jameson decisively argues, either "an imbecile or a schizophrenic."[7] These critical labors to organize the text testify to the fecundity of error in *Ulysses*, provoking not only scholarly corrections but further errors.

The critic who has most fully documented the specific errors in *Ulysses* is Fritz Senn. Finding it both "annoying and wholly appropriate" that Joyce's text is rife with "derailment[s], deviation[s], dislocution[s], omissions, chance delays, and collisions," Senn argues that such failures are "intrinsic" to the programmed "malfunction" of the work.[8] In his view, *Ulysses* both thematizes and performs the movement of erring; not only do its characters continually make mistakes and try to mend them, but their interpretive mishaps and corrections are mimed by the readers of *Ulysses*. Thus, his emphasis is not just on how characters in *Ulysses* err but, especially, on how they attempt to set these errors aright. The project of interpretive "righting" operates on four levels: in the activities of characters in the book (notably Bloom); in Joyce's revisionary artistic procedures; in the reader's interpretive "adjustments"; and in the text itself inasmuch as it "seems to try to right itself," each episode rewriting previous ones. According to Senn, the epistemological fumblings in *Ulysses* are guided by unspecified "corrective urges" that strive "towards systematic completion."[9]

Such a phenomenology of reading is explicitly directed by a teleology that is mystically built into Joyce's text, a belief upheld by what Vicki Mahaffey criticizes as "the myth of a mastermind."[10] Moreover, Senn's valuable local observations of epistemological failures in and of *Ulysses* are framed by his narrative of the reader's progress in which missteps lead ineluctably to correction. Error is the avenue to truth, just as the apparent mistakes of "a man of genius," according to Stephen, are in fact "portals of discovery" (*U* 9.228–29). Within this circular logic, interpretive lapses are always ultimately rectified, and *Ulysses* is celebrated as, in Senn's words, "a polytropic endeavor to comprehend all possible modes of being,"[11] including even mistaken readings of itself.

However gratifying such a belief in the all-knowing book may be, a book that tutors us in our misunderstandings of itself and waits for us to realize or actualize its truth,[12] such a notion bears a disquieting similarity to Bloom's belief in his comprehension of Molly. His attempts to teach her are largely unsuccessful, for her "deficient mental development" resists his efforts at correction. Yet Molly's mistakes ironically undercut Bloom's own assurance, for he, too, misquotes and mispronounces foreign words, commits errors of calculation, and exhibits naïveté, domestic and public. The reflection of Bloom's errors in what he condescendingly views as Molly's lapses might appear simply to mime once more the reader's errancy and thus to reiterate the self-reflexive mastery of this book, were it not that Molly's errors hold a special status in *Ulysses*. While Bloom's and Stephen's errors are represented as unsteady grasps at knowledge, Molly's mind is like a sieve, holding nothing, and her errors are presented as a nonteleological vagrancy, unconcerned with arriving at the truth. Bloom describes her responses to his attempts at "direct instruction" thus: "She followed not all, a part of the whole, gave attention with interest, comprehended with surprise, with care repeated, with greater difficulty remembered, forgot with ease, with misgiving reremembered, rerepeated with error" (*U* 17.698–702). The amusing mistakes and outright follies exhibited by other women in the text, such as Martha Clifford and Gerty MacDowell, thus reach their apotheosis in "Penelope," a text that seems to transcend the distinction between truth and error.

While other characters make mistakes, Molly inhabits error; whereas Stephen's and Bloom's slips simply indicate human epistemological frailty, Molly's monologue is, according to Phillip Herring, "a tapestry of contradictions" in which error and truth promiscuously mingle.[13] Previously dismissed as "formless" and "without style," "Penelope" has since been celebrated by some feminist critics as the conclusive statement of indeterminacy in *Ulysses*.[14] Molly's peculiar position on the margin of the text yet also as its culmination – the "clou" of the text, in Joyce's ambiguous term (*LJ* 1:170) – both places her outside its economy of righting/writing and calls upon her affirmative endorsement of it.[15]

It is by now a critical commonplace to link Joyce's disruption of linguistic and literary norms in his later texts, particularly *Ulysses* and *Finnegans Wake*, with his representation of a so-called feminine language in Molly's and ALP's monologues. More generally, Joyce's attempt to break out of patriarchal literary, social, and religious structures of authority hinges upon the interpretation of "Penelope" as offering an alternative to those structures. Molly thus assumes a crucial role as a figure of female otherness, both outside and subversive of masculine sexual and textual norms. Her feminine difference permits her, so *Ulysses* leads us to believe, a kind of errant liberty. Sexual and epistemological waywardness thus converge in the figure of a woman who, apparently free from patriarchal authority, also escapes the norms of truth. *Ulysses* suggests that the interpretive errancy wrought by its plethora of errors and by its general stylistic errancy is implicated with feminine alterity.

By aligning this fructive errancy with femininity, *Ulysses* is in keeping with the habits and norms of Western thought for thousands of years. Yet the relation between error and sexual deviance – in particular, homosexual desire – is far more equivocal and occluded. In the following section of this chapter, "Cheating on the Law of the Father," I address the ways in which Joyce represents women as at once beneath and beyond the symbolic order. This order, sustained by what Lacan calls the Law of the Father, is the regime of logic and language, whose transgression in Molly's monologue is often understood as Joyce's climactic celebration of femininity. Such a reading, while in some respects faithful to what Joyce might have believed, nonetheless confirms the very paternal law whose violation it supposedly applauds. Moreover, this reading of the meaning of gender difference in *Ulysses* often turns a blind eye to the imbrication of gender and sexuality. The relation between same- and cross-gender desire complicates any clearcut distinction between masculinity and femininity in *Ulysses*.

Sexual perversity, broadly speaking, and its relation to the many kinds of error in and of the text of *Ulysses* are much less frequently discussed issues than that of errant femininity. Just as the knowledge of homosexuality functions as a shameful secret in *Ulysses*, so, too, Joyce's critics have in general avoided mention of it. However, sexual difference and sexual perversity are bound up in all sorts of ways. Historically, the early twentieth century marked the beginning of an ongoing derangement of gender and sexual definition, in which male and female gender identities became linked in sometimes conflicting ways with the nature and direction of sexual desire.[16] Since then, for a man to identify too much with *either* other men *or* women puts him at risk of exposing a latent homosexuality. The emergence of the social and sexological categories of heterosexuality and homosexuality is at once a provocation of and a response to this crisis. Moreover, since the articulation of these separate categories of sexuality, a host of other sexual practices have tended to be grouped under these headings, so that perversions of all sorts now cluster around homosexuality. Indeed, the invention of the homosexual may be seen as an attempt to resolve the confusion of sexual definition by organizing sexual desire according to two, supposedly distinct, sexual orientations.[17]

*Ulysses* participates in the crisis of sexual definition that became especially acute about the turn of the century, in which the distinction between heterosexuality and homosexuality became the central axis that orders a variety of heretofore discrete sexual and nonsexual practices. Hence, the various sorts of sexual transgression represented in Joyce's work, including flagellation, sadomasochism, masturbation, fetishism, coprophilia, and so forth, are all directly or indirectly linked to the decisive and phobically charged division between heterosexuality and homosexuality. Moreover, this division is fundamentally implicated with the several types of error outlined above – interpretive, textual, and discursive errancy. Already a deviation from the sanctioned path of desire, homosexuality functions in *Ulysses* as a secret disclosed through slips, rumors, and misrecognitions.

The occluded, uncertain representation of homosexuality in *Ulysses* raises a host of questions concerning the interpretive capabilities and errors of the characters within *Ulysses*, especially Stephen and Bloom, who variously suppress or displace their knowledge of same-sex desire. Moreover, it casts considerable doubt upon the institution of Joyce criticism which, like Stephen and Bloom, has heretofore averted its gaze from the prospect of homosexual desire in the text. Finally, it broaches the troublesome issue of Joyce's authorial intentions as they have been embodied in various editions of *Ulysses*. The dispute over the Gabler edition has been in part fueled by the fact that this edition has offered a more ample reading of homosexual relations among its male figures.

The debate over the 1984 edition of *Ulysses* by Hans Walter Gabler has drawn attention to the issue of textual error and its relation to the interpretive possibilities and limitations offered by any edition of Joyce's text. Initially publicized as correcting over five thousand errors,[18] subsequent commentary on the Gabler edition, by Gabler himself and others, has made clear that, rather than correcting previous mistakes by printers and copyists, the 1984 edition is in fact the construction of an altogether new text, largely on the basis of Joyce's manuscripts.[19] Although, in Jerome McGann's words, Gabler's edition is an invention or "imagination of Joyce's work and not its reconstitution," based principally upon a "reconstruction" of Joyce's "documents of composition,"[20] the issue of truth and error remains. Now, though, the problem is transferred to the level of the indeterminacy of the text as a material document, which reflects the ambivalence and fluctuations of Joyce's intentions. In short, the Gabler edition and the attendant controversy over its fidelity to what Joyce meant to write or publish calls for a conceptual shift from *error* to *errancy*.

Narrowly conceived, textual error refers to the failure of copyists, printers, proofreaders, and others to record faithfully the text that the author meant to publish – in a word, to what is commonly termed "transmission error." Such a concept also includes Joyce's own lapses insofar as he mistranscribed his own work or overlooked the mistakes of others. John Kidd's attack on the Gabler edition focuses on the fact that Gabler did not correct such mistakes.[21] This narrow conception of textual error also assumes the purity and singularity of Joyce's final intentions – precisely what the variability of the prepublication documents exposes as a fiction.[22] Recognizing what he calls "the instability of the text in process," Gabler argues that "authorial intention cannot rightly provide a constitutive basis . . . for editorial performance. Instead, . . . authorial intention . . . requires to be editorially set forth . . . [A]uthorial intention is not a metaphysical notion to be fulfilled but a textual force to be studied."[23] In other words, the author's intentions, rather than a yardstick by which to measure the accuracy of an edition, must be interpreted just as is the text which issues from them. In place of textual error, then, *Ulysses* confronts us with textual errancy – a processive and vagrant text that, within the social and historical conditions of its composition and publication, does not permit its fixation into either an "authoritative" or a "correct" text. Textual errancy, as I use the term, therefore refers to the instability of any text as a material document and to the corresponding heterogeneity of the intentions that underwrite it – including not only the author's but those of all others who have a hand in its composition and production.

What does textual errancy, thus understood, have to do with the thematics of gender and sexuality in *Ulysses*? In the broadest terms, reconceiving *Ulysses* as a textual process rather than as a finalized work suggests that the representations of sexual difference and deviation within it are likewise unstable and internally differentiated. Instead of searching for a consistent theme regarding gender identity and sexual desire, readers of this heterogeneous text might better look for its interior fissures. Moreover, female alterity and same-sex desire constitute, in varying but overlapping ways, forms of straying from normative male heterosexuality. Insofar as *Ulysses* represents male identification with femininity and acknowledges, however equivocally, homosexual affection, it is a decidedly errant text within the modernist canon. The particular errancy of the text of *Ulysses* thus enacts, on a documentary level, the vagaries of Joyce's ambivalence toward women and homosexuality.[24]

In her discussion of the Gabler edition, Vicki Mahaffey points out that "one of the difficulties of editing *Ulysses* involves preserving the misprints that Bloom and Stephen register without allowing the misprints in *Ulysses* itself to upstage the inculcated awareness that . . . print itself can 'tell a graphic lie' (*U* 16.1232)."[25] Distinguishing between, on the one hand, inadvertent misprints or transmission errors and, on the other hand, apparently deliberate errors that Joyce strewed throughout *Ulysses*, Mahaffey argues that "Joyce's use of 'volitional errors' . . . provided him with a way of intertwining conscious and unconscious awareness, intentional and unintentional expression, individual purpose and an . . . appreciation of chance and coincidence."[26] Moreover, this "intertwining" of knowledge and nonknowledge, graphically inscribed in such slips of the pen as the telegram Stephen receives in Paris, "Nother dying come home father" (*U* 3.199), renders undecidable the precise relation between what a character wishes to say and what, against his or her will, struggles for a voice.

The undecidability of error that Mahaffey detects is particularly acute in sexual matters. Situated on the boundary between conscious intention and unconscious impulse, the representation of sexual desire, and especially homosexual desire, in *Ulysses* is fraught with epistemological uncertainty. Nor is this simply a matter of repression in the psychoanalytic sense. Rather, this uncertainty manifests the anxiety and doubt that, for well over a century, has marked the division between heterosexuality and homosexuality in our culture. In short, one of the principal sites of discursive errancy in *Ulysses* is the ambivalent knowledge and nonknowledge of sexuality, a (mis)comprehension constituted and deformed by homophobia.

With some important but highly debatable exceptions, the understanding of sexuality presented in *Ulysses* is that of male heterosexual subjects, especially Stephen and Bloom. Like their author, they are situated unstably on what Eve Kosofsky Sedgwick has called the "homosocial continuum" of male relations. Sedgwick argues that

at least since the eighteenth century in England and America, the continuum of male homosocial bonds has been brutally structured by a secularized and psychologized homophobia . . . [T]he historically shifting and . . . the arbitrary and self-contradictory nature of the way *homosexuality* . . . has been defined in relation to the rest of the male homosocial spectrum has been an exceedingly potent and embattled locus of power over the entire range of male bonds, . . . especially over those that define themselves . . . *as against* the homosexual. Because . . . certain intense male bonds . . . were not readily distinguishable from the most reprobated bonds, an endemic and ineradicable state of . . . homosexual panic became the normal condition [of heterosexual men].[27]

The obfuscation of homosexuality in Joyce's text is the result of the dangerous similarity between the dearest and the most despised forms of love among men. The ensuing "panic" thus gives rise to what I am calling discursive errancy in *Ulysses*.

Not only is the relation between Stephen and Bloom uneasily poised between venerated paternal affection and proscribed same-sex love, but the meaning of the numerous allusions to homosexuality in the novel as a whole is uncertain or errant; they may be either oblique indications of the truth of a character's perverse desire, albeit leaking out through a slip of the tongue, or just accidents or misunderstandings, whether by characters in the text or by readers of it. Moreover, the difficulty of interpreting the obscure signs of same-sex desire in *Ulysses* is compounded by the contradictions and fluctuations in the concept of homosexuality as well as by the lexical indeterminacy of the discourse concerning homosexuality over the past century. While I will discuss these problems in greater detail later, it is also important to note that homosexual errancy in *Ulysses* is to no small degree the result of the indeterminacy of the language used to designate same-sex passion, a polyglot assortment of obscene slang, sexological and psychiatric clinical terminology, and various gay subcultural codes and idioms.

*Ulysses* has often been analyzed as a tripartite structure, each section represented by Stephen, Bloom, and Molly, and loosely corresponding to Joyce's division of the book. I take up this approach in the second half of this chapter, arguing that these figures represent three distinct epistemological positions regarding homosexuality. Briefly, Stephen knows about homosexuality but wishes that he did not, reverting to the topic in his thoughts yet refusing to speak of it. By contrast, Bloom's knowledge consists of a willful ignorance that sanctions his unwitting confessions of the flesh. Protected from overt acknowledgement of same-sex desire both by his deliberate evasions as well as by the increasingly indeterminate styles of the text, Bloom at once gives voice to perversion and is distanced from its pathologizing effects. Finally, Molly apparently stands outside the orbit of homosexual knowledge as well as its panicked denial. Moreover, male and female same-sex desire in *Ulysses*, as in the historical discourse of homosexuality, are not simply parallel. Molly's indulgence in lesbian fantasies, while remaining exempt from the contaminating touch of the "love that dare not speak its name," does not, in my view, place her above the constraints of compulsory heterosexuality in a realm of unfettered pleasure. Rather, like Eliot's women and, as we shall see, Proust's Albertine, Molly is a phallic woman, an imaginary construction whose function in *Ulysses* is principally her introjection by male subjects as a potent figure of sexual indeterminacy.

## CHEATING ON THE LAW OF THE FATHER

In Joyce's now-famous words, the "Penelope" episode is "the indispensable countersign to Bloom's passport to eternity" (*LJ* 1:160). Molly Bloom's "last word" to *Ulysses* hardly ends the story, though, and the ambiguity of her signature is troublesome. Does Molly *underwrite* Bloom's Odyssean voyage, her affirmative flesh the "breasts, arse, womb, and cunt" (*LJ* 1:170) that warrant his immortalization in *Ulysses*? Or does she sign *counter* to Bloom's signature, her menstrual mark controverting the narrative that Bloom has endorsed? Or does she simply *write over* it, blotting with her famed indifference the story that Bloom tells? As Patrick McGee points out, Molly's countersignature could only be construed to legitimate Bloom's – if indeed it does – "because [his] first signature lacks authenticity without the second to endorse and recognize it."[28] Hence, Molly's signature, along with its representation of female sexuality, has the structure of a supplement in the Derridean sense, one which calls into question the authority and integrity of that "first signature."

The sexual economy of the novel is initially governed by Stephen's division of women into virgins and madonnas, on the one hand, and whores on the other, an economy reproduced in the debate over how many lovers Molly really has had and thus whether she is a "good" or "bad" woman. Yet the complications introduced in every episode undermine the confidence Stephen exhibits in a male eye that surveys and appraises female sexuality as well as in a unified male subject who takes woman as the vehicle for transcendence. Instead of a symmetry of sexual difference, *Ulysses* demonstrates that difference is reproduced *within* the regimes of gender, and that the apparently simple terms of the male/female opposition are internally divided. Among the effects of this doubling is that Molly's discourse cannot be appealed to as resolving – either in the sense of concluding or dissolving – difference within a monologue that has, for so many, been read as the conjunctive, incor- porative moment of *Ulysses*, as the utterance in which addresser and addressee acquiesce, in which "I" and "you" converge into a communal "we" and say "yes" to love.

Whether or not it is "the word known to all men," *love* is at least the word invoked by Bloom in his definition of justice as "the opposite of hatred" (*U* 12.1485). Bloom's vision of a community in which the addressers and addressees are able to utter divergent phrases, free from "insult and hatred" (*U* 12.1482), is ironically contrasted to the patriotic myth promoted by the Irish citizen of the pub for whom community is defined and legitimated by a "we" determined by race and nation.[29] "Love," on the other hand, is not national but international, articulated by the multiracial Bloom and Molly. Yet the equivocations raised both in "Cyclops" and "Circe" (e.g., the "new Bloomusalem") suggest that Bloom's "we" without a "them" is a utopian fantasy of harmonious assimilation. What *appears* to legitimate Bloom's defense of love as the basis for community, for a collectivity that would merge men and women as "children of nature" – "Free money, free rent, free love" (*U* 15.1693) in a union of differences, of "mixed races and mixed mar- riage[s]" (*U* 15.1699) – is Molly's discourse. Her "language of flow" (*U* 11.298), according to Bonnie Kime Scott, is like the "feminine lan- guage" of ALP in *Finnegans Wake* and "is what provides the umbilicus," circulating and recirculating among continuous subjects, thus "offer[ing] a new politics of relationship and authorship."[30] Such a notion locates the exchange and circulation of phrases in a homogene- ous language, thereby seeking redemption in a nonalienated site figured by women's bodies in much the same way as do Stephen and Bloom.

Stephen's self-constitution as a son is blocked by his deep ambivalence toward his mother. As the female "other," she is "the womb of sin," the Eve/Ann Hathaway who seduces and betrays. But, on the other hand, Stephen insists on the naturalness and immutability of the maternal bond as opposed to the arbitrariness and contingency of the "mystical estate" of fatherhood: "*Amor matris*, subjective and objective genitive, may be the only true thing in life. Paternity may be a legal fiction" (*U* 9.842–44). The symmetry of the objective and subjective genitive (the mother's love/love of the mother) would render this phrase the perfectly closed circuit of an addresser and addressee who exchange places and share the same referent: tautological and thus incontrovertible. However, it is the reproachful ghost of the mother whom Stephen cannot love as she would have him who destroys this myth. For motherhood is neither reciprocal nor "true" but is just as much of a "fiction" as that of the madonna "which the cunning Italian intellect flung to the mob of Europe" (*U* 9.839–40). Maternity is Stephen's nocturnal resource and his nightmare, a fathomless origin and fatal destiny, as though the mute female body gestured from beyond the pale of the symbolic order in some unspeakable, undecidable infinity. His enigmatic formula, "in woman's womb word is made flesh but in the spirit of the maker all flesh that passes becomes the word that shall not pass away" (*U* 14.292–94), renders the womb a figure for a nonfigurable origin, the source of eternal art in perishable forms, the material ground of the immaterial word. As such, the womb is, in McGee's explanation, "undecidable, even though Stephen tries to make a decision" between the Virgin and the whore,[31] between the spiritual and the fleshly woman, and between the first Eve by whom "we are linked up with by successive anastomosis of navelcords," who "sold us all . . . for a penny pippin," and the second Eve, who will save us (*U* 14.300–1). This difference between the good and the bad woman brings Stephen to an aporia. Although Bloom does not express himself in Stephen's theological terms, and while his attitude toward femininity is significantly more complex than Stephen's, he is likewise troubled and fascinated by the divergence between female carnality and, in his words, "sacred, lifegiv[ing]" motherhood (*U* 15.4648–49).

Both Stephen and Bloom, along with many of their critics, arbitrate sexual difference by enclosing difference within one of the parties – the female. The determinate male self is defined against the female, who embodies in herself the opposition between definition and indefinability, or between flesh and spirit. Thus, the difference that separates male and female – that long string of metonymies by which man distinguishes himself from his "other" – is transferred or displaced onto the female who contains an *internal* self-difference that renders her undecidable. Male subjectivity initially seems assured by such a move – he, at least, is what is known – but at the price of surrendering woman to an ungraspable zone beyond the symbolic order, to a region where, he fears and hopes, the Name of the Father does not govern.

Such a configuration of Stephen's and Bloom's relation to women is common to both traditional scholars and to some recent feminists, the latter of whom find in the feminine presymbolic what they consider an alternative space outside paternal authority. Thus, Scott endorses what she believes to be, employing Julia Kristeva's terms, the "semiotic pre-speech" of *Finnegans Wake* as well as, shifting to Hélène Cixous's figure, Molly Bloom's "writing the body," both of which spring from "generative principles positively associated with the river, the primordial mud, and the mother."[32] However, this positing of a female space not only provides no leverage with which to dislodge paternal authority but accepts on its own terms the Law of the Father and its supposed governance of the symbolic code. Furthermore, such a strategy reinstates precisely the sexual difference it set out to question, and in virtually identical terms. This recuperation is also at work in Patrick McGee's and Colin MacCabe's readings of *Ulysses*.

Describing the figure of the womb as the "unfinalized frame" as opposed to the defined male phallus, for the former "insists on the representation of what has been foreclosed by the symbolic construction of the body of man," McGee transfers this feminine undecidability onto the privileged male characters in the novel. Stephen is said to exist on the margins of the symbolic order, for "he subverts the law of the father not by standing in the place of its imaginary opposition [the female position as such], but by standing on the edge of the symbolic."[33] Likewise, as the "spermatazoon" in "Oxen of the Sun," "Bloom is a masculine figure, [yet] he enters into a process that is indeterminate as to sex. He is not the phallus . . . . because, in some sense, he is there [in the womb] as an indeterminate part of what frames and is framed."[34] In short, Bloom's identification with Mrs. Purefoy in her labors enables him to become like, or even "part of," the mother.

Indeed, these male characters become even better "women" than the female characters, at least those like Gerty and Mrs. Purefoy who are prisoners of their sex. Locked in her conventional discourse, "Gerty is finalized and imprisoned by the language that speaks for her," incapable of transcending the limits of her gender, whereas Bloom, according to McGee, is "unfinalized."[35] Framed – in every sense of the word – by Joyce's style into precisely the gender opposition that femininity as a trope supposedly transcends, Gerty occupies the *male* position of determinacy and definition, while Bloom is the "womanly man" (*U* 15.1799).

The location of the indeterminacy of gender difference in one of the parties to the opposition thus neutralizes the force of femininity and confirms the opposition between male and female that it set out to overthrow.

According to MacCabe, what enables Bloom to "become a woman" is his "perverse" acknowledgement of castration.[36] Rather than shielding himself from castration by taking refuge in the phallus as a fetish, as though it were a stable signified, Bloom releases himself to the movement of signification. "This submission to the signifier is a submission to writing, and writing functions . . . as the very exemplar of perversion. The crucial feature of perversion . . . is the instability of sexual position."[37] Thus, in "Circe," Bloom partially succumbs to the "pressure of the feminine," lets go of the fetishized potato, and gives voice to the woman within him. But the woman he becomes, as McGee correctly notes, is *"what he imagines a woman to be."*[38]

MacCabe's argument that the gender confusion of "Circe" constitutes a "bisexuality" through which Bloom transcends the limitations of his own gender to become a multivoiced subject is premised on the prior bisection of woman into a presymbolic, pre-oedipal maternal plenitude (a whole) and the castrated female under the Law of the Father (a hole). This ambivalent construction reproduces sexual difference *within* the female subject who is thus thought to contain a fundamental, internal undecidability, an inherent doubleness; the female is accordingly the very *untruth* of the truth of sexual difference, and *her* body is the privileged site of the "suture" or folding in upon itself of male and female.[39] This projection of difference onto the female in turn permits the male subject to appropriate female undecidability as a means of attacking the father *in the name of woman.* Becoming female in *Ulysses*, a gesture that reaches its apogee in "Penelope" when a male pen writes a woman's desire, is thus not a matter of denying or dismantling or even inverting sexual difference but of the male introjection of a projected femininity, which seems to stand ambiguously on the edge of paternal authority. Thus, Christine van Boheemen argues that Joyce's assault on the logic of sexual difference "paradoxically proves in the final analysis to be inspired by a desire for totality and wholeness which . . . hinges on appropriation and assimilation as an oral incorporative strategy."[40]

This move and the "bisexuality" (MacCabe) or "androgyny" (McGee) or "intermediate sex" (Richard Brown) that purportedly issues from it constitute a kind of male drag show.[41] In support of his claim, Brown quotes Joyce's praise of Ibsen and his female characters:

[H]e seems to know them better than they know themselves. Indeed, if one may say so of an eminently virile man, there is a curious admixture of the woman in his nature. His marvelous accuracy, his faint traces of femininity, his delicacy of swift touch, are perhaps attributable to this admixture. (*CW* 64)

Joyce suggests that Ibsen is a better woman than a woman, as Bloom is a better woman than Gerty. However, Ibsen's "delicacy" does not, Joyce stresses, compromise his essential virility while it gives him epistemological access to women's secrets and allows him the vicarious experience of femininity.

The strategic function of this drag style is evident in the scene of masochism in "Circe." This scene is often cited as evidence of Bloom's bisexuality – after all, he and Bella Cohen switch genders. Yet Bloom's "femininity," including his transvestism, is the masochist's script for rebellion against the father, not an "identification" with women or somehow becoming female. According to Giles Deleuze in his interpretation of Leopold von Sacher-Masoch's *Venus in Furs* – the subtext of the scene in *Ulysses* – the masochist abjures the father and transfers the paternal functions onto the mother, especially the oral mother. In order to challenge the father's authority and to exorcise the repression he exercises over sexuality, the masochist engages in an alliance with the mother. Having expelled the father, "the masochist experiences the symbolic order as an intermaternal order in which the mother represents the law . . . ; she generates the symbolism through which the masochist expresses himself. It is not a case of identification with the mother."[42] By investing the *mother* with the symbolic power of the law so that she becomes the "ideal phallus," the masochist in effect punishes the father, for, according to Deleuze, in the masochistic scene it is "*a father that is being beaten.*"[43] Masochism thus achieves an ironic, even humorous, overthrow of the paternal prohibition, for by strictly applying the law – now in the hands of the mother – the masochist is able to feel the pleasure that the law had denied. The mother remains plumped full of the riches of the pre-symbolic and yet assumes the authority of the symbolic law. My reading of Deleuze differs from that of Frances Restuccia, who believes that Joyce did not feel that "he had transgressed against the father" because he was allegedly "too shameless and radically rebellious to worry about such transgression." She claims that Joyce's masochism led to his "liberation" from the father, paradoxically concluding that the law of the father is "abolished" by the end of *Ulysses*, while the "Church – as a feminine (albeit phallic) body led by Mother Mary . . . – prevails," thereby revealing her misunderstanding of Deleuze's argument.[44]

Just as the masochist, by sealing a pact with the mother and investing her with the paternal law, tries to expel the father's authority, Joyce attacks the father in the name of the mother, thus appropriating maternal power in order to neutralize the father, but finally on the father's terms. This move succeeds in placing woman in cosmic exile from the symbolic, powerful only insofar as she can return *in the place of the father* as the fantasy of the woman with the whip. Molly and Bella are versions of the same woman – in Brown's words, "massive, potent, and self-possessed."[45] The similarity between the monstrous Bella and the effusive Molly suggests that we analyze the male subject who produces a vision of the female as both this side of and beyond the law of the father.

There are many ways of cheating at the father's game, including masochism, which laughs at the paternal proscription by scrupulously submitting to its rules. Another way, equally ironic in its pyrrhic victory, has been forging the mother's signature with the father's hand. Whether the author be male or female, the sanction of such *écriture féminine* is a system of gender difference in which woman is the limit and margin of the articulate. Such a writing obeys the law that it abjures.

Rather than conclude that there is no exit from the circuit of paternal authority, one might try a different move: questioning the status of the judge of this game – the law of the father. The judge is also a player in the game, yet he must disguise his play.[46] The penis in the masquerade of the phallus has been one of his more successful disguises, masking the discursive investments of what purports to be a metadiscursive "truth" of language. For the notion that sexual difference and concomitant access to the symbolic order are instituted by the law of the father rests upon the crucial distinction – and confusion – between the phallus and the penis, between the symbolic and the empirical. The basis of the Lacanian game, the phallus/penis distinction not only sacralizes the phallus as the privileged signifier but, according to Jean-François Lyotard, mystifies the *discursive* status of the phallus.[47] Unveiling the phallus by insisting on its corporeal reference deprives it of metalinguistic authority, revealing it to be, in Jane Gallop's terms, "one signifier among others, prey to the contingencies of the letter."[48] Joyce from time to time seemed to recognize the material contingency of phallic law and that sexual difference need not be acknowledged in terms of a lack. "Funny spot to have a fingey," Issy says in *Finnegans Wake* (144.35). Molly is equally dismissive of the phallus as the arbitrator of sexual difference and its pretension to place its signature on the female body: "they always want to see a stain on the bed . . . a daub of red ink would do" (*U* 18.1125–28).

Nevertheless, Joyce's attempt to write women's desire as though from the other side of the symbolic, like recent feminists' theorizing of an *écriture féminine*, plays along with the father by appearing to renounce the paternal symbolic through an alliance with the mother, yet that alliance is simply the reappropriation of an imaginary construction. This game of projection and introjection is the psychological equivalent of Joyce's textual strategy of incorporation. By including within itself its own measure, *Ulysses* does not thereby abandon the distinction between discourse and metadiscourse but installs itself as a self-interpretive supertext, a meta-metadiscourse. This operation depends upon the internal articulation of the "other" of the text, the creation of an interior alien, in a process analogous to the creation and incarceration of madness by and in the service of that which wishes to call itself reason. The forgery of Molly's discourse permits Joyce to include her as a sign of *Ulysses'* putative transcendence of sexual difference. The apparent relinquishment of phallic authority is thus managed by the invention and sublation of "woman."

Finally, the structure of masochism in which the phallic woman appears in Joyce's work offers an interesting point of comparison with T. S. Eliot as well as a useful way of contrasting the Deleuzean and Freudian models of masochism. As we have seen, the sexual relations in Eliot's poetry and prose suggest the Freudian paradigm in which the consciousness of female aggression serves as a displacement for the desire for the father's love. According to Freud, the male masochist's fantasy, formulated as "*I am being beaten by my mother*," is at bottom a wish to be beaten – i.e., to be loved – by the father; "*the beating-fantasy has its origin in an incestuous attachment to the father.*"[49] The masochist's guilt, so evident in Eliot's writings, stems, in Freud's view, from the introjection of paternal authority, producing a conscience whose sadistic demands are a "substitute for a longing for the father."[50] By contrast, the structure of masochism in *Ulysses* initially appears to fit more closely Deleuze's paradigm in which the *father* is beaten rather than administering the beating (or offering love), while the masochist's consciousness of female aggression veils his incestuous wish for the mother.

Perhaps oddly, Freud's theory is based upon a primary homosexual desire, evaded by switching the gender of the imaginary beater, whereas Deleuze's theory supposes a primary heterosexual desire. Yet neither Freud nor Deleuze offers a complete explanation for masochism in either Eliot's or Joyce's texts. In both of their works, same- and cross-gender desires coexist; moreover, the direction of sexual desire is not necessarily at odds with the direction of identification. Thus, Freud's claim that the male masochist has a "feminine attitude" and "feels like a woman in his conscious fantasies"[51] is consistent with Joyce's representation of masochism and largely contrary to Eliot's. To complicate matters further, Daniel Ferrer attributes the "masculinization" of women in *Ulysses* to the mother's assumption of paternal authority (like Deleuze), but he convincingly argues that "she stands between the union of father and son"; thus (like Freud), he claims that the "forbidden love" between father and son is the linchpin of the narrative.[52]

Despite the lack of an overarching theory of masochism that could account for *Ulysses*, the debate nonetheless points out the importance of understanding the figure of women in the text not simply in terms of heterosexual desire; indeed, cross- and same-sex desires intersect in *Ulysses* in numerous and often obscure ways. It is precisely the obliquity of homosexuality that concerns me in the next section, for the supposed deviation of homosexual desire from moral rectitude goes hand in hand with the errant mode of its representation in Joyce's text.

## HOMOSEXUAL SECRECY AND KNOWLEDGE

In the course of her monologue, Molly Bloom remembers an erotic moment she once shared with Hester Stanhope, her girlhood friend. "[W]e used to compare our hair . . . we were like cousins what age was I then the night of the storm I slept in her bed she had her arms round me then" (*U* 18.638–42). Later, when Hester departed, "she kissed me six or seven times didnt I cry yes I believe I did or near it my lips were taittering when I said goodbye" (*U* 18.672–74). Despite its air of Victorian innocence, Marilyn French detects a "homosexual tinge" in the scene.[53] *Ulysses* reveals quite a few homosexual tinges; indeed, the three major characters and a number of the lesser ones are all colored by a faintly queer hue. Harry Levin, among others, has observed that Stephen "hints" that his friendship with Cranly "may have had a homosexual tinge."[54] Frank Budgen was perhaps the first to notice Bloom's "homosexual wish to share his wife with other men"; his suspicions were confirmed by Joyce, who in a subsequent conversation with Budgen remarked, "You see an undercurrent of homosexuality in Bloom . . . and no doubt you are right."[55]

What are we to make of these hints and tinges of homosexuality in *Ulysses*? Recent critics continue to see homosexuality as a tint, but one within the multicolored fabric of human sexuality depicted in the novel. Richard Brown guardedly admits that "Stephen's relationships with Cranly and with Mulligan have sometimes been felt to display a latent or repressed kind of homosexuality," yet the latter, he adds, is one among "a variety of shades of sexual taste" represented in *Ulysses* and is "peripheral" to Joyce's "central" concerns.[56] David Fuller gives an ampler and more detailed assessment of homoeroticism in *Ulysses*, yet concludes that "Joyce infers the usually sublimated sexual element in male friendship without tipping this over into the fully homosexual feelings which would narrow his implications," which Fuller describes as "transsexual."[57] Although wishing to give homosexuality its due, Brown and Fuller assume that "fully homosexual feeling" is aberrant whereas partial homosexual feeling is a normal deviation within the larger spectrum of sexual desire.

The indirection of the signs of homosexuality in *Ulysses* might be taken to underwrite this assumption. Pervasive yet scarcely visible, the indications of same-sex desire in the novel both elicit and frustrate a reading of them as homosexual. Like D. B. Murphy in "Eumaeus" with the enigmatic number sixteen tattooed on his chest, *Ulysses* is laced with queer suggestions that are neither confirmed nor renounced. This peculiarity of homosexual signs is not unique to *Ulysses*; for the better part of this century, homosexual signs have worked by casting a doubt through the off-color remark, sly hint, or innuendo. Joyce's text therefore raises a number of crucial, long-standing questions concerning the interpretation of homosexuality: What is a sign of homosexuality? What does it mean to read such signs? What are the signs of homosexuality in *Ulysses*? Who knows about homosexuality and who can read it in *Ulysses*, including its characters, its possible readers, and its author? How do the signs of homosexuality operate in the text?

The question of what constitutes a homosexual sign in Joyce's texts and in the literary culture of the early twentieth century is especially vexing because, shrouded in shame and confusion, homosexuality calls for a definitional clarity that its very "unnatural" character precludes. Indeed, the perversity of homosexuality for those charged with policing it – and the problem for those who wish to speak in its defense – consists in its protean ability to mask itself or to remain invisible. The referent of homosexual signs is never finally verifiable nor deniable; indeed, one might claim that the referent of homosexual signs in modern literature is not the "fact" of homosexuality but a telling absence, a knowing ignorance, or the whisper of an unspeakable secret.[58] Its visible manifestations have included forms of moral and psychological degeneration, obscure disorders, and fatal illnesses evident in, for instance, Thomas Mann's *Death in Venice*, André Gide's *The Immoralist*, Marcel Proust's *Remembrance of Things Past*, and Djuna Barnes's *Nightwood*.

The signs of homosexuality are not only symptoms of an inner pathology but are themselves tainting, contaminating the subject who speaks of homosexuality with its pathogenic secret. The knowledge of homosexuality typically implies the subject's darker familiarity with it. The perceiver of homosexual signs is often believed to have a peculiar competence, exceptional powers of detection or, if nothing else, a dirty mind. One who can discern such signs is already a member of the cognoscenti, perhaps even a "friend of Dorothy's," acquainted with the passwords and double entendres of those "in the life."[59] Even the doctor who studies homosexuality is liable to the suspicion that, as Marcel Proust says, some "obscure inclination" or "dreadful fascination had made him choose that subject."[60] This double-edged sword of homosexual knowledge cuts both ways in *Ulysses*, for example, in Mulligan's adeptness at spotting homosexuals and Jews and in Stephen's mute association of Wilde's "love that dare not speak its name" with Cranly and Mulligan. In these cases and others, knowledge of homosexuality is bivalent – subjective and objective genitive.

To know about homosexuality is to be its accomplice. Because knowledge carries guilt, those privy to the secret of homosexuality are obliged to guard it – as Richard von Krafft-Ebing, for instance, was obliged to write much of *Psychopathia Sexualis* in Latin – yet the purpose of this suppression is not just to restrict information concerning homosexuality to those with professional expertise but also to broach it publicly as unintelligible and therefore in a sense as nonexistent. "The social function of secrecy," according to D. A. Miller, "is not to conceal knowledge so much as to conceal the knowledge of the knowledge."[61] Hence, the recent "don't ask, don't tell" policy of the United States military codifies homosexuality as an open secret, publicizing the military's refusal to know about it.

The obliquity of homosexual signs is bound up with the uncertain ontological status of homosexuality itself. From its conceptual birth in the late nineteenth century, homosexuality has referred both to, in Proust's words, "a race apart" – a sexual minority of those with Fuller's "fully homosexual feelings" – and to a race within: the tendency toward perversion to which everyone is susceptible. Sedgwick thus argues that, for the past century, the discourse about homosexuality has been locked in a "conceptual incoherence" marked by two major contradictions or "paradigm clashes."[62] The first clash is between the aforementioned minoritizing and universalizing paradigms. On the one hand, homosexuality is assumed to be the natural condition of a certain group of people who are truly homosexual by virtue of a genetic, hormonal, or other constitutional defect. On the other hand, such inverts have the potential to seduce and infect normal members of society; hence, homosexuality is a potential condition for heterosexuals, something they might catch. Krafft-Ebing therefore differentiated between "*perversion* of the sexual instinct," or the disease of sexual inversion owing to a "hereditary taint," and "*perversity* in the sexual act," or the vices into which otherwise sound people sometimes fall.[63] Krafft-Ebing's wish to distinguish between those with "acquired" and "congenital" inversion, despite the difficulty he encounters in doing so, is repeated in the insistence of recent theorists as well as those Joycean critics who are determined to separate polymorphous sexuality from true homosexuality. In both instances, reading the signs of homosexuality is underwritten at the start by the presupposition that homosexuality per se is a special case separate from the broader zone of sexually liberating (or at least excusable) perversity.

The second paradigm clash that Sedgwick notes in the modern discourse about homosexuality is between gender inversion and gender separation. In the first sense, same-sex desire is considered to be the result of a reversal of gender identity, so that, for example, a male homosexual is revealed by his effeminate manner. Cross-gender behavior has typically been seen as the surest sign of homosexuality, so that the pretty youth, the woman or man who cross-dresses, or the effeminate aesthete like Oscar Wilde – whose name, according to Joyce, "evoked . . . a vague idea of delicate pastels, of a life beautiful with flowers" (*CW* 202) – are all sexual suspects. In the second sense, same-sex desire is believed to be motivated by a rejection of the opposite sex and by a solidarity with one's own gender. Greek homosexuality was thus described at the turn of the century by John Addington Symonds as an ideal masculine love, discreetly emptied of explicit eroticism in favor of "noble" male comradeship.[64] The twin poles of this paradigm clash are evident in the library scene in "Scylla and Charybdis" and in the theme of transvestism that runs throughout *Ulysses*.

The uncertainty of knowing what homosexuality is has often led those who would read it into a paranoid search for elusive clues. Indeed, its signs seem to proliferate into a hypertrophy of ambiguous indices and referential illusions. The fecundity of the signs of homosexuality corresponds to what Freud described as the paranoid subject's excessive knowledge.[65] Because the idea of homosexuality has no definitional core, the attempt to specify it leads one into what Freud called "delusions of reference" involving a "hypercathexis of the interpretations of someone else's unconscious [behavior]."[66] In a sense, homosexual signs may be nothing more than *signs of paranoia*, symptoms of an individual or societal fear; more broadly, though, they proliferate in *a paranoia of signs*, a luxuriant production of equivocal signifiers. Harold Beaver's observation about "the homosexual reader" is equally true of the homophobic interpreter: "Every sign [for him] becomes duplicitous, slipping back and forth across a wavering line, once the heterosexual antithesis between love and friendship has been breached."[67]

The knowledge of homosexuality is therefore caught in a dialectic of concealment and exposure. On the one hand, as a contingent, possible attribute, homosexuality bears an underground existence as any subject's secret, possible desire, an interior alterity; on the other hand, homosexuality is the determinate essence of those who explicitly attest to themselves as gay. Yet each of these terms depends upon the other and, indeed, can be reversed: secrets are potent because they can be told, while the "fact" of homosexuality, by virtue of the general presumption of heterosexuality, is always already dissimulated. Even the most resolutely out-of-the-closet person must continually keep revealing herself as gay in order not to fall under that presumption. In short, homosexuality requires and elicits constant confession, while the interpretation of homosexual signs inevitably entails the enticement and virulence of a tabloid exposé.

There is perhaps no more striking and influential example of the dynamics of homosexual secrecy and knowledge than the case of Oscar Wilde. As he remains today, Wilde was for Joyce and for the modern period in general a metonymy for homosexuality. Moreover, he is the magnetic pole for the shameful yet fascinating knowledge of homosexuality in *Ulysses*. In his defense of Wilde's sexuality in his 1909 essay, "Oscar Wilde: The Poet of 'Salomé,'" Joyce was alive to the contaminating effects of homosexual knowledge and ambivalently tried to acknowledge yet ward them off. His sympathetic account of Wilde grants him a distinguished if fictive Irish genealogy and pleads his case as a misunderstood "scapegoat" to the hypocrisy of English morals.

Alluding to Wilde's trial, Joyce begins his essay with the disclaimer that "this is not the place to examine the strange problem of the life of

Oscar Wilde" (*CW* 203), but he proceeds to do so anyway as though it were impossible not to speak of homosexuality in connection with Wilde. He then attributes Wilde's "unhappy mania" both to nurture and to nature, playing both sides of the sexological coin. On the one hand, "in the eyes of some," his mother's disappointment that she had produced a son rather than a daughter feminized Wilde and may have "dragged him to his ruin" (*CW* 202). On the other hand, "heredity and the epileptic tendency of his nervous system can excuse that which has been imputed to him" (*CW* 203). Joyce ultimately blames Wilde's condition on the homosocial confinement of English schools: "the truth is that Wilde, far from being a perverted monster who sprang in some inexplicable way from the civilization of modern England, is the logical and inescapable product of the Anglo-Saxon college and university system, with its secrecy and restrictions" (*CW* 204).[68]

Joyce's interpretation of the causes of Wilde's homosexuality has usually been adduced as evidence of his frank realism, even his broadmindedness. After all, the intimate friendships among Oxford and Cambridge undergraduates are the stuff of British fiction and popular lore. Moroever, *A Portrait of the Artist as a Young Man* explicitly alludes to a sexual incident among the boys at Clongownes.[69] Yet Joyce's association of homosexuality with "secrecy and restrictions" strikes a phobic note that grows louder as the essay progresses.

Joyce charges that "the graffiti, the loose drawings, the lewd gestures of those people [the English]," as well as, more generally, "the life and language of men, whether in soldiers' barracks or in the great commercial houses," attest to the fact that not "all of those who threw stones at Wilde were themselves spotless" (*CW* 204). Joyce's condemnation of the fraudulence of English scruples is both historically wellfounded and ethically brave in contesting the duplicity of the open secret of homosexuality. Yet his admission of what everybody knows immediately redounds upon Joyce, who guiltily admits, "In fact, everyone feels uncomfortable in speaking to others about this subject, afraid that his listener may know more about it than he does" (*CW* 204).

Uneasy at the thought of his own implication in the secret of homosexuality, Joyce appeals to an "objective" judgment of the matter, for which the authority is Wilde himself:

Oscar Wilde's own defence in the *Scots Observer* should remain valid in the judgment of an objective critic. Everyone, he wrote, sees his own sin in Dorian Gray (Wilde's best known novel). What Dorian Gray's sin was no one says and no one knows. Anyone who recognizes it has committed it. (*CW* 204)

In fact, Wilde's letter to the *Scots Observer* reads, "Each man sees his own sin in Dorian Gray. What Dorian Gray's sins are no one knows. He who finds them has brought them."[70] Joyce slightly but tellingly misquotes Wilde in three ways: Dorian Gray's sins become singular; Joyce adds that "no one says" what that sin is; and Wilde's comment that "[h]e who finds them has brought them" is modified to Joyce's "[a]nyone who recognizes it has committed it." These alterations have subtle but significant effects. By singularizing Dorian Gray's sins, Joyce implies that his sin stands out among many others as the sin par excellence. This particular sin is unspoken as well as unknown. Finally and most damningly, one "recognizes" this sin in himself because he has "committed it" (instead of having "brought" it). Joyce's slips of the pen commit the reader to a greater guilt than Wilde had, suggesting his stronger internal realization of and implication in homosexual "sin."

Joyce's reading of Wilde's defense of *The Picture of Dorian Gray* can be interpreted in two ways: first, as an attempt to force Wilde's readers to face their own disavowed homosexuality and thus to accept their commonality with the disgraced Wilde or, second, by singling out Wilde's special sin, to throw it back against his accusers with the charge that "it takes one to know one." In short, Joyce ambivalently proposes both universalizing and minoritizing versions of homosexuality, with both antihomophobic and homophobic effects. In a similarly equivocal fashion, Joyce wrote in a 1906 letter to his brother Stanislaus that Wilde should have come out in *Dorian Gray* instead of hiding his homosexuality behind allusions and witticisms, yet he also says that Wilde did not hide his sexuality well enough.

> I can imagine the capital which Wilde's prosecuting counsel made out of certain parts of [*Dorian Gray*]. It is not very difficult to read between the lines. Wilde seems to have had some good intentions in writing it – some wish to put himself before the world – but the book is rather crowded with lies and epigrams. If he had had the courage to develop the allusions in the book it might have been better. I suspect he has done this in some privately-printed books. Like his Irish imitator:
>
> > Quite the reverse is
> > The style of his verses. (*SL* 96)

Joyce's private allusion here is to Oliver St. John Gogarty, with the less-than-hidden innuendo that Gogarty is Wilde's imitator in sexual inversion as well as in literary style. Joyce develops the allusion further in *Ulysses* by making Mulligan/Gogarty the voice of the lewd wisecrack, the one who accuses others of being perverts in a way that insinuates his own sodomical interests.

While at times generously allowing that homosexual desires are common and publicly refusing to condemn them, Joyce nonetheless keeps his distance from them. In *Ulysses* Joyce, like Wilde, largely conceals references to homosexuality "between the lines," while displacing explicit knowledge of perversion onto contemptible characters.

How are we to read the signs of homosexuality in *Ulysses*? If homosexuality is interwoven with other same-sex relationships, there is no simple line to be drawn between homosexuality and same-sex friendships (or rivalries), cross-generational bonds, or bisexuality. Indeed, the general heading of homosexuality is misleading insofar as it implies the dubious belief that same-sex desire is confined to those who are "really" gay. On the contrary, I read the equivocal signs of homosexuality not as indications of a character's true orientation but as part of larger discursive struggles over the meaning of sexuality. These contests take place on many levels: among the characters within *Ulysses*; across Joyce's texts, including his letters, essays, recorded conversations, and so forth; and throughout the modernist period. Interpreting homosexuality in *Ulysses* and elsewhere is not simply a matter of accuracy – as though we know what homosexuality is and could therefore identify it – but of attending to moments of expressive silence and knowing ignorance.[71]

*Ulysses* presents four episodes in which homosexual knowledge and utterance are especially at issue: "Scylla and Charybdis," "Circe," "Eumaeus," and "Penelope." Within each, Stephen, Bloom, and Molly display in differing ways the definitional incoherences of modern homosexuality. Stephen's panicked references to homosocial and homosexual relations have the horror of an open secret whose knowledge he admits and suppresses. Bloom's "undercurrent of homosexuality" in his dealings with Boylan, Stephen, and other men remains a covert suggestion whose implications are left to be drawn by the "knowing" reader – including the readers in the text, such as Mulligan and Murphy. By contrast, Molly's liaison with Hester Stanhope – mentioned in passing during her heterosexual reveries – never raises for her the fears attendant on Stephen's mention of Wilde's "love that dare not speak its name." I will take up these episodes in turn as sites of the question of homosexual knowledge.

Reading homosexuality is an explicit and recurrent concern in "Scylla and Charybdis." It keeps coming up during the discussion of Shakespeare's sonnets and in Mulligan's remarks about Bloom; it returns in Stephen's thoughts regarding Cranly; and it runs as a mute question throughout his speculations on the mystery of paternal love. Although homosexuality is frequently the topic of conversation among the men gathered in the library – a sort of intellectual locker-room scene – it just as often goes unspoken. Thus, we need to ask not only who knows about it but also who speaks about it and who is silent. My focus in this section is on these discursive dynamics, especially the ways in which the players in the scene read the signs of same-sex desire in Shakespeare and in each other. Later, I will touch on the sexual implications of the father/son relation between Bloom and Stephen as it is represented in "Eumaeus."[72]

Shakespeare's love for men is first discreetly alluded to by Lyster, the Quaker librarian who encourages Stephen to publish his ideas "for the enlightenment of the public," as have other Irish commentators. The one Irishman he fails to mention is Oscar Wilde, who in "The Portrait of Mr W. H." advanced a theory of Shakespeare's personal life as an explanation for his literary work.[73] Like Stephen's story about Shakespeare, "overborne in a cornfield" by Anne Hathaway, Wilde's biographical speculations, presented narratively through the character of Cyril Graham, tell a tale of Shakespeare's love for the boy-actor Willie Hughes, allegedly the "W. H." to whom the sonnets are dedicated. The Wilde/Graham theory, like Stephen's, is based upon textual conjecture mixed with rumor and, in the absence of objective evidence, relies for its persuasiveness upon its aesthetic coherence and subjective satisfaction. The connection between Wilde and Stephen is further strengthened when Best later suggests to Stephen that he "ought to make [his theory] a dialogue, don't you know, like the Platonic dialogues Wilde wrote" (*U* 9.1068–69). But the pure-minded Lyster omits any reference to Wilde and only hints at the possibility of Shakespeare's love for William Herbert, Earl of Pembroke (another "W. H."), as "what ought not to have been" (*U* 9.445).

"[T]hat story of Wilde's" is on everyone's minds, though; Best, Eglinton, and Mulligan bring it up several times during discussions of Shakespeare's sexuality in which Stephen is largely silent. The "charge of pederasty brought against the bard" (*U* 9.732) threatens to derail Stephen's discourse about Hathaway's perfidy, and he repeatedly tries to return the conversation to his own ideas. Yet Stephen's unvoiced thoughts during each of these interruptions indicate that he knows and fears more than he says about homosexuality. The three scenes of extended debate regarding Shakespeare and Wilde are marked by

Stephen's ambivalent identification with and abjection of these figures of male love.

In the first scene, Best is the spokesman for Wilde and is described in terms that taint him with Wildean aestheticism:

– The most brilliant [theory] of all is that story of Wilde's, Mr Best said, lifting his brilliant notebook. That *Portrait of Mr W. H.* where he proves that the sonnets were written by a Willie Hughes, a man all hues.
– For Willie Hughes, is it not? the quaker librarian asked.
  Or Hughie Wills? Mr William Himself. W. H.: who am I?
– I mean, for Willie Hughes, Mr Best said. . . . Hughes and hews and hues, the colour, but it's so typical the way he works it out. It's the very essence of Wilde, don't you know. The light touch.

His glance touched their faces lightly as he smiled, a blond ephebe. Tame essence of Wilde. (*U* 9.522–32)

Like Cranly's smile, Best's smile and touching gaze are curiously moving; indeed, Best is drawn much like the eponymous subject of Wilde's story, the youthful, effeminate, and magnetic Willie Hughes. Furthermore, Best's prepositional confusion in this passage (the sonnets were written *for* not *by* W. H.) implies the intermingling of Shakespeare's identification with and desire for Willie Hughes, an intermingling that Stephen takes up and repeats in his own desirous identification with the bard. Stephen's comparison of himself with Shakespeare ("Mr William Himself. W. H.: who am I?"), like his wish to be Shakespeare's son within a literary "apostolic succession," entails both *identification with* (being like) Shakespeare and *desire for* (possessing or incorporating) him. Yet this mingling of allo- and autoeroticism is precisely what is forbidden under the rule of normative heterosexuality, in which what a man wants to be and what he desires to have must remain distinct, on the pain of becoming an invert. Consequently, despite his momentary wish to be "W. H.," Stephen phobically paints Best in the hues of the queer and later imagines him as Shakespeare's and Socrates' boy-toy, "the douce youngling, minion of pleasure, Phedo's toyable fair hair" (*U* 9.1138–39). Stephen thus transcribes Best as another Willie Hughes, but Stephen, wanting to be another William himself, perversely implies his similarity to the abjected Best, for both are versions of W. H.

The sonnets have long been the locus of debate over Shakespeare's sexuality. In this episode, they are crucial for Stephen's theory that the poet was betrayed by his wife and, by extension, Mary Fitton as well as for Stephen's own psychosexual conflicts. He is thus divided between the accepted heterosexual version of Shakespeare's sonnets as presented by

George Brandes and Frank Harris, in which the poet's mistress Fitton was a "wanton" who seduced his friend W. H. (here William Herbert, Earl of Pembroke), and Stephen's covert suspicion that Wilde may have been right.[74] Not long after Best's remark, Stephen mentions the sonnets in a curious nonanswer to Mulligan's question: With "[w]hom do you suspect" Hathaway was fooling in Stratford? Stephen's reply phobically insinuates precisely the sorts of sexual desires from which Brandes and Harris had tried to protect Shakespeare.

– Say that he is the spurned lover in the sonnets. . . . But the court wanton spurned him for a lord, his dearmylove.
    Love that dare not speak its name.
– As an Englishman, you mean, John sturdy Eglinton put in, he loved a lord.
    Old wall where sudden lizards flash. At Charenton I watched them.
– It seems so, Stephen said, when he wants to do for him, and for all other and singular uneared wombs, the holy office an ostler does for the stallion. (*U* 9.657–64)

John Eglinton, who knows what the doctors have to say about homosexuality, puts in his oar to avert the implication that Shakespeare's love was anything other than what all Englishmen proverbially feel toward aristocrats. In so doing, he repeats not only Joyce's but also Frank Harris's opinion that "Shakespeare loved a lord with passionate admiration."[75] Indeed, the linchpin of Harris's chapter-long defense of the poet against what he calls the "foul accusation" of homosexuality is his claim that Shakespeare's avowals of love for Pembroke were nothing more than "snobbishness . . . heightened to flunkeyism" by "the hope of benefits" from a wealthy patron.[76] Although Eglinton is the voice of convention, he unwittingly implies another commonplace regarding the English character – the "English vice" of masochism or sexual flagellation – and perhaps suggests to Stephen the French slang term *anglaiser*, meaning to sodomize someone.[77]

Among the men gathered in the library, Eglinton plays the role of the "sturdy," "steadfast," "severe" guardian of healthy morals. However, in Stephen's mind this bachelor is a "dour recluse" who "has his cake," perhaps through masturbation (*U* 9.1138). In Mulligan's bawdy, off-the-cuff satiric verse, both Eglinton and Best, "Being afraid to marry, . . . / . . . masturbated for all they were worth" (*U* 9.1151–52). Like the bachelors Edward Martyn and George Moore, they come under a cloud of vaguely sexual suspicion (*U* 9.307–9).

Stephen appears to agree with Eglinton and Harris that Shakespeare loved a lord in the usual English fashion. However, his interpolated thoughts tell a different story, of Wilde's shameful, homosexual love and of his own, presumably homoerotic, voyeurism at Charenton, a town southeast of Paris where the Marquis de Sade, the notorious sodomite, was imprisoned. Stephen's refusal to say what he saw there, although he evidently "watched them" do the literally unspeakable in horrified fascination, has implications of fellatio which are reinforced by his recollection a few lines earlier of French prostitutes soliciting oral sex ("*Minette?*" [*U* 9.642]). Stephen's fearful pleasure at the implied spectacle of sodomy parallels Mulligan's projected homoerotic voyeurism at the end of the episode, when he whispers to Stephen about Bloom: "Did you see his eye? He looked upon you to lust after you" (*U* 9.1209–10). However, Stephen immediately suppresses his homosexual memory and converts Shakespeare into a hyperphallic heterosexual – Shakespeare's "office" to W. H. is to secure him a wife and progeny – which thus enables him to return to his favorite theme of the shrewish wife.

The topic of Shakespeare's homosexuality is brought up a third time by Mulligan, who regales the company with salacious rumors he has pried from Edward Dowden, a professor at Trinity:

– He died dead drunk, Buck Mulligan capped. . . . O, I must tell you what Dowden said!
– What? asked Besteglinton.
   William Shakespeare and company, limited. The people's William. . . .
– Lovely! Buck Mulligan suspired amorously. I asked him what he thought of the charge of pederasty brought against the bard. He lifted his hands and said: *All we can say is that life ran very high in those days.* Lovely!
   Catamite.
– The sense of beauty leads us astray, said beautifulinsadness Best to ugling Eglinton.
   Steadfast John replied severe:
– The doctor can tell us what those words mean. You cannot eat your cake and have it.
   Sayest thou so? Will they wrest from us, from me, the palm of beauty?
– And the sense of property, Stephen said. He drew Shylock out of his own long pocket. (*U* 9.726–42)

In this passage, Stephen, Mulligan, and the other men gathered in the library again compete for control over the interpretation of Shakespeare's sexuality, as well as, more broadly, for domination of the discourse concerning Shakespeare and the meaning of male homosexuality. Stephen's non sequitur, "[a]nd the sense of property," reflects his wish to own the poet, "wrest[ing]" him away from Mulligan, whose version of Shakespeare's perverse sexual practices and ignominious death is, to Stephen, a debasement. The poet has become popular property and discussion of him a commercial enterprise, which he labels "William Shakespeare and company, limited." Stephen's silent, derisive remark on the critical industry built up on the poet also alludes outside the text to the bookstore owned by the lesbian publishers of *Ulysses*, Sylvia Beach and Adrienne Monnier. Rather than simply a sly compliment to these women, as it has often been read, this extratextual reference reflexively implies the limitations of what Stephen and the other men think they know about same-sex love.

Here as elsewhere, Mulligan's mocking references to Shakespeare's pederasty and Dowden's effeminacy enforce the homosexual stigma and confirm his own status as a man's man or, as he later calls himself, "a Fertiliser" (*U* 14.660).[78] His remarks have the double effect of silencing "the love that dare not speak its name" and of putting it into discourse *as* forbidden and titillating. Mulligan's eagerness to talk about other men's same-sex desires is the obverse of Stephen's reluctance; they are two sides of the coin of sexual secrecy. Mulligan plays the leading part in "Scylla and Charybdis" of volubly labeling homosexuality as *non nominandum inter christianus*; he thus polices the boundary between deviance and normality, while Stephen veils his homosexual anxieties, expressing them in mute, phobic asides.

Stephen's unspoken "Catamite" seems poised between the accusation that Mulligan is himself a pervert and the charge that Mulligan has perverted, through his homophobic innuendoes, what Stephen would prefer to think of as "the palm of beauty." Stephen's contest with Mulligan is thus a debate over the meaning of male friendship. Like the doctors to whom "ugling Eglinton" refers in a sobering fashion, including "the new Viennese school" of Freud (*U* 9.780), Mulligan has distorted the significance of male love that Best, in Wildean fashion, refers to as "the sense of beauty," and that Stephen desperately fears "they will wrest from us, from me." The pathos of the question of "what those words mean" – including the high life of Shakespeare's Renaissance, the beauty of male friendship, the ugliness of the doctors' diagnosis of homosexuality, the filthiness of the term "catamite," and, at bottom, the unutterability of "the love that dare not speak its name" – infuses this passage and motivates Stephen's attempt to steer the conversation away from the whole matter and to talk about the innocuous topic of Shakespeare's commercial transactions.

The expert in perversion, Mulligan cautions Stephen that Bloom "is Greeker than the Greeks. His pale Galilean eyes were upon [the statue's] mesial groove" (*U* 9.614–15). Mulligan is right and wrong – Bloom is a Jew, is interested in anality, and, like Swinburne, enjoys flagellation – but his warnings to Stephen here and at the end of the episode are so obviously homophobic and anti-Semitic that we are apt to underread Stephen's own homophobia. In response to Mulligan's warning, Stephen thinks, "Manner of Oxenford" (*U* 9.1212). His association of Bloom with homosexual practices at schools such as Oxford and Clongowes is comic in this context, although the fact that Gogarty, the model for Mulligan, attended Oxford in what Joyce implied was an imitation of Wilde (*SL* 96) suggests that Stephen's remark is a slap at Mulligan.

Although Stephen's understanding of homosexuality may be more ambivalent than that of Mulligan, Best, or Eglinton, it is, like theirs, locked in contradictions. The phobically charged epistemology of homosexuality that underlines "Scylla and Charybdis" is based upon the conflicting paradigms outlined by Sedgwick. Homosexuality is the fate of aesthetes like Best as well as rakes like Mulligan; it is marked both by effeminate delicacy and excessively robust masculinity. Although Stephen battles with Mulligan for control of the discourse about Shakespeare and his sexuality, he shares with Mulligan these contradictory yet virulent assumptions. Hence, in "Oxen of the Sun," where a group of men sit around telling sexual jokes, Stephen repeats Mulligan's quotation of Dowden's words. Discussing Beaumont and Fletcher, Stephen says, "they had but the one doxy between them . . . in delights amorous for life ran very high in those days . . . Greater love than this, he said, no man hath that a man lay down his wife for his friend" (*U* 14.358–62). The triangle that Stephen describes in "Oxen," in which two male friends form a bond by sharing a woman, anticipates the bond that he will make with Bloom when the latter brings him home to Eccles Street and offers him his wife – the classic homosocial triangle.

It is a commonplace of Joycean scholarship that Stephen views male friendship with suspicion and sees in it treachery at every turn. To what extent is his distrust motivated by disavowed homoeroticism? Stephen's repeated thoughts of Cranly in association with Wilde's unspeakable love constitute a simultaneous acknowledgement of his love for Cranly, albeit tacit, and a denial of that love. Not only does his love go unvoiced, it is typically converted into resentment at Cranly's alleged betrayal. Thus, Cranly serves as the model for other brother-betrayers, especially Mulligan, onto whom he displaces the homosexual desires he repudiates.

When Stephen thinks of Cranly, he almost always remembers Cranly's arm and his smile – corporeal metonymies of his body that carry a sexual charge. For instance, early in *Ulysses* Mulligan, joking with Stephen about the cracked shaving mirror ("If Wilde were only alive to see you!"), tells him, "if you and I could only work together we might do something for the island. Hellenise it." Stephen's reaction is silent: "Cranly's arm. His arm" (*U* 1.143–44, 157–59). He rejects Mulligan's offer of an artistic alliance just as he wants to get rid of his shoes, which "spoil the shape of my feet" (*U* 9.947–48). Stephen is wearing Mulligan's cast-offs, and in "Proteus" he reflects on the intimacy entailed in fitting his feet into the "leather wherein another's foot had nested warm." Stephen thinks, "foot I dislove . . . Staunch friend, a brother soul: Wilde's love that dare not speak its name. His arm: Cranly's arm. He now will leave me" (*U* 3.447–52). The blame that Stephen attributes to Mulligan parallels the infidelity with which he charges Cranly, comparing him to a faithless wife to whom he had given his "soul's youth, . . . night by night," but who has left him to hunt for other lovers (*U* 9.39).[79] Stephen's jealousy and resentment at what he perceives as treachery fit Freud's description of the persecuted paranoiac, who sees in others an enmity which

is the reflection of his own hostile impulses against them. Since . . . it is precisely the most loved person of his own sex that becomes his persecutor, . . . this reversal of affect takes its origin . . . [in] ambivalence, [which serves as] a defence against homosexuality.[80]

The theme of the brother-betrayer is broadly associated in *Ulysses* with homosexuality, epitomized by Wilde, the victim of his love for the faithless Lord Alfred Douglas, as well as by Shakespeare, played false by his brothers and the elusive W. H. Indeed, love between men is especially untrustworthy in *Ulysses*. Eglinton's cynical remark elicits the memory of Cranly's grin: "Have you found those six brave medicals . . . to write *Paradise Lost* at your dictation? . . . Smile. Smile. Cranly's smile" (*U* 9.18–21). The memory of Cranly's smile attests to the fear and desire that energizes Stephen's riven fraternal bonds, although sometimes disavowed by critics whose interpretive strategies mime Stephen's own disavowals and displacements.

As we have seen, knowledge of homosexuality in "Scylla and Charybdis" is divided between the vocally homophobic Mulligan and the silent, ambivalent Stephen, whose preoccupation with "the love that dare not speak its name" itself goes unspoken. These two characters represent symmetrically opposed poles in the discourse of sexuality and together form a chiasmus: on the one hand, a public knowledge of homosexuality that scarcely conceals its ignorance and, on the other hand, an apparent ignorance that conceals private knowledge. The epistemology of sexual perversion in "Circe" is also chiasmically structured, although with two major differences. First, the formal shift from a narrative dominated by Stephen's interior monologue to "Circe's" drama, whose phantasms float free from any individual consciousness, collapses the public/private distinction. "Circe" exposes the private(s); its theatricalization of sexuality exteriorizes the inner, sexual truth of the subject and satirizes the sciences devoted to its study, producing a camp perversion. The second, related difference between the two episodes is that, in "Circe," subjectivity is staged in such a manner that the questions I have asked thus far – Who knows and who speaks about homosexuality? – are shifted to another register. Although the episode does not represent the silence of characters who possess psychological depth, "Circe" is pervaded by other silences harder to hear under the din of its extravagant, three-ring circus of perversion. These differences notwithstanding, "Circe's" sexual discourse is organized around a similarly paradoxical opposition between knowledge and ignorance whose poles are comprised of, on the one hand, Bloom's many accusers and torturers, along with assorted sex doctors and others who collectively subject Bloom to instruction, and, on the other hand, the object of this pedagogy and diagnosis, Bloom. Although the former possess authority and even, in the case of Bella/o Cohen, have carnal knowledge of Bloom, he is the source of the guilty secrets that everybody – including the reader – wants to find out. Bloom seems to confess to everything, his sins ranging from fetishism to coprophilia. Missing from his list of transgressions, however, is sodomy.

It has frequently been observed that "Circe" is a spectacle – indeed, makes a spectacle – of perversion. For years critics believed that the purpose of this spectacle was to expose Bloom's repressed desires or even those of Joyce himself. "Circe," Mark Shechner claimed, is Joyce's "self-revelation as slapstick" within a book that "is an act of continuous confession."[81] Readers less willing to implicate Joyce in Bloom's confessions have nonetheless believed, like Marilyn French, that "Joyce's approach to sexuality was primarily one of exposure,"[82] although precisely what he exposed remains a question. Kimberley Devlin, for instance, has recently asserted that "'Circe' . . . exposes the instability of [Bloom's] assumed position of mastery" as a man.[83] By contrast, I argue that in "Circe," as in "Scylla and Charybdis," the appearance of revelation serves to maintain sexual secrecy.

Bloom's seemingly coerced disclosures take place within staged interrogations during which his accusers or torturers elicit from him his deliciously dirty secrets. "Puke it out!" Bella/o orders Bloom. "Say! What was the most revolting piece of obscenity in your whole career of crime? Go the whole hog . . . Be candid for once" (*U* 15.3042–43). Bella/o's command, repeated again and again during the episode, is an incitement to Bloom to tell all, to recite in elaborate detail his every shameful desire, the telling of which is itself a sexual act. The confessional scenes that she/he directs combine elements of the Catholic ritual of the "confession of the flesh" and the rhetoric of pornography, especially that of Sade and Sacher-Masoch. Michel Foucault has shown the similarity between the priest's and the pornographer's injunctions to penitent and initiate to speak of their forbidden lusts, and he has described how the confession, as a "ritual of discourse," "unfolds within a power relationship, for one does not confess without the presence . . . of . . . the authority who requires the confession," who punishes and forgives, while the person confessing must overcome "obstacles and resistances" until, by his verbal admission of guilt, he is unburdened or relieved.[84] The supposed knowledge or insight produced by the confession is nothing other than an effect of the "sexualization of power" – the pleasure excited by examining, watching, or forcing, as well as by resisting or exposing.[85]

The confessions in "Circe" may be usefully compared with Stephen's confession in *Portrait* and with Gerty MacDowell's "confession album" (*U* 13.636) in which she writes poetry. Indeed, *Ulysses* is rife with staged confessions. Bloom tries to induce Martha Clifford to plead for him to confess his desires; recalling her letter, he thinks, "How will you pun? You punish me? . . . Tell me I want to. Know" (*U* 11.890–92). Despite or perhaps because of his own confessional urges, Bloom often imagines confession as a masochistic, feminine act, performed before a dirty-minded priest: "Confession. Everyone wants to. Then I will tell you all. Penance. Punish me, please. Great weapon in their hands . . . Woman dying to" (*U* 5.425–27).

The confession incorporates the twin, contradictory obligations to conceal sexual secrets and to admit them, and it indulges temptation while repulsing it. Thus, in response to Bella/o's command, Bloom's protest ("Don't ask me!") heightens the sexual charge by raising the bar against divulgence. Bella/o continues, "I insist on knowing. Tell me something to amuse me . . . Where? How? What time? With how many?" (*U* 15.3049–54). Her/his demand for information extracts Bloom's admission ("I rererepugnosed in rerererepugnant") – confession being a form of elimination – as well as Bella/o's detailed list of exquisitely filthy punishments. Rather than revealing the concealed truth of Bloom's psyche, however, the ritual of torture, disclosure, and discipline comprises a discourse in which sex is hidden so that it can be rediscovered, then ostentatiously displayed as a dirty secret.

The scene of interrogation in "Circe" is performed many times. At his mock trial early in the episode Bloom is accused of all sorts of crimes, including "unlawfully watching and besetting." As the trial proceeds, it becomes evident that his misdeeds center on the buttocks. Three aristocratic women – Mrs. Yelverton Barry, Mrs. Billingham, and the Honorable Mrs. Mervyn Talboys – claim that Bloom sent them indecent letters asking them to horsewhip him, which they, in graphic language, threaten to do to him as punishment. Talboys asserts that Bloom watched her "from behind," just as he had praised Bellingham's "nether extremities" (*U* 15.1051, 1064). Bloom seems to have gotten farther with Mary Driscoll, his former maid, who alleges that "[h]e surprised me in the rere of the premises," and did something unspecified to her, leaving her "discolored in four places as a result" (*U* 15.885–87).

What did Bloom do, and does it matter? J. J. O'Molloy, his attorney, pleads for him on the grounds that the "misdemeanor was due to a momentary aberration of heredity, . . . such familiarities as the alleged guilty occurrence being quite permitted in my client's native place, the land of the Pharaoh" (*U* 15.944–47). O'Molloy's defense hints strongly, albeit confusedly, at homosexual sodomy, a sexual practice common in Arabia, according to Richard Burton, but that Krafft-Ebing claimed was caused by a "hereditary defect."[86] Bloom is later accused of "debauchery, recalling the cities of the plain" (*U* 15.1756), and while transformed into a woman is instructed by Bella/o in "Gomorrahan vices" (*U* 15.3122), but whatever he did to Mary was at least heterosexual. The question is neither whether Bloom really committed sodomy nor what is his true psychosexual character but how abjected desire is represented and known. Bloom is given the burden of confessing to shameful sexual acts, the most degrading and exciting of which are anal, yet he never confesses to sodomy. His anal, even sodomical desires are always heterosexually framed. This discourse that pretends to show all, and that tells it as horribly and delightfully unspeakable, nonetheless discreetly veils the scene of Bloom's sodomy.

Bloom's conversation with the statue of a nymph, whom he had approached in the museum "from behind," centers on her nonexistent anus. She tells him what he already knows and a little more: "We immortals, as you saw today, have not such a place and no hair there either" (*U* 15.3392–93). The hirsute bottom assumes special importance in "Circe." In Bella/o's fantasy, Bloom is hairless, in contrast to Boylan's conspicuously hairy butt ("A shock of red hair he has sticking out of him behind like a furzebush!" [*U* 15.3141–42]). Bloom's sexual practices with women seem to involve all but anal penetration ("I have paid homage on that living altar where the back changes name" [*U* 15.3405–6]). With Bella/o, Bloom crosses that line but only in disguise.

Bella/o notoriously forces Bloom to avow his anal desires by word and deed. A "[d]ungdevour[ing]" "[a]dorer of the adulterous rump," Bloom is metamorphosed into a woman, yet is soon thereafter again referred to as a man.[87] Though recognizably and grotesquely masculine in his female clothing, Bloom confesses to having dressed up in the "naughties" he bought from Mrs. Miriam Dandrade and, "behind closedrawn blinds," according to Bella/o, imagined himself "in various poses of surrender" (*U* 15.2990–96). Bello (in this passage consistently male) narrates Bloom's fantasy of a gang rape, taking over his voice as well as the power and guilt of the gaze: "You were a nicelooking Miriam when you clipped off your backgate hairs and lay swooning . . . across the bed as Mrs Dandrade about to be violated" (*U* 15.2999–3001). The list of those "about to" sodomize Bloom as he pretends to be a woman consists of a series of men (including the Trinity crew team), a dog, and a duchess, a group whose significance lies in their heterogeneity and anonymity. They are everybody and nobody, thus further occluding the already deferred scene of sodomy.

At one point in "Circe" the veil is almost lifted. In his female guise, Bloom is repeatedly subjected to anal penetration by Bello, who threatens to "skewer" Bloom, shoves a cigar into his ear, squats in his face, "thrusts out a figged fist" (an obscene Italian gesture), mounts and rides him like a "cockhorse," "corks" a buttplug in himself for good measure, "pokes" his fan into Bloom's "haunches," and, finally, fistfucks him. Although up to now Bloom has been referred to as male, he is suddenly for an instant female with an anatomically correct body. Bello "*bares his arm and plunges it elbowdeep in Bloom's vulva*," taunting, "There's fine depth for you!" (*U* 15.3089–90). At the moment of penetration Bloom is regendered; Bello's fist goes into his "vulva," not his anus, thus sparing Bloom the degradation of explicit homosexual sodomy. Moreover, here and throughout the episode, Bloom is passive, responding to the accusations and submitting to the desires of others. For instance, he disingenuously blames his cross-dressing on "dear Gerald," who "converted me to be a true corsetlover when I was a female impersonator in the High School play *Vice Versa*" (*U* 15.3009–11). In short, Bloom can serve as the vehicle for the expression of perversion without suffering from its stigma because he seems not to be in control of or even to know quite what he is doing. That knowledge and responsibility are borne by "dear Gerald," Bella/o, Mulligan, Virag, and others in "Circe."

Solicited by Bloom to give medical testimony on his behalf against charges of "debauchery," Mulligan and his fellow doctors are "sex specialists" whose diagnoses of Bloom comprise a parody of contemporary sexology. Their pronouncements echo and ridicule, among others, Krafft-Ebing's notions of congenital and acquired homosexuality (the former is caused by "hereditary degeneracy" often signaled by epilepsy; the latter, by masturbation). They also allude to Otto Weininger's theory of homosexuality, in which male homosexuals possess the "anatomical characters" of women and are thus similar to Jews, who are "saturated with femininity," and to Freud's concept of a primordial bisexuality, which is inverted in "Circe" into the phrase "bisexually abnormal."[88] "*[V]irgo intacta*," with his "*fetor judaicus*" and malformed male genitals, Bloom is a walking caricature of inversion. The sexologists' defense of Bloom consists of describing him in terms of homosexuality; far from offering him as a model of androgyny, sexual "ambidexterity," or the feminist "new womanly man" – however much those terms have since been transvalued – Joyce's satire is directed at those doctors who would interpret Bloom as a homosexual. Presumed to know about sexuality, they are more ignorant than Virag.

Astute at noticing Bloom's underwear fetish and his attraction to women in "male habiliments," Lipoti Virag knows both too much and too little about sex. The author of the sensational "Fundamentals of Sexology or the Love Passion," Virag is a quack doctor with expertise in insect sex, aphrodisiacs, and cures for warts. Despite his vulgar, animalistic view of sex, his often mangled language, and his obviously limited epistemological grasp – the last word he utters is "Quack" (*U* 15.2638) – Virag has the inside story on the Virgin Mary's liaison with Panther, the Roman centurion, and has "disclosed the Sex Secrets of Monks and Maidens. Why I left the church of Rome. Read the Priest, the Woman and the Confessional" (*U* 15.2546–48), a book which argues that the act of confession has a corrupting influence on women.[89] His finger on the pulse of "Circe's" main artery, Virag's popular expertise both contrasts and parallels that of Private Compton, who calls Stephen a "blighter" or sodomite. The stupidity of Compton's blustering, man-on-the-street sexual knowledge, like the sexologists' theories parodied by Virag, wards off the homosexual implications that surround Bloom and Stephen by voicing them through discredited characters.

Bella/o, Virag, Compton, and Mulligan and his fellow doctors all, in one way or another, claim to know about homosexuality, while Bloom is presented as ignorant. Joyce's parody of professional and popular sexual expertise might suggest that he refuses any clear distinction among the varieties of sexual desire and gender behavior, leading to the judgment that "Circe" endorses a pluralistic vision of human sexuality. However, in my view the dynamics of sexual knowledge in the episode lead to a different conclusion. Although the signs of sexual deviance are clustered around Bloom, he is protected by his ignorance, for the meaning of those signs is left to the sex experts and to his confessors. Bloom is compelled to admit his lusts, but he does not name them. The meaning of his desires is left to others. Bloom's obliviousness and passivity incite the reader to nominate and interpret his desires, yet they shelter him from the guilt that attaches to knowledge. By shifting the epistemological weight onto Bloom's readers in the text and onto the readers of *Ulysses*, Joyce saves him as a site of innocent, polymorphous desires in spite of his innumerable sins, whereas, in a curious reversal, his interrogators, bent on discovering his vices, expose their own depravity.

"Circe" parades a cornucopia of perversions whose diagnostic labels include transvestism, fetishism of various kinds, sadomasochism, voyeurism, coprophilia, and so forth. The distinction between homosexuality and heterosexuality is rarely alluded to, however, and does not play a significant part in the episode. Instead of the division between same- and other-gendered desires, "Circe's" carnival of vices is organized around the division between appropriate gender behavior aligned with genital sexuality (e.g., the robustly masculine Boylan and Compton) and inappropriate or reversed gender behavior aligned with nongenital sexuality (e.g., Bella/o and virtually every other character in the episode). Cross-dressing, sadomasochism, and anal obsessions turn gender and sexual norms upside down; indeed, "Circe" has often been read as governed by the principle of reversal. These inversions, far from being linked to what Carl Westphal in 1869 called "contrary sexual feeling"[90] and that has subsequently been termed homosexual, are generalized in the novel as part of a plenum of perversity. One might

rather reverse the question and ask why Circean inversions are *not* articulated with that other inversion. Indeed, the historical relation between
male homosexuality and transvestism, sadomasochism, anal sexuality,
and related phenomena is highly overdetermined.

To ask the question of homosexuality is to place oneself in the unenvi-
able position of Joyce's suspicious editor, George Roberts, who, Joyce
records,

asked me very narrowly was there sodomy also in *The Sisters* and what was
"simony" and if the priest was suspended only for the breaking of the chalice.
He asked me also was there more in *The Dead* than appeared. (*LJ* 2:305–6)

If "sodomy" is an inadequate name for male same-sex desire in both
*Ulysses* and *Dubliners* it is because Joyce evades its specific implications,
generalizing perversion while pinning sodomy in the narrow sense on
contemptible figures. Thus, in "Circe's" Black Mass scene, for instance,
the backside of Father Malachi O'Flynn – a composite of Mulligan and
Father Flynn from "The Sisters" – is exposed by Haines, *"revealing his grey
bare hairy buttocks between which a carrot is stuck"* (*U* 15.4705–6). Yet, by con-
fining knowledge (in both senses of the word) of homosexual sodomy to
Mulligan and his kind, Joyce preserves Bloom as the hero of his domestic epic.

Bloom's journey home begins in "Eumaeus," an episode that is often
thought to be the low point, emotionally and stylistically, of the entire
book. According to Richard Ellmann, "Joyce told Linati that the
episode's signification was 'The Ambush at Home,'" referring to
Bloom's "ambush" by the sailor, who, extending the Odyssean analogy,
is supposed to be "Ulysses Pseudangelos, that is, Ulysses the false messenger."[91] Thus poisoned at the well, "Eumaeus" has been more or less
written off as an instance of weary, bad language and of duplicitous,
seedy characters. Yet the very agreement of critics on what Kenner calls
the falsity of its diction and what others have termed its "banal locu-
tions" and "deadly language" of clichés – indeed, its "forgery of Bloom's
voice"[92] – suggests that "Eumaeus" is fruitful ground for an investigation
of Joycean errancy, both discursive and sexual.

"Eumaeus" is not only famous for its proliferation of grammatical,
syntactical, and rhetorical errors, but, according to Gabler, it contained
the greatest number of textual mistakes in the 1922 edition.[93] Gabler's
corrections have made the episode even more errant, allowing and even
soliciting what Senn calls "misreadings, wrong leads," and continual
readjustments as the reader tries to make sense out of its now more

garbled syntax.[94] Again, the reader's struggles with the botched syntax in "Eumaeus" are thought to mime Bloom's frustration with texts, including the *Evening Telegraph*'s "usual crop of nonsensical howlers of misprints" (*U* 16.1262–67). Bloom tries to sort things out and makes pathetically unsuccessful attempts at linguistic propriety, even elegance, yet he also engages in misrepresentation and evasion. As Derek Attridge points out, "Eumaeus" demonstrates "the impossibility of fixed . . . significations when the structures of language are permeated by the dissolving energies of erotic desire."[95] Although Attridge offers a subtle, detailed anatomy of the various kinds of linguistic error in the episode, demonstrating precisely how its language "permits slippage and uncertainty, deception and detour" that "go beyond a particular character's mental condition,"[96] he stops short of articulating the erotic forces that are co-implicated with the episode's linguistic errancy.

The textual and discursive errors in "Eumaeus" are bound up with the broader question of errant knowledge, especially homosexual knowledge. The central problem of "Eumaeus" is epistemological – that is, how to put together fragmentary and dubious bits of information or, in Bloom's words, "pieces of intelligence" into a body of knowledge. Not only is the narrative voice, which is aligned with Bloom in the free indirect style, a tour de force of mistakes, but the sources of information at Bloom's disposal are corrupt. The newspaper ("tell a graphic lie") is as unreliable as are the numerous accounts purporting to explain various characters' identities. The rumored genealogy of Lord John Corley, allegedly descended in an irregular fashion from the Lords Talbot de Malahide, is an early example of a pattern repeated throughout the episode in which knowledge of a character is uncertain because it is based upon gossip, doubtful "facts," and possibly fraudulent documents. The identities of the characters in the cabman's shelter are mysterious, illusory, and probably fabricated.

These epistemological dilemmas are typically presented in the narrative as Bloom's problems. Yet Bloom's judgment also comes under suspicion, particularly in regard to sexual matters. Playing the detective, Bloom is intrigued by the sailor, D. B. Murphy. "Sherlockholmesing him up" (*U* 16.831), Bloom tries to figure out who Murphy is, yet he avoids reading the homosexual clues that surround the sailor. In short, the conclusions that Bloom draws about Murphy and his judgments in general are as dubious as those of other characters. Rather than simply opposing the Odyssean Bloom to Murphy as the "false messenger" or the pseudo-Ulysses, "Eumaeus" develops a series of parallels between the two that, undermining the domestic closure of the "Nostos" or the return home and thereby constituting a countercurrent to the structural movement of the plot, are also in keeping with the homosexual subtext of *Ulysses* as a whole. To begin with, we need to ask, paraphrasing Senator Howard Baker, what does Bloom not know, and how does he not know it?

Error is a way of knowing. Neither an accident nor simply the effect of repression, error is productive and enabling. Thus, Bloom's mistakes and misjudgments comprise a knowing ignorance of sexual perversion that structures the episode and that sanctions and even sanctifies its concluding epithalamion: the nonperverse union of Stephen and Bloom. Far from correcting Bloom's blunders, I argue that his mistakes and moments of incomprehension permit him *not* to know about homosexuality – the particular, unspeakable perversion whose articulate silence is the condition of Bloom's knowledge.

The epistemological dilemmas of "Eumaeus" focus on D. B. Murphy, the enigmatic sailor whom Bloom tries to decipher, but they include to a lesser degree the keeper of the shelter and a host of minor figures. "[S]aid to be the once famous Skin-the-Goat, Fitzharris," a member of the invincibles (*U* 16.323–24), the keeper is the mouthpiece for nationalist polemic and is thus, in Bloom's view, the representative of what one may call political perversion. However, it is Murphy who dominates the scene and whose tall tales of his exploits across the seas magnetize his audience. The crux of Murphy's mystery is not his salty yarns but his obscure sexuality, which hints vaguely at homosexuality. In short, Murphy is the locus of sexual perversion in the episode, a perversion that extends beyond him to touch other characters, especially Stephen and Bloom.

In general, knowledge circulates in "Eumaeus" by means of indirection and innuendo, as the possession of insiders, concealed like a dangerous weapon and revealed through circumlocutions, oblique clues, or inadvertent slips of the tongue. This paranoid epistemology is especially prominent when the conversation skirts the highly charged topics of homosexuality and, to a lesser extent, subversive political conspiracy. Indeed, both sexual perversion and political subversion function as "open secrets," officially nonexistent and known only to those who have been initiated into their obscure mysteries.

A minor but telling and amusing example of this paranoid epistemology occurs early in the episode, following Murphy's story about the man whom he saw knifed in Trieste by "an Italian chap." One of the other men in the shelter, "somebody who was evidently quite in the dark," according to Bloom, puts in that the Italians are "great for the cold steel . . . That was why they thought the park murders of the invincibles was done by foreigners on account of them using knives" (*U* 16.589–92). Bloom, who fancies that he knows about the Phoenix Park murders and who believes himself to be an astute observer of human character, enjoys a smug sense of superiority over this unenlightened fellow and draws Stephen into his circle of the cognoscenti.

> At this remark passed obviously in the spirit of *where ignorance is bliss* Mr B. and Stephen . . . both instinctively exchanged meaning glances, in a religious silence of the strictly *entre nous* variety however, towards where Skin-the-Goat, *alias* the keeper, not turning a hair, was drawing spurts of liquid from his boiler affair. His inscrutable face which was really a work of art, a perfect study in itself, beggaring description, conveyed the impression that he didn't understand one jot of what was going on. Funny, very! (*U* 16.593–600; emphasis Joyce's)

The joke, however, is on Bloom, his inflated language undercutting his overweening confidence in his knowledge of political secrets.

In sharp contrast to his claim to have gotten Skin-the-Goat's number, Bloom is evasive regarding Murphy and what Murphy knows. Certain that he is "bogus," Bloom does not seem to want to understand who Murphy really is, though, and when insinuations of his possible sexual perversity arise, Bloom changes the subject, looks out the door, ignores the matter, or denies it. Nevertheless, Bloom's own version of "where ignorance is bliss" regarding homosexual knowledge coexists with his constant references to homosexuality, often apparently innocent.

The free indirect style of "Eumaeus" places the narrative voice at an indeterminate distance from Bloom, yet inasmuch as this voice is aligned with him, it reveals his equivocal familiarity with homosexuality. "Eumaeus" contains a startling number of off-the-cuff phrases with ambiguous connotations, such as "the genus *homo*" (*U* 16.328), to "fag out" (*U* 16.251), "queer sights" and "queer things" (*U* 16.464, 465–66), "a gay sendoff" (*U* 16.1247), and the "queer suddenly things" that Stephen pops out with which "attracted the elder man" (*U* 16.1567–68).[97] The uncertainty of grasping precisely what these words mean – whether they are just throwaway phrases or whether they are slips of the tongue that expose Bloom's covert cognizance of sexual perversion, the overt awareness of which he avoids – reflects the epistemological instability of sexual knowledge in "Eumaeus" as a whole. This instability is itself "queer" in the sense that the signs of homosexuality function in the episode like counterfeit money, or as a kind of cheat or trick.

This queer linguistic undercurrent contributes to the paranoia in which the subject of homosexuality is enveloped, both in "Eumaeus" and in modern literature in general. As we have seen in "Scylla and Charybdis," the knowledge of homosexuality functions as a contaminating secret that proliferates through multiple, ambiguous indices and delusive references. The semiotic duplicity that pervades "Eumaeus" – including the fraudulence of personal identities, the errors of language, and the interpretive misprisions of its characters – can be seen to issue from a generalized homophobia or, more precisely, in Sedgwick's term, homosexual panic.[98] In this sense, the equivocal signs of homosexuality in "Eumaeus," rather than indicating the sexual orientation of any of its characters, indicate the *fear* of the possibility of being thought homosexual. Moreover, this fear is not reducible to the personal anxiety of any particular character, although Bloom is its focus in this episode; instead, it is a general fear that pervades the episode, operating on the discursive level to disrupt the certainty of sexual identity and to obscure the objects of desire. "Eumaeus" is thus a crucial site in the larger struggle over the meaning of sexuality in *Ulysses*, its paranoid proliferation of the signs of homosexuality signifying not a determinate sexual orientation but the indeterminacy of homophobia.

The general structure of perverse knowledge in "Eumaeus" breaks down along the following lines: Murphy, the experienced outsider, possesses the dark, inner secrets of perversion, learned in the East and *non nominandum inter christianos*, yet inscribed enigmatically upon his chest; whereas Bloom, the domestic Dubliner whose dreams of adventure consist of taking the ferry to Holyhead, tries not to or at least pretends not to know the unspeakable secrets symbolized by Murphy's tattoo. As a consequence, Murphy remains an internal exile in the episode, the great imposter, while Bloom, by virtue of his seeming innocence, is free to attempt to lure Stephen into a frankly homoerotic triangle with Molly.

"Eumaeus" is thus comprised of two, opposed and reversed representations of homosexuality: on the one hand, the explicit, albeit mysterious, portrayal of perversion embodied by Murphy, who is, broadly speaking, the homosexual abject of "Eumaeus," and, on the other hand, the implicit, domesticized portrayal of male same-sex affection embodied by Bloom and Stephen, who walk off arm-in-arm at the end of the episode *"to be married by Father Maher"* (*U* 16.1887–88), protected from homophobic retribution by their apparent ignorance. Indeed, Bloom's preoccupation with the theme of adultery in the second half of the episode may be interpreted as a screen that shields him from what Frank Budgen observed is his "homosexual wish" to share his wife with other men.

One of the crucial moments in "Eumaeus" is the tattoo scene. Murphy introduces himself as a native of Carrigaloe, with a "little woman" at home "waiting for [him]," whom he has not seen for seven years (*U* 16.415–21), producing as evidence of his identity his discharge paper from the *Rosevean* (*U* 16.450–52). Elaborating on the "queer sights" and "queer things" (*U* 16.464–66) that he has seen in his career as a sailor, Murphy pulls out "a picture postcard" which, he claims, "a friend of mine sent me," featuring "a group of savage women in striped loincloths . . . amid a swarm of infants," under which is the printed inscription, "*Choza de Indios* [Indian huts]. *Beni, Bolivia*" (*U* 16.471–77). As a number of critics have noticed, the inscription does not, strictly speaking, correspond to the picture. Bloom's doubts are raised when he turns over the card to find that it is addressed not to Murphy but to "*Senor A Boudin, Galeria Becche, Santiago, Chile,*" and that it contains no message (*U* 16.489–90). "[H]aving detected a discrepancy between his name (assuming he was the person he represented himself to be and not sailing under false colours . . . ) and the fictitious addressee of the missive," Bloom "nourish[es] some suspicions of our friend's *bona fides*" (*U* 16.494–98). Murphy's questionable postcard parallels the photograph of Molly that Bloom later produces as his own *bona fides* for Stephen. Both pictures show women in various stages of undress; the bare-breasted Indian women of the postcard pose *National Geographic*-style, while Molly's dress is "cut ostentatiously low . . . to give a liberal display of bosom" (*U* 16.1429–30).

These pictures of women are passed around the group of men not simply for the purpose of sexual arousal but also in order to form bonds with each other in the time-honored fashion of men exchanging women. Indeed, the circulation of the postcard and photograph in the cabman's shelter is a typical male homosocial ritual.[99] Bloom's exhibition of Molly's picture apparently confirms his own heterosexuality while concealing within that display his scarcely acknowledged wish to lure Stephen to himself. Although Bloom's gesture is designed to attest to his normality as well as to induce Stephen to come home with him, Murphy's similar gesture provokes Bloom's anxiety.

The dubious character of Murphy's identity immediately takes on an explicitly sexual cast when Murphy bares his "manly chest" to reveal his tattoo. Murphy's self-exposure reiterates the exposure of the chests of the Indian women and of Molly, with the crucial difference that the breast he bares for their viewing pleasure is a hairy, masculine one. He does so to oblige the members of his audience, who – in the grip of his stories about crocodiles, magical Chinese pills, a man knifed in Trieste, and a certain Simon Dedalus who shot "two eggs off two bottles at fifty yards over his shoulder" (*U* 16.389) – are so transfixed that they stare at Murphy's chest while he scratches lice. "Seeing they were all looking at his chest he accommodatingly dragged his shirt more open so . . . they had a full view of the figure 16 and a young man's sideface looking frowningly rather" (*U* 16.673–76). Later in the episode, Bloom gazes at Stephen's "sideface," thus reinforcing the structural parallel between him and Murphy.

Murphy explains that the tattoo was done by "Antonio, . . . a Greek" (*U* 16.679). When asked, "[W]hat's the number for?" he does not answer; instead, he directs a knowing "half smile" toward the questioner and repeats, "A Greek he was" (*U* 16.695–99). Antonio is not, of course, a typical Greek name, suggesting that his emphatic Greekness has to do with nonracial characteristics connected with the number sixteen. Although Murphy never tells his secret, *Ulysses'* annotator, Don Gifford, informs us that the number sixteen signifies homosexuality in European slang and numerology.[100] In a word, Antonio's Greekness apparently lies in the Greek vice.

While all the other men in the shelter congregate around Murphy, admiring his tattoo, Bloom remains detached. His inchoate awareness of the homosexual implications of Murphy's tattoo is curiously displaced onto a streetwalker who happens to poke her head through the doorway of the shelter at that moment, looking for business. She finds no takers, for all the men are grouped around and gazing at "Murphy's nautical chest" (*U* 16.725–26). Bloom is embarrassed by the fact that he had met her earlier that day when she had "begged the chance of his washing." That recalled incident compels him to "admit" that "he had washed his wife's undergarments when soiled" (*U* 16.712–17), and he is consequently relieved when she leaves. His coprophilic confession immediately induces a reverse discourse: a brief, highly ethical lecture to Stephen concerning the need for the regulation and medical inspection of prostitutes "by the proper authorities, a thing, he could truthfully state, he, as a *paterfamilias*, was a stalwart advocate of" (*U* 16.743–44).

The regulation and inspection of prostitutes was the primary purpose of the Criminal Law Amendment Act of 1885, which linked prostitution with male homosexual behavior, attributing both to unbridled male lust as the "corrupter of youth."[101] Section 11 of that act, which outlawed male homosexuality, recurs in Bloom's mind a few pages later while ruminating over an incident involving O'Callaghan in a sexual indiscretion. He recalls how the latter "had to be spirited away by a few friends . . . so as not to be made amenable [*sic*] under section two of the criminal law amendment act" (*U* 16.1191–94), evidently misreading the Arabic numeral 11 as the Roman numeral II. Bloom's mistake, in keeping with the episode's errant style, sustains his putative ignorance and innocence of homosexuality as well as maintains the ambiguity that obscures the homosexual theme throughout *Ulysses*.[102] While reflecting on O'Callaghan, Bloom "put[s] two and two together" and comes up with "six sixteen," yet, as with Murphy, "he pointedly turned a deaf ear" to the conclusion of his own calculations (*U* 16.1195–96).

Bloom's digression from Murphy's tattooed chest to the prostitute is overdetermined by his preoccupations with women's soiled underwear and public hygiene.[103] Moreover, wanting to present himself as a respectable "*paterfamilias*" to Stephen and thus as someone to whom he can safely entrust himself, Bloom's vagrant interest in the streetwalker also safely deflects his awareness of his intentions toward Stephen. Most of all, the digression draws attention away from Murphy's intriguing tattoo.

Bloom's account of Murphy is colored by his skepticism of the latter's veracity; indeed, he feels that "there was something spurious in the cut of his jib that suggested a jail delivery" (*U* 16.832–33). Murphy is likely a criminal, maybe even a murderer. On the one hand, Bloom's detective speculations render Murphy a melodramatic figure, for in his imagination Murphy looms larger than life. Indeed, Bloom admits that "the lies a fellow told about himself couldn't probably hold a proverbial candle to the wholesale whoppers other fellows coined about him" (*U* 16.845–47). Yet, on the other hand, the "whopper" that Bloom plainly avoids is Murphy's possible homosexuality; he argues instead, for instance, that "the Antonio personage," the Greek tattoo artist, bears "no relation to the dramatic personage of identical name who sprang from the pen of our national poet" (*U* 16.839–40). The friendship between Antonio and Bassanio in Shakespeare's *The Merchant of Venice* has often been thought to have a homoerotic aspect which Bloom, by his disavowal, merely underscores. Indeed, Bloom's comment ironically takes the form of *paralepsis*, the rhetorical device by which a speaker emphasizes a point by pretending to pass it by.

Within the cabman's shelter, Bloom's repeatedly voiced doubts about Murphy's character and truthfulness serve largely to cement, at least in Bloom's mind, the bond between himself and Stephen. Confiding "*sotto voce*" to Stephen, Bloom remarks that "our mutual friend's stories are like himself. . . . Do you think they are genuine?" (*U* 16.821–22). Bloom's reference to Dickens's novel, itself laced with homophobic and homosexual themes, is ostensibly intended to draw Stephen into his confidence, allying them together against the deceptive and sexually suspicious Murphy, while tacitly alluding to the homosexual aspect of their collusion. Murphy thus mediates the relationship between Bloom and Stephen, much as Molly will do in the following episode.

In Bloom's account, Murphy is plumped full of imaginary strangeness and power. Mysterious and exotic like Sinbad the Sailor of *The Arabian Nights*, Murphy is a fantasmic figure, larger than life. Furthermore, he is the object of Bloom's projections both of homosexual perversion and of an intimidating masculinity. His urination, as described by Bloom, is of epic proportions, awakening Gumley in the sentrybox and a horse in the cabrank. Moreover, it prefigures Bloom's and Stephen's mutual micturition in "Ithaca" and exceeds theirs in its display of virility. Despite Bloom's scorn for his "sixchamber revolver anecdotes" and "the usual blarney about himself" (*U* 16.1632, 1635), Murphy commands authority in the cabman's shelter as a real man's man, especially through his abilities as a raconteur. Bloom's equivocal admiration for Murphy is evident when he tries to compete with Murphy through repeated references to his own witty repartee back in Barney Kiernan's pub.

Most of all, Murphy is charged with the allure of the hidden knowledge of homosexuality. His status as the subject who knows secrets, especially sexual secrets, is confirmed late in the episode when he puts on "greenish goggles" to read the newspaper (*U* 16.1672). These green eyeglasses, resembling those of Joyce, render him an author surrogate of sorts. His esoteric and heterogeneous reading habits bear a curious similarity to those of his creator. According to Murphy, his favorite books are *The Arabian Nights Entertainment*, the collection of stories containing the notorious "Terminal Essay" concerning Eastern homosexual practices among men, and *Red as a Rose Is She* by Rhoda Broughton, a sentimental love story with a heavily moral lesson.[104] Sir Richard Burton's translation of *The Arabian Nights* served as a metonymy in late Victorian culture for perverse sexuality in general, contributing to the commonly held belief that the Orient was the seat of sexual license and the origin of corrupting – or, alternatively, liberatory – homosexual practices, evident in fictional works and memoirs by André Gide and T. E. Lawrence.

"Eumaeus" ends with Bloom and Stephen walking home together, the older man full of plans to install the younger one in his house and, perhaps, in his wife's bed. While the father/son dynamic of their relation and its structural significance for the narrative of *Ulysses* have received ample commentary, the eroticism of their union has only recently been given notice. Yet Frank Budgen's early observation, "that his wife is possessed by other males gives [Bloom] physical contact with them at second hand,"[105] is born out by Joyce's remarks on a similar homosocial triangle in *Exiles*, this time between Richard Rowan, his wife Bertha, and his friend Robert Hand. In his notes for the play, Joyce describes Richard's motives in staging a sexually charged, late-night meeting between his wife and his friend.

The bodily possession of Bertha by Robert, repeated often, would certainly bring into almost carnal contact the two men. Do they desire this? To be united, that is carnally through the person and body of Bertha as they cannot, without dissatisfaction and degradation – be united carnally man to man as man to woman? . . . Richard . . . wishes . . . to possess a bound woman Bertha through the organ of his friend. (*PE* 351–52)

In his notes Joyce also imagines Bertha cooperating in his venture: "Bertha wishes for the spiritual union of Richard and Robert and *believes (?)* that union will be effected only through her body" (*PE* 350; emphasis Joyce's). In the play, though, she is more circumspect and resists her husband's attempts to lure her into an adulterous liaison. Richard's staging of this triangle in *Exiles* culminates in a scene of interrogation and confession worthy of Bella/o Cohen. At bottom, the triangles in *Exiles* and *Ulysses* reflect the injunction that Joyce copied from Stanislaus's diary and inserted into "A Painful Case": "Love between man and man is impossible because there must not be sexual intercourse."[106]

Of course, Stephen leaves 7 Eccles Street that night and so defeats Bloom's schemes, but not before the two of them urinate together, "their organs of micturition" conspicuously out of sight, their eyes lifted toward the light in Molly's bedroom window (*U* 17.1186–90). Molly thus serves as both the pretext and the symbol of their conjunction, "the reciprocal flesh of theirhisnothis fellowfaces" (*U* 17.1183–84). Yet the following episode takes Molly far beyond her role as mediator between Bloom and Stephen. By virtue of its unique style, "Penelope" radically reframes the question of (homo)sexual knowledge. Moreover, it explicitly poses the issue of female same-sex desire.

Molly Bloom is famous for telling all; her monologue is a confession of the flesh seemingly free from punitive authorities, guilt, and penance. Moreover, her graphic descriptions of her bodily pleasure attest to her impeccable heterosexual credentials. Yet the spectacle of Molly's body ought not blind us to the ways in which her sexuality shades into the homoerotic; indeed, she is the only one of *Ulysses'* main characters to admit to having had a homoerotic experience. The signs of perversion in "Penelope" fall into two categories: the lesbian and the phallic. While the former signs are rare and muted, associated exclusively with Hester Stanhope, the latter are frequent and emphatic.

Reading lesbianism is, in general, difficult given the historic invisibility or denial of female sexual desire; furthermore, female homosociality and homosexuality were not sharply distinguished until the twentieth century.[107] Molly's relationship with Stanhope might thus be viewed as an intimate friendship whose emotional and erotic energies had not yet been pathologized. The fact that they address each other in letters in Circean terms as "dog" and "my dearest Doggerina" casts only a slight shadow on their relationship. Molly's night with her could plausibly include hugging and kissing and playing with each other's hair and still retain the putative innocence of a slumber party. Yet the scene is also mildly titillating in a soft-porn way and forms part of the larger narrative of Molly's sexual self-exposure. Moreover, the real-life Lady Stanhope was a cross-dresser and explorer of the exotic whose adventures were scandalous.

Although Molly seems quite unaware of the possible implications of her friendship, Joyce surely was not. In the notes for *Exiles*, he describes a similar relationship between the young Bertha and her departing girlhood friend, Emily Lyons. "*A faint glimmer of lesbianism* irradiates [Bertha's] mind" while thinking of Emily, an "older, stronger" woman who is "a prophecy of a later dark male" (*PE* 350; emphasis mine). The structure and tone of the scene in these notes are close to those in "Penelope," with the significant exception that Molly does not betray the slightest knowledge of lesbianism.

In contrast to this particular ignorance, Molly knows quite a lot about heterosexuality and speaks freely of it. Her discourse is energized by her aggressive sexuality, transsexual fantasies, and command of the gaze – all phallic attributes – which serve to excite the reader rather than to stigmatize Molly. While "Penelope" as a whole places Molly's body on display for its readers' viewing pleasure, she also possesses the power to look. Conventionally referred to as the male gaze, this spectatorial power, according to Lacan, signifies having the phallus, as opposed to being the object of the gaze – the supposedly feminine position.

Molly does not simply reverse the masculine and feminine positions of the gaze but plays both sides of it. Most often, she exhibits herself for men, yet she also looks at men, at women, and at herself. Molly notices and compares her hair with that of other women, such as Mrs. Galbraith, a "lovely woman [with a] magnificent head of hair on her down to her waist tossing it back like Kitty OShea." Describing her voyeuristic pleasure at watching Galbraith, Molly also notices the other woman's autoerotic pleasure: "in Grantham street 1st thing I did every morning to look across see her combing it as if she loved it" (*U* 18.479–80).[108] Proud that her bust is larger than that of Kathleen Kearney and other Irish actresses (*U* 18.885–86), Molly also gazes at her own breasts and takes sensual delight in them. "I loved looking down at them," "shaking and dancing about in my blouse" (*U* 18.850–51); "so plump and tempting . . . they excite myself sometimes" (*U* 18.1378–79).

Molly's carefree homoeroticism and autoeroticism seem poles apart from Bella/o Cohen's transsexual performance in "Circe," which stages the most depraved perversions. Yet the sexually adventurous Molly, like the virile Bella/o, imagines switching genders, if only for fun and with another woman: "I wouldnt mind being a man and get up on a lovely woman" (*U* 18.1146–47). Again, she wishes she had a penis but in a way that enhances instead of threatens phallic power: "I wished I was one myself for a change just to try with that thing they have swelling up on you so hard and at the same time so soft when you touch it" (*U* 18.1381–83). As phallic women, Bella/o and Molly tap the same erotic current, yet they must be kept clearly distinct in *Ulysses* for Molly to be an acceptable object of the reader's and Bloom's desires. However, the continuity between the degraded Bella/o and the sexy Molly suggests the continuity between the lesbian and the phallic.

The boundary between the two is further eroded by Molly's association with the many transvestite women in *Ulysses*, of whom Bella/o is only the most notorious instance. Mrs. Bandmann Palmer, the actress who plays Hamlet (*U* 5.196) and who provokes the question of whether "the prince was a woman" (*U* 9.519), is the first in a series of cross-dressing women in the novel. Cissy Caffrey, for example, "dressed up in her father's suit and hat and the burned cork moustache and walked down Tritonville road, smoking a cigarette" (*U* 13.276–77). Mrs. Dignam wears her late husband's trousers and boots when she turns up in "Circe" (*U*

15.3841). Virag taunts Bloom, "have you made up your mind whether you like or dislike women in male habiliments?" (*U* 15.2397–99); indeed, the night before Bloom "dreamed . . . a strange fancy of his dame Mrs Moll with red slippers on in a pair of Turkey trunks" (*U* 14.508–9), literally and figuratively wearing "the breeches" (*U* 13.1241).

Unlike Bella/o, Molly's transvestism remains safely within a heterosexual context. Yet much of the sexual appeal of the cross-dressed woman derives from the perverse exoticism of the reversal of sexual roles. While homosexuality in women was supposedly difficult to detect, the surest sign of it, according to turn-of-the-century sexologists as well as the popular wisdom, was the inversion of gender characteristics resulting in what Krafft-Ebing called "viragines."[109] Molly's graphically depicted, manifestly female body thus apparently places her within the pale of heterosexuality while offering the titillation of the woman with a penis or the kitten with a whip.

The spectacle that is made of Molly and that she makes of herself, including her equivocally lesbian scene with Hester Stanhope, is an incitement to the reader's pleasure. Yet the desire aroused by her frank disclosures is permitted by her peculiar sexual ignorance. The virtually mythic figure of visible, affirmative flesh, Molly is represented as innocent of the knowledge of lesbianism which, if it is not entirely denied or invisible in "Penelope," appears only as a "faint glimmer" in Joyce's and the readers' imaginations. As a reader of her own sexuality, she is at once worldly wise and resolutely naive.

Moreover, Molly is a woman without secrets, a woman who tells all. If homosexuality operates according to a dynamic of secrecy and exposure, so that, for instance, the "Gomorrahan vices" of "Circe" achieve their exciting effect as the promise of the disclosure of hidden vice, Molly's easy revelations play both upon the spectacle of lesbianism and upon its putative innocence. As such, she raises and evades the question of homosexuality, at once representing female same-sex desire and eluding the stigma of sexual inversion as a minority perversion. Molly seems to straddle the divide separating the heterosexual from the homosexual, resisting or simply ignoring the minoritizing pull of the homosexual stigma.

It seems that, in *Ulysses*, ignorance is bliss. Unlike Stephen, who has a phobic knowledge of the love of which he cannot speak, and unlike Bloom, who has a flirtation with sodomy, the knowledge of which he avoids, Molly suffers no anxiety over the implications of her desires and is apparently exempt from the stigma of homosexuality. Yet not knowing is a labor throughout *Ulysses*, a labor that Joyce's characters share with their author and with a society that maintains the pretense that it does not know what it knows. For the price of pretending to be ignorant includes the expenditure or abjection of those who know too much, which always, in one way or another, means oneself.

# CHAPTER 4

# Sexual/textual inversion: Marcel Proust

We would like to have [the author] give us answers,
when all he can do is give us desires.
        Marcel Proust, *Remembrance of Things Past*

*Remembrance of Things Past* is usually read as the record of its hero's journey from misperceptions to intuitive insight, from the forgetfulness of voluntary memory to the indubitability of involuntary memory, from error to epiphanic truth. The novel's "long path of error," according to Roger Shattuck, leads finally, like a detective story, to "the solution," thus giving hope to its readers who must persevere in "the sucession of errors which is our lot."[1] Perhaps every reader of the *Remembrance* has wondered why the trip takes so long, though, and has found herself rather dispirited by the many blind alleys encountered along the way. Responding to early complaints regarding the vagrant, piecemeal construction of *Swann's Way* (before the addition of the Albertine volumes), Proust justified his style because he had chosen to "recreate" the "evolution of a mind," and "so I am forced to depict errors, but without feeling bound to say that I hold them to be errors. So much the worse . . . if the reader believes I hold them to be the truth." The "last volume will clear" up this "misunderstanding," Proust explained. *Time Regained* has certainly been taken as confirmation that, as Proust claimed in this February 1914 letter to Jacques Rivière, "[a]s an artist I considered it more scrupulous and more tactful not to reveal . . . that I was embarking on the search for Truth."[2]

Why did Proust engage in confessedly systematic, scrupulous deception? According to Vincent Descombes, it is because "*the search for Truth necessarily takes the form of a depiction of error.*"[3] However, I propose that we interpret Proust's self-exculpation in the spirit with which he offers it: as a tactful and tactical lie in keeping with the doubleness and duplicity of his hero/narrator. The erroneousness that pervades *Remembrance*, including the erratic narrative and the errant itinerary of its narrator's putative journey to truth, represents it as an unfinishable epistemological task and gives a specific, sexual motive for both the enterprise and its failure. Marcel's jealousy drives his wish to grasp the unknowable Albertine, whose lies are a paradigm for his own as well as for the mendacity of the narrative. Rather than searching for truth, the hero is possessed by a voyeuristic passion for revelation. Antoine Compagnon frankly asserts that the "search for truth is a disguise imposed on the reader."[4]

Before turning to an examination of how and why Proust palms off the search for truth as the raison d'être of *Remembrance*, it may be useful to recall that such an understanding of Proust's novel resembles traditional accounts of Joyce's *Ulysses* and Eliot's *Waste Land*. Their formal fragmentation is said to mime their readers' epistemological errors yet ultimately to bring them to the truth in Eliot's spiritual conclusions or Molly Bloom's corporeal epiphany. Confronted by the manifest textual errancy of these works, critics have been quick to seize upon the possibility that some kind of mind governs and unifies them. F. R. Leavis's belief that *The Waste Land* is "the product of an inclusive consciousness"[5] and David Hayman's confidence in *Ulysses*' "Arranger" are paralleled by the many claims that *Remembrance* issues from a narratorial consciousness which transcends the limitations of its hero. For instance, Gerard Genette insists upon the distinction between the hero and narrator – "the voice of error and of tribulation cannot be identified with that of knowledge and wisdom" – despite what he allows as "transgressions" between the two.[6] The narrative "I" of *Remembrance*, characterized by belated knowledge (the "plus tard, j'ai compris" formula), is said to be the prospective author of the book one holds in one's hands, announcing his intention at the end of *Time Regained* to write a book about time.

The self-reflexivity of Proust's text, like Eliot's self-consciously literary citations and Joyce's incorporation of readers' errors into *Ulysses*, have conspired to promote the notion that these monuments of modernism are, as it were, "total" books, texts that strive for (or achieve) an essence of literariness inasmuch as they include within themselves a critique of the literary values and readerly strategies upon which they are based. Although Proust presents *Remembrance* as a preface to such a book, a prophecy of its coming, whose arrival is postponed into an impossible future, the infinite deferral of the advent of the full book parallels the equally romantic belief that the reader's grasp of it is perpetually deferred by the finitude of her comprehension, leaving her like Moses, who can only catch a glimpse of its Promised Land of textual plenitude. Critics of *The Waste Land*, like those of *Ulysses* and, especially, *Finnegans Wake*, are given to similar pronouncements of the transcendent nature of these texts. Their circular structure, in which the end appears to initiate a return to the beginning, like that of *Remembrance*, buttresses the conviction that these are all-encompassing texts. Such an understanding of these icons of modernism – what Proust calls idolatry – says much about the desires of certain readers and less about the works themselves. The future of these and other modernist works in a postmodern age depends not so much upon assimilating them to up-to-date literary values but upon questioning tacit assumptions concerning the essence of art, regardless of whether the latter is located in modernity or in postmodernity, or whether it takes the form of high or mass culture.

Focusing upon errancy is one way to investigate those aesthetic assumptions, especially insofar as they intersect with the uneasy sense, common throughout the twentieth century, that there is something fundamentally strange, even wrong, with prevailing gender and sexual arrangements. Nowhere is this more apparent than in *Remembrance*, in which the hero's mistaken perceptions are bound up with the narrative's compulsive digressivity. Marcel's interpretive errors are thoroughly imbricated with the novel's textual errancy, both of which are motivated by and engaged in a struggle with sexual errancy, centered upon the problem of Albertine's desire. The elaboration of her "lies" concerning her possible lesbianism produce not only the expansion and transformation of the text of *Remembrance* but plunge the search for truth into an interminable, futile wandering, which cannot end except by means of the deus ex machina of the madeleine. Far from being simply a theme in the novel, the ambiguity of Albertine's desire lies at the crux of the problems it poses concerning the narrative's coherence and closure as well as the narrator's self-consciousness, control, and veracity.

Even more to the point, though, is the question for which Albertine is presented as the answer: Why is she the cause of the novel's epistemological and textual errancy? Compagnon observes "the disparity between the question the work asks and the answer it provides," noting that "putting the literary event back into history would mean demonstrating how the question tries to catch up with the answer."[7] The historical dimension that Proust's work shares with those of Eliot and Joyce is the mystification of female sexuality as an unfathomable monstrosity and the fearful proximity of masculine affection with femininity. Both of these involve an intermingling of the sexes or, in Proust's idiom, the intermediacy of the man-woman of Sodom and Gomorrah. Unlike Sodomites, who are given a detailed genealogy and a precise physiology, Gomorrahans as a whole and Albertine in particular are presented as an unknowable alterity, as though their generalized errancy were the pretext for the failure of Proust's purported "search for Truth."

As every reader of *Remembrance* realizes somewhere in the middle of its thousands of pages, that search goes nowhere. The novel's indirectness, digressions, and deferral of the epiphanies of *Time Regained* point to what Richard Goodkin calls its "avuncular" principle, the sidetracking of the parental narrative axis which calls for a return to the "home" of narrative closure. "Proustian error" entails "missing the mark, not reaching the goal, or even being disappointed if ever one does arrive at it."[8] The parallels that Goodkin draws between *Remembrance* and Homer's *Odyssey* apply equally to Joyce's *Ulysses* and to Eliot's early poetry. D. B. Murphy of "Eumaeus" is patently an avuncular figure, a lying pseudo-Odysseus who waylays Bloom's homecoming, while the homelessness of Eliot's Prufrock characters in his early poetry prefigure Harry's rejection of home in *The Family Reunion*. In all of these cases, "postponement is a blessing," according to Goodkin, just as Proust's endlessly prolonged sentences, analyzing the internal divisions of time, expand each moment to infinity. Moreover, the narrative's burgeoning "growth from the middle" in its revisions between 1913 and 1922, "undermin[e] the very conclusions that Proust's rampant digressions postpone," namely, the conclusive, involuntary memories of *Time Regained*.[9] Albertine hardly seems an avuncular figure, though her disregard for moral and narrative rectitude places her within Goodkin's scheme. Understanding Albertine calls for attention to the erotic investments of reading.

## THE EROTICS OF READING

For the two angels who were posted at the gates of Sodom to learn whether its inhabitants (according to *Genesis*) had indeed done all the things the report of which had ascended to the Eternal Throne must have been, and of this one can only be glad, exceedingly ill chosen by the Lord, who ought to have entrusted the task to a Sodomite. Such a one would never have been persuaded by such excuses as "I'm the father of six and I've two mistresses," to lower his flaming sword benevolently and mitigate the punishment. (*R* 2:655)

Proust's burlesque account of the escape of the Sodomites, whose lies go undetected by the guardians sent to contain them within the condemned city, affronts the straight reader in and of *Remembrance*. Taking as her task the decipherment of sexual and gender identity, such a reader is like the narrator who, in his efforts to discover the truth of Albertine, tries to distinguish delusive appearances from true identity. Drawing the line between heterosexuals and the "cursed race" of Sodom and Gomorrah, or between the natural and unnatural, turns out to be as difficult for the narrator as for the hapless angels sent by God to divide the saved from the damned. The amusing confusion between truth and lies in this passage is reiterated on nearly every page of *Remembrance*, in which signifiers repeatedly turn out not to be the dress of signifieds but their drag disguise. In particular, the deceitfulness of signification arises in terms of the duplicity of sexual identity that mystifies the straight man in the text, Swann, that appears ambiguously to the ambivalently situated narrator, and that is known best to the master manipulator of masks, Charlus.

Homosexuality seems to invade and eventually to take over the novel. In the later volumes, so many characters become or are revealed to be gay that *Remembrance* takes on a apocalyptic tone, comic yet sad, as though the novel represented a slightly tawdry, fin-de-siècle coming-out party. Proust's novel represents on a grand scale the turn-of-the-century shift in sexual paradigms that, as Michel Foucault has argued, transformed same-sex love into a pathological inversion, and sodomites into homosexuals.[10] Yet the revelations of the homosexual orientation of so many characters are rendered in a fashion that acknowledges the darker, painful aspects of this generalized "outing" – that is, the stratagems of concealment to which newly designated homosexuals resorted and the forceable exposure of their desires. What makes Proust's novel so intriguing is that it participates in the modern impulse to tell what is supposed to be the truth about sexuality, sharing the idioms and the epistemological aims of sexual science, while, at the same time, it irretrievably complicates and undermines that impulse. The narrator's relentless observations, his methods of scientific analysis, and his rhetoric of the objective evaluation of evidence are shown to issue from a jealous and hence insatiable passion. The desire to know is, as a consequence, bound to err.

In modernist texts, homosexuality poses a particular epistemological problem and, hence, bears an intimate relationship to error. Whether conceived as a moral straying or as a biological or psychological aberration, homosexuality is paradoxically both interior and exterior to the "natural" sexual order. This peculiar status of homosexuality is compounded by its concealment. Like the Jews with whom they are so frequently compared in modern literary as well as scientific works,[11] homosexuals are often undetectable. Eliot's attempts to purge literary criticism of error are confounded by the equally insidious quality of both sexual perversion and Jewishness. Joyce gives more ample play to the secret of homosexuality, including the fascinating if dangerous proliferation of its indeterminate signs, and the seductive if paranoid urge to expose the secret. Not surprisingly, the male character in *Ulysses* who comes closest to admitting same-sex desire is a Jew, Leopold Bloom. Proust's comically ironic analogy between the "race accursed" and the chosen people hinges upon what the narrator claims is the hereditary yet camouflaged nature of both conditions. Among the shifting scientific paradigms of sexual inversion in the early years of the twentieth century, a common feature was that it was attributed to, in Krafft-Ebing's words, a "congenital abnormality"; like Jewishness, in Proust's view, inversion was biologically caused and revealed by involuntary, often occluded yet ultimately telltale signs. Proust's references to Racine's dramas link the motif of disguise and transvestism with his analogy between inverts and Jews.

Proust's botanical theory of homosexuality, elaborated by the hero after his eyes are opened by the unseen spectacle of Charlus and Jupien's encounter in the Hôtel de Guermantes, endorses the belief that the male invert has, in Karl Heinrich Ulrichs's notorious phrase, "the soul of a woman in the body of a man." The origins of the "race of inverts" lie, according to the narrator, in an archaic "hermaphroditism of which certain rudiments of male organs in the anatomy of women and of female organs in that of men seem still to preserve the trace" (*R* 2:653). While Proust openly espouses what he calls a "congenital essentialism," Compagnon claims that the "botanical metaphor" is neither a condemnation nor a justification of homosexuality but simply describes it as a morally neutral, natural phenomenon. In a daring move, he argues that inversion is the product of the fundamentally "non-deterministic intermittency" of racial memory. The same-sex desire which erupts within and seizes the male invert is "the reincarnation of a female ancestor," rendering him a duality poised between the sexes. This eccentric notion of transmigration accounts for the aleatory, even fortuitous intersection of genesis and event in the occurrence of homosexuality.[12] Although Compagnon focuses almost exclusively upon the "menwomen" of Sodom, as does Proust in *Cities of the Plain*, and although he underplays its pathological valence in the novel as a whole, he usefully draws attention to inversion as a whimsical aberration of nature. Its unpredictable errancy in producing inverts is repeated by the "initial error on the part of society" that segregrates inverts (*R* 2:645), and it is repeated again in the "initial error" of readers who always misinterpret the object of their desires (*R* 3:671). As Malcolm Bowie observes, desire unerringly errs, so that nature's deviations – its "initial hermaphroditism" and subsequent throwbacks – converge with the mistakes to which all desiring readers fall prey and with the errancy of discourse in general.[13]

The theme of sexual inversion that preoccupies so much of *Remembrance* is bound up with erotically charged textual and stylistic inversions. The most pervasive instances of the latter are Proust's interminable and digressive sentences, diverting and inverting proper syntax, and the epistemological reversals of what has been called "Proustian impressionism." Like Elstir, Proust, "instead of presenting things in their logical sequence, that is to say beginning with the cause, shows us first of all the effect, the illusion" (*R* 3:385).[14] Even what Leo Bersani terms the "banal thematization" of inversion in *Cities of the Plain* is inverted, so to speak, by the possibility, broached by Proust, that homosexuality discloses a universal, internal dehiscence within the self, in one's relation to the alterity of one's desires.[15] In this light, the representation of homosexuality in *Remembrance* is compromised by the errancies of textual representation itself, so that the hero's drive for knowledge is at once impelled and defeated by the impossibility of any sure grasp of the enigmatic text of the other's and one's own desires. Despite the reassuring closure of intuitive understanding offered by involuntary memory in *Time Regained*, Proust's novel as a whole records epistemological failure and the deconstitution of sexual identity.

In the utopian version of such a reading, Proust's novel would reveal gender and sexual identity as self-deconstructing, phallogocentric fictions. Sodom and Gomorrah, instead of the topographical loci of a reductive homosexuality, would name the unspecifiable elsewhere of desire, its hopelessly divided nature, and its continual transformations. This reinstallation of the "truth" of Proust's novel at the level of the paradoxical "lie" of homosexuality is encouraged by the narrator – perhaps a reason to view it with suspicion – and hinges upon the asymmetrical opposition of Sodom and Gomorrah. The gender difference between these poles of homosexuality, so crucial to the novel and to the question we have raised – Why is Albertine the motive of the novel's errancy? – was fundamental to modernist understandings of lesbianism and male homosexuality. As we have seen in Joyce's *Ulysses*, male and female same-sex desire operate in quite different modes and discursive registers. The divergence between the two has been insufficiently examined by critics of *Remembrance*.

Advancing Bersani's suggestion, Eve Kosofsky Sedgwick argues that the tortured center of the novel lies in the tension between homosexuality as the particular condition of a minority of people and the diffusion of same-sex desire as a universal human possibility. The "indissoluble, incoherent yoking" of these concepts is such that the "effectual animus of [the] diffusion [of homosexuality] depends unstably on the underlying potential for banal thematization; while the banal thematization . . . displays . . . the sheer representational anxiety of its reductive compaction."[16] In simpler terms, the novel is, on the one hand, driven by centripetal forces toward a definite knowledge of homosexuality and the identification of homosexuals. Thus, Charlus is presented as the exemplary homosexual with an elaborately depicted set of characteristics that signify his perversion. On the other hand, the novel is energized by the centrifugal force of same-sex desire with the capacity of touching everyone, able to infiltrate every sign of desire or even of indifference. Albertine is the epitome of this generalized same-sex desire that permeates and undermines signification – in short, the dispersal of same-sex desire across the sign function. The reading of Proust is, in Sedgwick's view, caught between these conflicting hermeneutic demands in which the discursive generality of homosexuality is policed or controlled by the specificity of the perverse theme.

Because Charlus so visibly incarnates homosexuality while Albertine's lesbianism remains an unresolved enigma, and because the narrator's speculations on the primal origins of inversion overtly concern male homosexuality, critical discussions of homosexuality in *Remembrance* have gravitated, as it were, toward Sodom rather than Gomorrah. Following Proust's lead, Sedgwick and others typically take the Baron as the novel's homosexual prototype, consigning lesbianism to an inarticulate and unarticulable alterity, often failing to consider female same-sex desire in a theoretically sustained fashion. Margaret Gray, a recent critic who does do so, concludes that "Gomorrrah's only history is speculation deriving from its association with Sodom. For the narrator, female homosexuality is not only unknown, it is . . . unknowable."[17] Contributing to the tendency to collapse same-sex desire into male homosexuality and to ignore the female variety as inchoate or insignificant is the long-standing practice of reading Albertine as a man in disguise, a screen for Proust's chauffeur and the object of his affections,

Alfred Agostinelli.[18] The widespread interest in Proust's social life, concomitant with the habit of reading the novel as a roman-à-clef, is based upon the common belief that its interpretive key is the author's homosexuality.

Lesbianism not only comprises a major theme and poses perhaps the overwhelming interpretive dilemma within *Remembrance*, but it also structures the crucial narrative distinction between the narrative voice – the "I" that is fleetingly called "Marcel" within the novel – and the authorial "I" with whom the narrative voice is so closely aligned. Throughout much of the novel these two voices seem to blend or even blur with each other so that, as Leo Bersani argues, "we are constantly tempted to confuse the two; it is as if Proust were trying to make us forget the differences between Marcel and himself." Bersani's view is premised upon the fact that, throughout much of the novel, the narrator possesses the ability to peer into and conjecture in an authoritative manner about the motivations of other characters. The reader is thus lured into the mistaken belief, as Bersani puts it, that "the narrator's *je* has the full authority of the author's *je*."[19] The conspicuous exception to this rule is his lack of knowledge concerning Albertine's sexual desires.

Albertine's possible lesbianism drives a wedge between the narrator and the author. Her sexuality is what the former endlessly labors to learn yet never succeeds in doing; it marks the limits of his knowledge and thus the difference between himself and Proust. This rupture also prevents the novel from being read as a bildungsroman concerning the hero's growth from a naive youth into a disillusioned but wiser old man. His instruction in life does *not* include his education into the mysteries of lesbianism. The two volumes of the novel – *The Captive* and *The Fugitive* – devoted to his failed attempt to discover the facts of Albertine's sexuality are sometimes disparaged as a tedious hypertrophy, even as the nadir of the novel, but they are its crux insofar as they force the uncomfortable recognition that Albertine's sexuality introduces an ongoing and irresolved disjunction between the three levels of narration: "Marcel" the character, the narrator, and the author. The uncertainty regarding her sexuality generates a fundamental asymmetry within the narrative structure, a confusion underscored by the fact that "Marcel" is named as such within the novel by Albertine. In these volumes, the question of her lesbianism incites the jealousy that Bowie calls "the quest for knowledge in a terrifying, pure form," and the search for truth becomes lost in the labyrinth of desire.[20]

*Remembrance* is structured by the opposed axes of desire symbolized by

Sodom and Gomorrah. The former represents male same-sex desire as inversion, a relatively fixed sexual definition marked by cross-gendered behavior and desire and typified by Charlus, who, Brichot jokes, should be appointed to "a Chair of Homosexuality" (*R* 3:311). By contrast, Gomorrah is the locus of mobile, indefinite, female desire, of boyish girls like those in the little band at Balbec or like Odette, dressed up as Miss Sacripant in Elstir's painting and typified by Albertine, who admits that she once "dressed as a man, just for a joke" (*R* 3:340). In the hero's eyes, the dandyish style and amorphous sexuality of girls like Andrée is a far cry from the effeminacy of Charlus, which he views with revulsion. Whereas the women are almost always the objects of desire, Charlus is placed, like the hero, as a desiring subject. When, like Mlle Vinteuil, they become desiring subjects, they are virilized and degraded as sadists; by the same token, the Baron's descent into a passive or "feminine" sexual position is the road to masochism. In the *Cities of the Plain*, the nature of inversion is dissected under the heading of Sodom, whereas Gomorrah is spread out through the text and is never given a theoretical explanation. Although the hero's discussion of these "men-women" nominally includes female as well as male inverts, he subsequently admits that "love between women was something too unknown, whose pleasures and nature nothing enabled me to imagine with certainty." In short, Sodom seems to be the locus of masculine knowledge, and Gomorrah, of feminine mystery.

However, this opposition is misleading inasmuch as there are, in fact, many crossovers between the two poles in the novel. Not only does Mlle Vinteuil migrate toward Sodom as she is masculinized, but there is never any doubt about the nature of her friend's desires; the hero calls her "a practising and professional Sapphist" (*R* 2:1153). Both Saint-Loup and Morel, as sexually fluid characters yet whose masculinity is unquestioned, tend toward Gomorrah. On the theoretical level, the hero's fantasy of Gomorrah as an unknowable alterity eventually reifies it as an absolute Other; by the end of the novel, the homoerotic girls of Balbec have been transformed into an occult abstraction. By contrast, the apparently static figure of the hermaphroditic Sodomite, as Compagnon has shown, turns out to give free play to chance "intermittencies" of homosexual desire. In Gilles Deleuze's formulation, it serves as a trope for the "coexistence" within the individual of "fragments of both sexes [as] *partial objects*," in short, for a "transsexuality . . . based upon the contiguous partitioning of the sexes-as-organs" instead of "sexes-as-persons."[21]

These crossovers between Sodom and Gomorrah suggest that we attend to the imbalances of this opposition. Observing that Proust typically "sets forth symmetries only to slant them; he establishes poles and then brings them together," Compagnon argues that it is the "in-between" which "is essential to Proust's work."[22] For our purposes, this will mean taking with a grain of salt the hero's pronouncements concerning Gomorrahan unknowability. Nonetheless, distinguishing between Sodom and Gomorrah has the merit of foregrounding the radically different status of male and female homosexuality in Proust's texts as well as in the modernist milieu that he shared with Joyce and Eliot. For all of these writers, male homosexuality occupied the nadir of sexual degradation, while lesbianism often represented an enticing eroticism, by turns pure and wicked, either – or both – a sapphic heaven or a Baudelairian hell.

Before turning to *Remembrance*, it may be useful to digress to Proust's essays on Ruskin and reading where he adumbrates a theory of reading as a passionate forgetfulness motivated by the reader's love for the text, but a passion that in turn consumes the reader. This exchange of places between the desiring reader and the desired text, in which the subject, instead of taking possession of the object, surrenders to it, is analogous to the relation between penetrator and penetrated in the economy of sodomy. The parallel between these textual and sexual economies is significant because it clarifies Proust's understanding of male same-sex desire and offers a way of interrogating the notion of homosexuality as such, including the question of whether there exists such an "as such." Proust's essays cast into doubt the belief that a text or a beloved person can be grasped by the penetrating reader. The particular discursive disruption marked by homosexuality sheds light on reading as a whole by broaching the question of how to read its errant signs, a question to which all of the answers are wrong yet which, as a lie, "can open windows . . . for the contemplation of universes that otherwise we should never have known" (*R* 3:213). The erotic relationship between reader and text, and the problem of misreading in general, are illuminated by the mendacity and illegibility of the homosexual text.

## ERRORS OF AFFECTION: RUSKIN, VENICE, AND READING

The assumptions of the proper aims and methods of reading that inform Proust's early writings are the commonplace ideas that reading is a mediated recollection of the author's thoughts, as the latter are transcribed in the written text. A faithful reading is true to the author's intentions and is, in effect, an act of homage that reanimates his meanings. Proust's critical essays therefore assume a filiative model of reading similar to Eliot's. The point in Proust's career at which he most clearly articulated these assumptions and began to question them was the moment when he tried to be faithful to an author with whom he explicitly affiliated himself, John Ruskin, in his translations of *The Bible of Amiens* and *Sesame and Lilies*, the prefaces to which have been translated, together with his notes, in *On Reading Ruskin*.

Proust's prefaces to Ruskin's essays delineate the latter's hermeneutics yet depart from them even as he tries to reanimate or, in his words, to "restore" the "tomb" of Ruskin's text. Rather than breathing life into the form of the dead letter, Proust finds himself, almost against his will and certainly against his stated aim of remembering Ruskin's work or "giving it back to us through recollection," forgetting Ruskin (*ORR* 61). He strays from the latter's intentions instead of, as Ruskin had demanded of the reader, "annihilating" himself in order to "resurrect" the text. In the end, Proust's passion for Ruskin leads him not only to disavow the latter's authority but to reject the notion of reading which had formed the basis of that passion. He ultimately implies that reading is as faithless and vacillating as love and, like love, inevitably betrays the object of its desire. In Proust's analogy between reading and love, David Ellison argues, impassioned reading produces a "cycle of errors."[23] The errant erotics of reading traced by Proust in the course of what he calls his "infatuation" and subsequent disillusionment with Ruskin's text becomes the basis for the enactment of reading in *Remembrance of Things Past*.

Ruskin writes in *The Bible of Amiens* that his method of reading was formed by reading the Bible: "the duty enforced upon me in early youth of reading every word of the gospels and prophecies as if written by the hand of God, gave me the habit of awed attention" (*ORR* 20). This passage, according to Proust, is "the center of gravity of Ruskinian aesthetics," for Ruskin's "religious feeling [not only] directed his aesthetic feeling," thereby subordinating art to moral ends, but his "religious fervor" was "the sign of his aesthetic sincerity," protecting him from the "foreign encroachment" of ulterior pleasures (*ORR* 36). The central problem in Ruskin's thought, Proust argues, is that religious feeling, or sense of awe at the sacred, is both the guardian *and* the product of art, at once the guarantor of moral truth *and* the effect of beauty. As a consequence, Ruskin's aesthetic passion mingled promiscuously with his Christian enthusiasm, the former constantly threatening to take over or betray its guardian and thus rendering true belief indistinguishable from idolatry. Ruskin's ambivalence toward the religious image and the feelings it evokes is present throughout his work but is addressed directly in appendix 10 of *The Stones of Venice*, entitled "The Proper Sense of the Word Idolatry." There he claims that "idolatry is . . . the serving or becoming the slave of any images or imaginations which stand between us and God, and it is otherwise expressed in Scripture as 'walking after the *Imagination*' of our own hearts." Despite his vehement condemnation, he admits that, "in this sense, which of us is not an idolater?"[24]

In *The Seven Lamps of Architecture* Ruskin had interpreted the cathedral of Rouen as an instance of a preindustrial, nonalienated relation of the laborer to his work; according to Proust, the cathedral exemplifies Ruskin's "belief in the necessity of free, joyful, and personal work without the intervention of mechanization" (*ORR* 44). To demonstrate that relation Ruskin described a tiny figurine over the Porch of the Booksellers. However, Proust's reading of Ruskin's description of that figurine passes over the latter's interpretation and fixes upon the figurine itself. "Seized with the desire to see the little man" (*ORR* 45), Proust travelled to Rouen where, catching sight of it, he was moved to a rapture by it, not as an exemplification of the joyous work of the medieval artist nor as a finely crafted work of art ("there was nothing truly beautiful" about it), but as a fetish object in his personal cult of Ruskin. Singled out and "named" by Ruskin, "the little man" had been "at the call of Ruskin . . . resurrected in its proper form" (*ORR* 47). Proust's apotheosis of Ruskin as the savior of this "monstrous little figurine" implies that the ultimate object of idolatry is Ruskin himself, the beauty of whose prose has seduced him and into whose heart and mind he seeks to penetrate.

Proust's preface to *The Bible of Amiens* begins by following the instructions laid down for reading by Ruskin himself in *Sesame and Lilies*. In order to understand "great" authors "[y]ou must love them, and show your love in these two following ways: First, by a true desire . . . to enter into their thoughts," and then "to enter into their Hearts . . . that you may share at last their . . . Passion." Hence, "what is rightly called 'reading'" is "putting ourselves always in the author's place, annihilating our own personality, and seeking to enter into his, so as to be able assuredly to say, 'Thus Milton thought,' not 'Thus *I* thought, in misreading Milton.'"[25] Proust adopts Ruskin's notion that reading is an act of devotion involving empathetic identification and submission, the reader emptying himself out in order to be filled by the author and, concomitantly, to "enter" into the latter. However, Proust's reading of Ruskin, no less than the latter's reading of Milton, is far from a disinterested effacement of the self. His love for Ruskin cools remarkably later in the preface as he moves from reverential appreciation to angry rejection and, finally, to a calm recollection of his now-dead infatuation.

At first, Proust forgives what he considers to be Ruskin's misjudgments by arguing that the general truths of art that he adumbrates are independent of the aesthetic qualities of particular works of art or assessments of them. "The beauty of his erroneous judgment is often more interesting than the beauty of the work being judged and corresponds to something which, in spite of being something other than the work, is no less precious" (*ORR* 48–49). Ruskin's mistakes thus lead or "correspond" to aesthetic truths, which are revealed to the inspired observer, not the dispassionate judge. Indeed, Proust argues that the truth of an interpretation of an artwork is determined not by the artwork itself but by the response it engenders in its viewer or reader: "it is perhaps enthusiasm in art that is the criterion of truth" (*ORR* 48). In short, he abandons the referent of literary or aesthetic interpretation altogether and embraces a theory of reading as desire.[26] Yet Proustian passion is highly unstable, oscillating between ardor and disillusion, as does his love for Ruskin. The concluding section of the preface, written several years after the earlier sections, opens with a broadside attack on Ruskin, charging him with the very idolatry that he had condemned in his *Lectures on Art*, from which Proust quotes:

Such I conceive to have been the deadly function of art in its ministry to what . . . is truly, and in the deep sense, to be called idolatry – the serving with the best of our hearts and minds some dear and sad fantasy which we have made for ourselves, while we disobey the present call of the Master, who is not dead, and who is not fainting under His cross, but requiring us to take up ours. (*ORR* 50)

Proust accuses Ruskin of having been lured from his vocation – the work of social and moral justice that Ruskin tirelessly argues is the sole justification of art – by aesthetic blandishments. Ruskin succumbed, not in his deeds, but in his heart, "in those profound, secret regions" where lust hides, and which forced him to "a continual compromising of conscience" (*ORR* 50–51).

The story of Ruskin's corruption presented by Proust is a seduction narrative. Moreover, because he refused to admit that he had been seduced, Ruskin tricked out his aesthetic predilections in the appearance of religious devotion – a double inversion of his avowed moral values.

"The doctrines he professed were moral doctrines . . . yet he chose them for their beauty. And since he did not wish to present them as beautiful but as true, he was forced to deceive himself about the nature of the reasons that made him adopt them" (*ORR* 51). Ruskin's "*unavowed aesthetic preference*" therefore forced him into repeated and "addict[ive]" deceit, a "sin" whose secret and compulsive character and whose inversion of Ruskin's stated hierarchy of morality over beauty point toward that nadir of sexual decadence and hypocrisy: Venice.

In his condemnation of Ruskin, Proust adopts the position of the straight man, offering as an instance of Ruskin's "trickery" a passage from *The Stones of Venice* that he finds "most beautiful." The example cited by Proust of Ruskin's seduction is itself a story of seduction and moral inversion. Furthermore, this "error of affection" is the effect of another misreading – the refusal of the Venetians to read the truths written on the walls of their cathedral.

Never had [a] city a more glorious Bible. Among the nations of the North, a rude and shadowy sculpture filled their temples with confused and hardly legible imagery; but, for her, the skill and treasures of the East had gilded every letter, and illuminated every page, till the Book-Temple shone from afar off like the star of the Magi . . . [T]he sins of Venice . . . were done with the Bible at her right hand . . . And when in her last hours she threw off all shame and all restraint, . . . be it remembered how much her sin was greater, because it was done in the face of the House of God, burning with the letters of His Law. (*ORR* 51–52)

Against Ruskin's jeremiad, Proust argues that the vices of the Venetians were no worse for their having had a beautiful church in their midst. Yet his objections are themselves disingenuous. Proust wishes to condemn Ruskin for violating his own principle of the subordination of "aesthetic feelings" to "moral feelings," but he admires the beauty of that violation and finds its very falseness alluring. Indeed, his pleasure in the deceptive beauty of Ruskin's prose resembles the "impure" joys of the narrator of *Remembrance* as he stands in the mysterious darkness of St. Mark's. His sensual delight is intensified and corrupted by the sacred texts inscribed on its walls, for the cathedral's luxurious sensuality is a kind of profanation of the holy. Like "the mosaics of its style that dazzled in the shadows," Ruskin's prose mingles verbal lasciviousness with Biblical quotations (*ORR* 53). This erotic defilement prefigures the scene between Mlle Vinteuil and her female lover at Montjouvain in which they spit on the image of Mlle Vinteuil's father to incite their pleasure.

In *Remembrance*, Venice is one of the enchanted scenes of the hero's imagination. It is thus fitting, in terms of the economy of passion and power in the novel, that his father suggests a trip to Venice but immediately withdraws the proposal after the narrator, "raised to a sort of ecstasy" at the thought of "penetrating" this city of his dreams, contracts a fever and is sent to bed by his doctor-father (*R* 1:426–27). Thereafter, until late in the novel, Venice remains a name pregnant with magic. Ruskin is only rarely, yet significantly, mentioned in connection to it. Like Ruskin, though, who was "amazed at the secret virtue there is in a word," for whom it was a "flask full of memory" (*ORR* 157), the hero delights in the word "Venice."

Indeed, Venice has the status of what Roland Barthes calls a "Proustian Name," designating a milieu steeped in reveries as well as a precious object that contains hidden pleasures. The hero makes this quite clear when, imagining the trip to Italy, he thinks "of names . . . as a real and enveloping atmosphere into which I was about to plunge," while "the life not yet lived, the life, intact and pure, which I enclosed in them gave . . . to the simplest scenes the same attraction that they have in the works of the Primitives" (*R* 1:423). Longing to enter into and to be entered by the world signified by "Venice," he has a Cratylean faith in the power of the name. Accordingly, Barthes argues, the name undergoes a "semic dilation" in *Remembrance*, functioning both paradigmatically (containing within it the essence of a place or person) and syntagmatically (linking together several scenes, which thereby comprise a narrative).[27] But what sort of "semantic monstrosity," in Barthes's words, does Venice represent and what story does it tell?

The many references to Venice throughout *Remembrance* form an itinerary of deferred desire. As Tony Tanner points out, "not-getting to Venice is one of the recurring preoccupations and themes for over five-sixths of the book."[28] The hero's excuse for not going is that doing so would entail losing Albertine. In short, Venice and Albertine are posed as mutually exclusive choices. When he does visit the city it is with his mother, after Albertine's death, although she is repeatedly revived in his memory and in a mistaken telegram. One reason for keeping Venice and Albertine physically separate is that, in terms of the narrative structure of the novel, they represent the same thing: the impossibility of penetrative knowledge. The hero's "Venetian imaginings" (*R* 3:420) locate desire in a distant, inaccessible, aestheticized place – a Gomorrah.

Yet he does, finally, go to Venice and delve into its convoluted depths. His explorations of the city and his liaisons with prostitutes tell a very different story – indeed, two different stories – which will lead us back to

Ruskin. On the one hand, Venice is the locale of a peculiar geograph-
ical and erotic fluidity, while, on the other hand, it carries strong implications of an orientalized homosexuality. Nissim Bernard's intrigue with
the byways of the Grand Hotel where he seeks out homosexual liaisons
prefigures the hero's interest in Venice and, moreover, links the former's
Jewishness with his perversion:

He loved . . . all the labyrinth of corridors, private offices, reception-rooms,
cloakrooms, larders, galleries which composed the hotel at Balbec. With a strain
of oriental atavism he loved a seraglio, and when he went out at night might be
seen furtively exploring its purlieus. (*R* 2:874)

In its "semantic monstrosity," Venice is a paradigm for the divergent
directions of sexual desire in the novel.

Elstir had remarked of Venice as depicted in Carpaccio's paintings
that "you couldn't tell where the land finished and the water began, what
was still the palace or already the ship" (*R* 1:959). The indeterminacy of
Venetian typography represents a blurring of the boundaries of nature
and culture, and of categories of identity in general. For instance, the
hero achieves sexual satisfaction by imagining himself both *as* and *with*
Albertine; in Venice, he says, "I accosted plebeian girls as Albertine
perhaps had done, and I should have liked to have her with me" (*R*
3:642). Bowie argues that Venice is "a privileged site for phantasy and
. . . transformations of desire" and hence is "a model not only of desire
in perpetual displacement but of the sublimating and desublimating
exchanges that occur between the sexual and the cultural realms." An
example of such an exchange, Bowie observes, is Albertine's Fortuny
cloak, worn by a male figure in a Carpaccio painting, which undergoes
a series of gender and sartorial transformations.[29]

The hero's bisexual phantasies are suggested by the description of his
gondola ride through the small canals. "Like the mysterious hand of a
genie leading me through the maze of this oriental city, they seemed . . .
to be cutting a path for me, . . . barely parting, with a slender furrow,
. . . the tall houses with their tiny Moorish windows" (*R* 3:641). The
Eastern cast of the hero's vision of Venice and of the sexual license it
thereby offers are underscored by a series of references, here and
throughout the novel, to the *Arabian Nights*. With its tales of exotic sexual
practices, the book was a topos of sexual perversion in modernist literature. In *Ulysses*, D. B. Murphy's preference for reading the *Arabian Nights*
is an indication of his sexual preferences, just as for André Gide, as for
many European men, the East offered the opportunity to engage in

homosexual pederasty.[30] A few pages before we are told of Nissim Bernard's penchant for labyrinthine corridors, we learn that the hero is engaged in reading the *Arabian Nights* at Balbec.

Proust's references to the book and to its famous "open sesame" often allude, playfully and ironically, to Ruskin. For instance, late in the novel, the hero visits Jupien's brothel and denounces it as "a veritable pandemonium. I thought that I had arrived, like the Caliph in the *Thousand and One Nights*, . . . to rescue a man who was being beaten, and in fact it was a different tale" – that is, he witnesses the Baron engaged in a masochistic sex scene. Jupien replies to his outrage by citing another book that he has seen at the Baron's house, a translation of Ruskin's *Sesame and Lilies* which the hero had sent Charlus. He invites him to come to his brothel some night where his open window is "my private Sesame. . . . As for Lilies, if they are what you seek I advise you to go elsewhere" (*R* 3:862). By means of such allusions, Proust suggests a subterranean confluence between a series of seeming opposites: between the moralistic and the sensual Ruskin, between the *Arabian Nights* as a collection of stories of heroism and a collection of tales of perversion, and between the straight hero and the queer Baron. Indeed, the former confesses that the latter's "desire to be bound in chains and beaten, with all its ugliness, betrayed a dream as poetical as, in other men, the longing to go to Venice" (*R* 3:870).

The hero's ambivalent yearning "to go to Venice" is linked to his hesitation between the two poles that Venice represents: erotic and cultural polymorphousness, and homosexual perversity. The latter is apparent in his account of his nocturnal wandering through the city, which is described as an allegory of anal sex.

I went out alone, into the heart of the enchanted city where I found myself in the middle of strange purlieus like a character in the *Arabian Nights*. It was very seldom that . . . I did not come across some strange and spacious *piazza* of which no guidebook, no tourist had ever told me. I had plunged into a network of little alleys . . . packed tightly together . . . Suddenly, at the end of one of these alleys, it seemed as though a distension had occurred . . . A vast and splendid *campo* . . . spread out before me surrounded by charming palaces silvery in the moonlight . . . [I]t seemed to be deliberately concealed in a labyrinth of alleys, like those palaces in oriental tales whither mysterious agents convey by night a person who, brought back home before daybreak, can never find his way back to the magic dwelling. (*R* 3:665)

Unlike his casual, afternoon pleasures with female prostitutes, the hero's solitary, night-time venture leads him into wayward, hidden alleys. Thrusting into those "tight," rectal passageways, he suddenly discovers an opening that offers ecstatic pleasure, a strange, voluptuous delight unknown to all but those who have been taken captive by their "oriental" powers.

The sodomite subtext of Venice is hinted at obliquely in a glancing reference he makes to "some work [he] was doing on Ruskin" immediately before he visits St. Mark's (*R* 3:660). If we return to *The Stones of Venice*, to a passage that Proust does not cite in his essays, we find that Ruskin explicitly links the sins of Venice to those of Sodom and Gomorrah. The inversion of the aesthetic order in these cities is directly attributed by Ruskin to their inversion of the proper sexual order, described in lurid terms.

[Y]ear after year, the nation drank with deeper thirst from the fountains of forbidden pleasure, and dug for springs, hitherto unknown, in the dark places of the earth. In the ingenuity of indulgence . . . Venice surpassed the cities of Christendom . . . ; and as once the powers of Europe stood before her judgment-seat . . . , so now the youth of Europe assembled in the halls of her luxury, to learn from her the arts of delight . . . It is as needless, as it is painful, to trace the steps of her final ruin. That ancient curse was upon her, the curse of the cities of the plain . . . By the inner burning of her own passions, as fatal as the fiery rain of Gomorrah, she was consumed from her place among the nations; and her ashes are choking the channels of the dead, salt sea.[31]

Ruskin's denunciation of aestheticism finds its fitting vehicle in the figure of Sodom and Gomorrah, which he decries in a torrent of language that permits the expression of his censored aesthetic desires.

The rhetorical hellfire that Ruskin rains upon Venice informs not only Proust's claim that Ruskin practiced the vices that he disavowed but also his representation of homosexuality. In *Remembrance*, Charlus's sexual orientation, which he calls an "aesthetic" preference for boys, is explained by the hero in terms that echo Ruskin's condemnation of the inversion of moral and aesthetic values: "Society is like sexual behavior, in that no one knows what perversions it may develop once aesthetic considerations are allowed to dictate its choices" (*R* 3:236). The structure and effects of Ruskin's dissimulation are similar to those of Charlus, as seen by the hero, whose vices betray him precisely through the means he employs to hide them. For "the various compromises to which he had been driven by the need to indulge his taste and to keep it secret . . . had the effect of bringing to the surface of his face precisely what the Baron sought to conceal" (*R* 3:206). Indeed, Ruskin's strategy of negation resembles that of Joyce's Stephen Dedalus. Like Joyce, Proust depicts overt male homosexual desire mostly in the form of contemptible figures. In an ironic fashion, Proust sets up his hero as another Ruskin, as a self-righteous and hypocritical commentator on other people's sexual mores.

The failure of the Venetians to read "the letters of [God's] Law," like Ruskin's misreading of Venice, according to Proust, issued from wayward affections, from loving beauty more than the truth. However, in the final pages of the preface to *The Bible of Amiens*, Proust acknowledges his own errant affection for Ruskin as well as the fact that such ardor was the enabling if superseded condition for his grasp of Ruskin and his translation of his text. For only by "subjecting [his] mind" to Ruskin and to "that longing without which there is never true knowledge" (*ORR* 58) – in brief, only through "idolatry" – was Proust able to understand the world as Ruskin saw it. Nonetheless, such love destroys its object, leaving the corpse of a "cold memory" and the suspicion that his passionate reading was an error, Ruskin's text having been only a pretext for his own "unavowed aesthetic preferences."

The preface to *Sesame and Lilies* develops Proust's critique of idolatry. Entitled "On Reading," it is divided into two sections: the first is a narrative recollection of scenes of reading from Proust's childhood, and the second, a discursive essay warning against the dangers of reading and its overvaluation. So strongly does Proust argue against reading, and so thoroughly does he depart from Ruskin's essay, devoted to what Ruskin calls "the treasures hidden in books," that readers have often been confused by the preface.[32] In his diatribe, Proust empties reading of content and cognitive value in order to reinvest it rhetorically with an erotic charge that admits precisely the idolatry that he denies on the thematic level.

The apparent triviality of Proust's elaborately detailed descriptions of the scenes of his childhood reading seems to underscore his claim that "[r]eading should not play the preponderant role in life that Ruskin assigns to it" (*ORR* 110). Contradicting Ruskin's assertion that the reading of "good books is like a conversation with the most cultivated men of past centuries who have been their authors" (*ORR* 111), Proust scorns the belief that one finds the truth in them. In contrast to Ruskin's angry indictment of the economic privations that prevent the working class from having the opportunity to read and his Arnoldian vision of the morally uplifting power of "great literature," Proust is interested in the psychology of reading, of "lingering in those flowery and out-of-the-way roads" (*ORR* 111) of reverie induced by popular novels, and, especially, in the secluded, self-indulgent pleasure of solitary reading. The locale of reading is the private space: the "wild and mysterious depths of the park" near his home, whose "labyrinth" of bushes and trees "sheltered [his] reading," or the "secret" hours when he would slip away to the "inviolable" solitude of his bedroom (*ORR* 107–8, 100). These scenes of hidden reading are similar to those in *Remembrance* where the hero's furtive reading in the lavatory is recounted as a masturbatory delight (*R* 1:13, 172). Indeed, his reading in the water closet suggests both the closeted pleasures of reading and a reading of his own closet.[33]

Not only do sexual and textual activities take place in similar locations but they operate in a similar manner. Typically in Proust's work, the enclosure of the book or the room – or the labyrinthine Venetian canals – discloses an exorbitant interior. This inner space is the site of a desire that breaches its boundaries and consumes that which holds it. One of the "fundamental figures" in *Remembrance*, according to Gilles Deleuze, is that of *"encasing"* or *"envelopment."* Books are like containers that, when explicated, reveal "an excessive content."[34] Similarly, in the preface, the happiness of opening and taking possession of a new book is described as like that of entering a hotel room where,

> when one opens the door . . . , one has the feeling of violating all the life that has remained scattered there, of taking it boldly by the hand . . . ; to sit with it in a kind of free promiscuousness on the sofa . . . ; to touch everywhere the nakedness of that life . . . , by pretending to be the master of that room full to the brim with the soul of others and which keeps . . . the imprint of their dreams . . . ; one has then the feeling of shutting in with oneself this secret life when one goes, all trembling, to bolt the door; of pushing it in front of one into the bed and finally lying down with it under the large white sheets. (*ORR* 106–7)

The interior, erotic site is here turned inside out. The body of the text, originally the enclosure of the self and the site of masturbatory pleasure, is fantasized as the body of the other, penetrated and mastered by a desire that circulates according to the economy of sodomy. The reader's body, seduced and incorporated into the text, reverses its position and in turn attempts to penetrate the text.

The axis of desire in Proust's text is, in this regard, faithful to the classical discourse of sodomy, which is structured according to the positions of the actors (penetrator/penetrated), rather than the modern discourse of homosexuality, which is based upon the sameness of their gender.[35] The dynamics of sexual/textual sodomy in Proust's essay are marked by a fundamental oscillation, determined not only by the uncertainty of the reader's dominance ("*pretending* to be the master of that room") but by the ambivalence of a desire that suspects its mastery to be only a more complete enslavement. Thus, the reader and the text, or the penetrator and the penetrated, continually exchange places in an endless, futile attempt to possess fully, and thus to read, the other.

This sodomite dynamic is at odds with the other prevailing libidinal model in *Remembrance*, associated with lesbianism and characterized by the inaccessibility of the beloved. In textual terms, this Gomorrahan model is marked by an original error from which all other (mis)interpretations ensue. The hero's misreading, in Venice, of a telegram that he had supposed to be from the dead Albertine is representative of what Bowie calls the general shift from "factual *erreur*" to "textual *errance*" in the novel.[36] Whether the hero's mistake stems from the ornate and sloppy handwriting of the actual author of the telegram, Gilberte, or from distortions introduced by a careless telegraph clerk, or from his own wishful thinking, does not matter. Like the imbrications of textual corruption, transmission error, and interpretive misunderstanding in *Ulysses*, these multiple and ever-multiplying mistakes confront the narrator with the ineluctability of error. They all add up to the unknowability of the other.

> We guess as we read; everything starts from an initial error; those that follow (and this applies not only to the reading of letters and telegrams, not only to all reading) . . . are quite natural. A large part of what we believe to be true . . . springs from an original mistake in our premises. (*R* 3:671)

The hero's first mistake is to try to get to the bottom of Albertine, whose illegibility is a paradigm for the errancy of all texts and whose lesbianism epitomizes the elusiveness of every object of love. As we shall see, Proust complicates these two libidinal models, represented by Sodom and Gomorrah, in *Remembrance*.

No doubt the most amusing passage in Proust's preface to *Sesame and Lilies* is his analysis of the perils of reading, all of which amount to inversions of value homologous to what he calls idolatry. The first and most common error is to substitute reading for the "life of the spirit," believing that truth is not realized within one's mind but is "a material thing, deposited between the leaves of books like honey ready-made by others" (*ORR* 118). A related but "less dangerous" mistake is to conceive of truth as "far off, hidden in a place difficult of access." Proust's remarks inadvertently poke fun at professors applying for sabbatical leaves: "What happiness, what repose for a mind tired of seeking the truth within to tell itself that it is located outside, in the leaves of a folio jealously preserved in a convent in Holland . . . No doubt we shall have to make a long trip," conduct research, and engage in interesting and picturesque adventures, all for the ostensible purpose of "taking possession of the truth – of the truth which for greater prudence, and so that we do not risk its escaping us, we shall jot down" in a notebook (*ORR* 118–19).

In both of these cases, the reader's mistake is to believe that truth resides in a material entity – in a book or a place – and thus to venerate the signifier over the signified. Ruskin's insistence on the necessity for books "with . . . stout leather binding[s]," "every volume having its assigned place [on the shelf] like a statue in its niche," manifests such error.[37] Proust dwells lovingly and at length on the pleasures of travelling to Holland, whose delusiveness he later examines in terms of the hero's infatuation with the idea of Balbec in *Remembrance* and whose disappointments are analogous to those of love. Indeed, they are "not different disappointments at all but the varied aspects which are assumed . . . by our inherent powerlessness to realise ourselves in material enjoyment or in effective action" (*R* 3:911). In short, the love of persons and of places are both fictions of reading. The "guise of truth" presented by novelists, whose landscapes make a "far stronger impression" on the reader's mind than an actual one, creates the illusion that one can "break out into the world" (*R* 1:92–93). Likewise, the "fascination of [the] book" is, according to the narrator of Proust's novel, a "magic" (*R* 1:94) that obliterates the reality which it allegedly represents. In his essay, Proust condemns the literary man's "fetishistic respect for books," which are for him "motionless idol[s]." Yet his reproach of "bibliophilism," which renders the book "a source of death" (*ORR* 120), suggests that it touches upon his seduction by Ruskin as well as upon the seductiveness of his own narrative of seduction, whose pleasures belie the charges he levels against them. As he wrote of Ruskin, an "unavowed aesthetic preference" forces him into compromises and brings about the return of the outlawed desire – in short, the return of the deceitful, errant charms of language.

Proust surrenders to the delights of textual passion in the famous passage on "Incitement." What the author offers as his conclusions serve the reader only as a stimulus: "We feel quite truly that our wisdom begins where that of the author ends, and we would like to have him give us answers, when all he can do is give us desires" (*ORR* 114). The virtue of reading is the longing it induces in the reader to penetrate the surface of the text, whose beauty leads to a fervor for the author and the places he describes. "This appearance with which [authors] charm and deceive us, and beyond which we would like to go, is the very essence of that

thing without thickness . . . – mirage fixed on a canvas – that a vision is."
Combining his Sodomic and Gomorrahan aesthetics, Proust imagines
that this hymenal "mist which our eager eyes would like to pierce is the
last word of the painter's art" (*ORR* 115). The incitement that the author
gives to his readers, at once a seduction and a deceit, is directly linked to
the epistemological model advanced in *Remembrance* in which the jealous
desire to know is essentially voyeuristic. In effect, the narrator of the
novel induces a similar voyeurism in its readers while refusing to provide
"answers," or, at best, misleading ones.

What Proust describes here as a beneficent vice (and elsewhere calls
an "intellectual sin") is a pleasure in which he indulges in the concluding pages of the essay: the illusion of entering the space to which the text
or image transports us. Not surprising, that place happens to be Venice.

How many times . . . have I known that impression of having before me,
inserted into the present actual hour, a little of the past, that dreamlike impression which one experiences in Venice on the Piazzetta, before its two columns
of gray and pink granite . . . [I]n the middle of the public square, . . . a little of
the twelfth century . . . springs up in a double, light thrust of pink granite . . .
[T]hose high and slender enclaves of the past are . . . in another time where the
present is forbidden to penetrate. Around the pink columns, surging up toward
their wide capitals, the days of the present crowd and buzz. But, interposed
between them, the columns push them aside, reserving with all their slender
impenetrability the inviolate place of the Past . . . appealing . . . to the mind,
overexciting it a little, . . . yet there, in our midst, approached, pressed against,
touched, motionless, in the sun. (*ORR* 128–29)

The phallic intrusion of the past into the present masters and penetrates
it even as the past is enclosed within and "pressed against" by the spec-
tator's vision. Indeed, the past is itself an "inviolate" enclosure, doubling
and reversing the relations of container and contained.

These flesh-colored columns enclosing a lost time articulate a
sodomite erotics of reading – the reversible exchange between penetrator and penetrated – which, in *Remembrance*, is traded for a lesbian model.
There, the hero's attempt to immure Albertine is caught in what Deleuze
calls a "curious torsion" by which his imprisonment of her in order to
pry open her mystery winds up trapping him in her strange universe.[38]
More broadly, his construction of the objects of his perception is rendered doubtful by a hidden alterity in those objects which engulfs the
perceiver, an invisible otherness whose proper name is Albertine.
However, this name is itself dubious, more an incitement to desire than
an answer to it.

In both its male and female guises, the phenomenon of homosexuality is coextensive with a discursive crisis in modern literature since it requires signs for what should not exist. As a negation of the natural order, same-sex desire is a concealed nothingness, a deprivation or privative mode of existence. Writing about the love for another of the same sex entails the production of signs with phantom referents, which lie when they speak of the truth of that desire and which lie when they do not. Inasmuch as a sign is such because it can lie, homosexual signifiers are signs par excellence. As a consequence, same-sex desire has been and continues to be, especially for women, always deniable and often denied. The problem of homosexual representation is therefore not a regional issue but a convulsion of language, one response to which has been to claim that homosexuality is a specific psychosexual disorder, to insist that, with homosexuality, a *legible* mistake has been made. For these reasons, it is not surprising that Proust argued that the gay people are the natural, albeit bizarre, products of a hermaphroditic error. His theory of homosexuality as a biological aberration normalizes it but at the price of consolidating heterosexuality as the true norm. Like Eliot's efforts to purify literary criticism of deviant elements, and like Bloom's wish to distance himself from the perversion to which he is susceptible in *Ulysses*, Proust's hero abjects male homosexual desire, but just as unerringly that errant desire returns. Perhaps the continuing appeal of the novel lies in the disparity between its stated aims and the errant effects of the narrative, in the duplicitous gap between what the narrator should know and what the hero says. The deconstitution of homosexuality in *Remembrance* begins with an account of the failure of consciousness to grasp its objects, including itself, or, through memory, to frame a story of that failure.

## REMEMBRANCE OF THINGS PAST

Proust's novel stages its hero's attempt to understand his life by recovering "lost time." Remembering is not simply the reminiscence of past moments in their sensuous immediacy – e.g., the taste of the madeleine – but is a systematic effort of self-reading coextensive with a retrospective narration that recapitulates the present moment in its genesis.[39] In the concluding pages, the hero announces with a thrill, "I seemed to see that this life that we live in half-darkness can be illumined, this life that at every moment we distort can be restored to its true pristine shape, that a life, in short, can be realised within the confines of a book!" (*R* 3:1088).

That book, Proust implies, is *Remembrance* itself, whose moment of writing has been postponed throughout the novel yet is allegedly coextensive with it. This conclusive gesture imposes a retroactive unity and circular structure upon the book, whose end is its beginning and vice versa, as well as posits its transcendent aesthetic value. The prospective book will not only "restore" life to its "true pristine shape," but life is not really lived at all until it is actualized within a fiction. Finally, Proust's conclusion advances the distinction between what Hans Robert Jauss calls the "remembering 'I'" and the "remembered 'I.'" [40]

Do the thousands of pages that precede *Time Regained* support this idealized image of the book and the fundamental split between narrator and protagonist? The hero's remarks immediately after his vision of literary self-realization cast a shadow upon the matter: "the writer feeds his book, . . . but afterwards it is the book that grows, that designates its author's tomb" (*R* 3:1089). The promised book, nurtured by its writer who seeks to read within it the clarified image of himself, turns out to be his grave. The surprising recurrence of incarceration figures throughout *Remembrance* suggests that writing is a kind of necrophilia, Serge Doubrovsky argues, manifested in the hero's "lethiferous love" for Albertine, a Poe-like fantasy familiar to readers of Eliot and not uncommon in modern literature.[41] Moreover, the trope of textual inversion, of interment in the work to which one simultaneously gives birth, recalls the thematics of sexual inversion.

The hero's wish to write a book in which he can read himself is inspired by the déjà vu experience of involuntary memory. The distinction between it and voluntary memory is another of the symmetrical oppositions that Proust erects, like that between Sodom and Gomorrah, which is promoted by the hero but which Proust silently subverts throughout the novel. An extension of perception, voluntary memory is limited to the presentation of an image that is little more than a "snapshot" or an "identity card photograph" (*R* 2:5) used for practical purposes and suffering the vicissitudes of time. By contrast, involuntary memory is epiphanic and atemporal. At odd and unexpected moments, such as when the hero slips on a paving stone and experiences a sensation like that which he felt in St. Mark's, the entire experiential context of the past moment is resurrected with "the exact, forgotten, mysterious, fresh tint of the days" that heretofore one could only recall in the "undifferentiated tones of voluntary memory" (*R* 2:5–6). The latter forms an "artificial impression," whereas involuntary memory, bestowed by chance but with the force of a compulsion, gives "the real impression." However, these "extra-temporal" moments in which one "enjoy[s] the essence of things" are locked in "sealed vessels" that are "absolutely different one from another"; they are isolated fragments which cannot form a bridge to each other or to the present moment but remain discrete "bits of time" (*R* 3:903–4).

The difference between these two kinds of memory – empirical and transcendental – is crucial for claims that the hero undergoes a spiritual transformation at the end of *Remembrance* and that the novel itself achieves its search for the truth in an aesthetic vision, somewhat akin to Stephen Dedalus's quest in *A Portrait of the Artist as a Young Man*, abandoned in *Ulysses*. Nevertheless, these claims obscure or overlook the fact that both types of memory are intermittent and fragmentary. As Deleuze points out, they are equally comprised of disparate images that coexist contingently, often without communicating or connecting, making up an ensemble of heterogeneous universes between which the hero shuttles.[42] These multiple, detached fragments, whether in the impoverished mode of "snapshots" or in the richness of "sealed vessels," can be recalled only in their isolated states. Forgetfulness is therefore caused not simply by the gradual erosion of memories but by faults and gaps within consciousness. Benjamin observes that involuntary recollection is a way of forgetting,[43] obliterating the discontinuities upon which it is based.

The paired oppositions upon which traditional readings of *Remembrance* are based – the difference between voluntary and involuntary memory, the homology between the novel and the novel-to-be-written, and the separation of the narrating from the narrated "I" – are not fully sustained by text. This disparity between what the text says and what it does leads Descombes to conclude that, in effect, Proust was wrong. Because the "thoughts reported *in* the narrative do not coincide with the thoughts that may be communicated *by* the narrative," Proust's philosophy of the novel contradicts his philosophy within the novel.[44] However, such an internal divergence is problematic only if one wishes to establish a true text. One of the bones that Descombes picks with Proust concerns his figure of "mental optics," the metaphor of the mind as a glass through which one sees the world, which is central to the theme of errancy in the novel and to the problem of its narrative voice. The hero tirelessly repeats that mistakes of judgment result from the unique standpoint and visual equipment of every viewer and, hence, are optical illusions. By contrast, Descombes points out that corrections of error in the novel do not proceed by a change in perspective – that is, by adopting the viewpoint of another – but by disenchantment, by abandoning "the exquisite mirage which love projects" (*R* 3:696). Although love does not figure in Descombes's analysis, and he quickly moves to assert that Marcel achieves his artistic vocation by journeying beyond his "misguided social career" to the "religious experience" of the epiphanies in *Time Regained*,[45] he inadvertently suggests the significance of passionate voyeurism in Proust's optical figure.

That figure may shed fresh light on the old problem of the narrating/narrated "I" and its relation to the reader. On the brink of writing "this" book and thereby reading his own life, the hero mirrors the reader of *Remembrance*, who is likewise, "while he is reading, the reader of his own self" (*R* 3:949). Presenting himself as a model reader, the former's successes and failures seem an instructive allegory for those who take up Proust's novel. He explicitly offers his text as an "optical instrument . . . to the reader to enable him to discern what . . . he would perhaps never have perceived in himself," adding that "the recognition by the reader in his own self of what the book says is the proof of its veracity" (*R* 3:949). Even if the hero's interpretations are consistently mistaken, his vision distorted by jealousy, those losses can be recouped as a reflection of the human condition; hence, for Shattuck, the optical imagery shows "the *errors* of our vision . . . Error establishes itself as one persistent principle of Proust's universe."[46] However, the hero is less quick to admit that he might be wrong. Ruminating on the book he is about to write in which his own life will be "realised," he allows that readers might not see things quite the same way:

For it seemed to me that they would not be "my" readers but the readers of their own selves, my book being merely a sort of magnifying glass . . . – it would be my book, but with its help I would furnish them with the means of reading what lay inside themselves. So that I should . . . ask them . . . to tell me whether "it really is like that," I should ask them whether the words that they read within themselves are the same as those which I have written (though a discrepancy in this respect need not always be the consequence of an error on my part, since the explanation could also be that the reader had eyes for which my book was not a suitable instrument). (*R* 3:1089)

This intrusion of the narrative voice foregrounds the persistent question of who is speaking in the novel – the hero Marcel, the narrator, or Proust himself. These narrative layers render the novel an eminently deniable text, what Bersani calls a "nonattributable autobiographical novel,"[47] permitting all three from being implicated by its perverse spectacles.

The narrator of *Remembrance* is, in Genette's view, depersonalized and anonymous, the voice of anybody who reads it, not because he is Everyman but because he is an empty term, subjectivity stripped of a subject. He claims that "Proust renounces the all too well centered 'he' . . . for the decentered, equivocal 'I' of a Narrator who is not precisely either the author or anyone else, . . . a self without foundation, a self without a self."[48] The structural opposition between the narrating and the narrated "I" parallels another well-worn, dubious distinction: the phallus and the penis. In principle, the phallus, the symbol of the Law of the Father, is irreducible to the penis, an anatomical entity, yet they bear an uncanny resemblance to each other. Distinguishing between an abstract subjectivity (the narrator) and an empirical subject (Marcel) protects them and Proust from certain embarrassments. The passion for revelation in the novel – the constant, jealous searches for secret truths, the voyeuristic gazes, the involuntary, shameful disclosures – alludes endlessly and alluringly to Proust but without directly exposing him. By contrast, Gray argues that the hero, the narrator, and Proust "cohabit" within the "je." "The narrator's moralizing 'truths' emerge as patent cover for his own failure to understand the world," disingenuously shifting from *je* to *on*, not to differentiate between "the mystified hero and the knowing narrator" but in order to conceal the "futility" of the latter's knowledge, particularly his inability to grasp Albertine.[49]

The doubling of the narrative voice initiates a series of specular relations between homologous sets of readers within the text. Just as the narrator reads the hero, so the latter reads Albertine. Furthermore, the "optical instrument" of the text implies that the reader is placed in a specular relation to the hero/narrator. Because these relations are reversible (the lens becoming a mirror), the narrator and the hero cannot ultimately be distinguished. Indeed, the hero (or, if one wishes, the narrator) is not sure if he sees anything other than himself, suspecting that Albertine is "an inverted projection" of his own imagination (*R* 1:955). Besides pointing to the self-reflexivity of the novel, which Genette rightly observes is like a "Moebius strip in which the inner and outer sides, . . . ceaselessly turn and cross over" in a "reversible circuit,"[50] these series of specular relations show the power of the gaze in the novel. The reader is likewise caught up in its voyeurism, titillated by Proust's seeming self-disclosures in its narrative instrusion.

Proust toys with this prospect endlessly. In the following passage, for instance, the hero is placed simultaneously inside and outside the text, imagining himself as a discarded character in the hands of an indifferent novelist.

The . . . suspicion . . . was that I was not situated somewhere outside Time, but was subject to its laws, just like those characters in novels who, for that reason, used to plunge me into such gloom when I read of their lives . . . [M]y father had suddenly made me conscious of myself in Time, and caused me the same kind of depression as if I had been . . . one of those heroes of whom the author . . . says to us at the end of a book: "He very seldom comes up from the country now. He has finally decided to end his days there." (R 1:520)

On the level of the fiction, the speaker's anxiety is plausible, yet, on the level of the work, the passage is incoherent. The atemporality of fictional characters induces in him, a fictional character, an awareness of his mortality, which supposedly becomes the motive for his authorship of a novel in which he is a character subjected to the vicissitudes of time. According to Maurice Blanchot, the conflation of the time of narration and the narrative of time in Proust's novel makes it impossible to discern not only "to which time the events he evokes belong" – either in the story or "before" it – but also the identity of the speaker, who "is no longer either the real Proust or the writer . . . but the shade into which they have been metamorphosed . . . Proust has become inaccessible."[51]

"Proust's" concealment depends upon that of Albertine. His inaccessibility is advertised and his secret life as the author or possibly the hero is flaunted in the scene where Albertine, poised between sleeping and waking, names the hero as "Marcel." Flirting with the reader, he affirms and denies the autobiographical "I": "Then she would find her tongue and say: 'My —' or 'My darling —' followed by my Christian name, which, if we give the narrator the same name as the author of this book, would be 'My Marcel,' or 'My darling Marcel'" (R 3:69). Such moments of the text's ontological oscillation are likewise those when Albertine's sexual desires are inscrutable. She not only names Marcel, but she is also the one who, as it were, unnames him. She calls Marcel (Proust) by name, but her sexuality is precisely what Marcel-the-narrator never knows and thus what prevents him from being taken as the author of Remembrance. Albertine's ambiguous confession of lesbianism (R 2:1152) broaches the possibility of her double life, which not only mimes but makes possible the double life of Remembrance as an autobiography/novel. The ambiguous factual/fictive status of the text is thus directly linked to the enigma of lesbianism. This is not to say that the hidden truth of the novel is Albertine's or Proust's "real" homosexuality. Rather, by posing female same-sex desire as an occult mystery, Proust fictionalizes fact and factualizes fiction, making it impossible to account for one in terms of the other. The text generalizes the hero's desire for homosexual disclosure (his wish to "get to the facts" of Albertine) by placing the reader in the same uneasy position. In short, *Remembrance* incites in its reader the passion for looking that it so amply represents while rendering its own narrative "eye" inaccessible – the perfect voyeuristic scenario.

Proust toys with the double life of *Remembrance* in many amusing asides in which the hero directly addresses the reader. For instance, he interrupts the narrative to announce that, "[i]n this book in which there is not a single incident which is not fictitious, not a single character who is a real person in disguise," he is compelled by patriotism to tell the true story of the Larivière couple (*R* 3:876). His insistence on the fictional status of the text even as he intervenes in order to mention one fact induces precisely those doubts regarding its status that the intervention pretends to lay to rest. Such self-reflexive and self-canceling references occur with remarkable frequency in the novel. According to Genette, this doubling of the narrative seems to be a "door . . . leading to something other than the work."[52] Instead of sending us beyond the text to external sources, though, the "dizzy rotation" provoked by its non-identity to itself points to the double lives of its characters. Just as the hero pretends, from time to time, to break through fiction to real life, so the people he describes are characterized by duplicity, especially when they confess their genuine desires. Beneath the surface of society in *Remembrance* exists a hidden world of Sodom and Gomorrah which, in its concealment, seems to offer the truth yet which only generates more illusions. The "something other" to which Genette refers is thus not outside the novel but an interior alterity. In particular, it is not homosexuality as a fact, discoverable by investigating extratextual sources, but homosexuality as an otherness within the text. Like the "noxious power" of Albertine's "vice," same-sex desire "infect[s]" the world of the novel. Watching the scene at Montjouvain, the hero had "perilously allowed to open up within [him] the fatal . . . Knowledge" of homosexuality (*R* 2:1152), which leads to a pervasive "inversion of symbols" (*R* 2:1157) and a paranoid proliferation of signs. If understanding the self entails deciphering an "inner book of unknown symbols" (*R* 3:913), Albertine is a closed book.

The impossibility of knowing the Other is accounted for by Proust in terms of perceptual laws that do not immediately imply a sexual alterity. The absence of either a stable viewpoint or perceptual object defeats the possibility of exact comprehension. Each perception of a person is belated and inaccurate, "for while our original impression of him undergoes correction, the person himself . . . changes"; whenever "we think that we have caught him, he shifts, and, when we imagine that at last we are seeing him clearly, it is only the old impressions . . . when they no longer represent him" (*R* 1:934). The nonidentical and adventitious particles of which perception is composed render unitary presentations of both the self and its objects mirages on the brink of dissolution. "Every person is destroyed when we cease to see him; after which his next appearance is a new creation, different from that which immediately preceded it, if not from them all." Because each perception is a "rectification" or "revised version" that erases the previous memory (*R* 1:978–79), these endlessly redrawn images, temporally and spatially superimposed upon each other produce, as Genette puts it, a palimpsest.[53] This plethora of images would be a blessing, each day bringing fresh wonders, if perception were not motivated by desire. The subject's longing to know is frustrated not only by changes in perspective and the mutability of the object but by the very interest that provokes it. The images of those we do not love are fixed in our minds, "[w]hereas the beloved model does not stay still; and our mental photographs of it are always blurred" (*R* 1:528). The hero harps on the theme that, in order to grasp Albertine, he "should have to immobilise [her], to cease to live in that perpetual state of expectancy ending always in a different presentiment," for only when we have lost interest in people do there emerge, "from the false judgment of our intelligence, . . . well-defined, stable characters" (*R* 3:58, 60). To be sure, his attempts to imprison Albertine and to control the fluctuations of her image are doomed to failure since she is immobile only when asleep, when she becomes a blank screen upon which he projects his wishes.

Albertine's character is presented as either a proliferation of multiple possibilities or an empty, opaque space. On the one hand, she signifies too much – she is semiotically excessive, generating a metastasis of signs. Like "a many-headed goddess" (*R* 2:379) with ten faces and preternatural powers of transforming herself into various shapes, Albertine is legion; she is everywhere. Her shapes possess no unity and, like the other luminous girls of the little band at Balbec, each time she appears she "so little resembles what she was the time before . . . that the stability of nature which we ascribe to her is purely fictitious" (*R* 3:59). The luxuriance of her signs prevents the narrator from attaching to her any distinct character except the variability of a mirage. According to Samuel Beckett, "the *pictorial* multiplicity" of Albertine at Balbec "evolve[s] into a *plastic* and moral multiplicity, no longer a mere shifting superficies and an effect of the observer's angle of approach . . . but a multiplicity in depth, a turmoil of . . . immanent contradictions over which the subject has no control" and even less knowledge.[54] On the other hand, Albertine signifies nothing at all. She is merely a dumb "stone which encloses the salt of immemorial oceans," and one can no more touch her than open a "sealed envelope" (R 3:393). Her semiotic fecundity finally issues in semantic impoverishment or senselessness.

Because Albertine is more or less "a collection of moments" corresponding to aspects of the narrator's consciousness, when he tries to free himself from her memory after her death he finds that "in order to be consoled I would have to forget, not one, but innumerable Albertines" (R 3:487). Even worse, "[i]t was not Albertine alone who was a succession of moments, it was also myself," so he must bury the "composite army" of selves that parallel each piece of Albertine (R 3:499, 540). These fragmentary perceptions leave him with sets of conflicting images from different times, since memory "record[s] photographs independent of one another, eliminat[ing] every link" (R 1:936). These discordant memories comprise noncommunicating temporal lines that occasionally intersect but fail to coalesce into a synthetic image. The hero is unable to form a coherent picture of an object, for "if one tries to take a snapshot of what is relatively immutable in it, one finds it presenting a succession of different aspects . . . to the disconcerted lens" (R 3:332).

What ultimately disconcerts the lens, though, is that the image it seeks to capture is only a projection of the "magic lantern" itself. The figure of the photographic image also signifies the inverted, projective nature of the imagination. Thus, the pictures taken by the hero are not even partially accurate representations but are always already distorted presentations which require the acid of reflective "development" – an interpretive reversal – before they reveal their truth. Describing his pleasures with the girls at Balbec as those of a photographer, the hero remarks that "[w]hat we take, in the presence of the beloved object, is merely a negative, which we develop later . . . [in] that inner darkroom" of the self (R 1:932). The repeated references to the mind as a "darkroom encumbered with innumerable negatives" (R 3:931) increasingly seem to allude to unconscious forces that, far from retrospectively correcting perceptions, distort them. Trying to discover the truth of Albertine's lesbian inclinations requires reversing appearances, somewhat like reading backwards or developing negatives, and even inverting one's own emotions: "what one feels is like a negative which shows only blackness until one has placed it near a special lamp and which must also be looked at in reverse" (*R* 3:933). Getting at the truth calls for negating negatives, attending to disavowals and inverted statements – in short, exposing the falsity of one's beliefs about oneself.

*Remembrance* is eloquent on the subject of lying to oneself. Far from transparent or authentic, the internal discourse of the self is laced with deceit. The massive textual production of love – "our feverish projects of letters and schemes," "all that we have not ceased . . . not only to say to the loved one but . . . to repeat endlessly to ourselves" – comprises "an oblique interior discourse" whose "rectification" requires "the task of a . . . translator" (*R* 3:926). The hero is no better at translating than at developing photographs, though, and persists in his "passionate dialogue." Albertine's supposed falsehoods are matched by his evasions and betrayals. He confesses to "placing features, for instance, . . . upon the face of a woman seen in the street, when instead of nose, cheeks and chin there ought to be merely an empty space with nothing more upon it than a flickering reflection of our desires" (*R* 3:1103). An accurate representation of a person would be a projection of one's own multifarious passions and thus wear a "hundred different masks" (*R* 3:1104). Such a person would be a monster, as, indeed, Albertine assumes demonic proportions; she is the vacant site of desire, "a vast, vague arena" in which the hero exteriorizes his jealousies (*R* 3:505). In effect, Albertine does not exist. As Beckett notes, "The person of Albertine counts for nothing. She is not a motive, but a notion . . . removed from reality," the locale of the hero's internal struggles.[55]

Within this drama, Albertine figures as a "sealed vessel" that the hero, with the force of an obsession, attempts to open. For Proust, to read is to desire, and the reader's desire is always for the Other who is concealed within the sign. Albertine becomes "no longer a woman but a series of events on which we can throw no light, a series of insoluble problems, a sea which, like Xerxes, we scourge with rods in an absurd attempt to punish it for what it has engulfed" (*R* 3:100). This description effects an inversion of the figure of the container/contained so common in *Remembrance*, in which the unintelligible sign swallows its puzzled reader. This inversion occurs not by chance in the course of the hero's attempt to disclose the mystery of Albertine's lesbianism. The truth that he avoids as much as he seeks, the locus of his projected fears and desires and the privileged site of deceit in Proust, is lesbianism. According to Deleuze, "all the deceptive signs emitted by a loved woman converge upon the same secret world: the world of Gomorrah, which itself no longer depends upon this or that woman . . . , but is the feminine possibility *par excellence.*"[56] In a word, the interpretive dilemmas posed by the text, ranging from the hero's efforts to read himself in the specular relationship between the narrating and the narrating "I" to his efforts to read Albertine and, by extension, to the reader's efforts to interpret the narrator (he is our Albertine), are confronted by lies, which in *Remembrance*, Deleuze asserts, "are organized around homosexuality." However, he mystifies Gomorrah as "the deepest expression of an original feminine reality,"[57] thereby repeating the hero's own obscuration.

In a similiar but less mystical vein, Mieke Bal argues that, because Albertine is the focus of its "exploration of alterity," the "libidinal model" of *Remembrance* is not male homosexuality but lesbianism. The narrator's "epistemological anxiety is constantly fed by glimpses of her ontological difference: she is unknowable because, as a woman and as a lesbian, she *is* doubly other."[58] Unlike Joyce, for whom the "faint glimmer" of lesbianism appears as a more or less enticing male heterosexual fantasy, Proust confronts what Bal calls the "painful inaccessibility" of female same-sex desire for a man. However, locating absolute Otherness in lesbianism, or privileging homosexuality as a master trope for sexual and textual errancy, will prove to be another mistake. The hero attributes this mistake to Charlus but flirts with it throughout the novel.

What is most striking in the representation of Albertine, evident in the contradiction between her semiotic proliferation and her semantic vacancy, could be termed her inverted signature: the negativity or the inversion of the signs in which she is encoded. While she shares "the happy aptitude for a lie" with many other characters in *Remembrance* – for instance, with Odette – Albertine's lies are distinguished not by their intentional nature, which remain in question, but by the way in which lying constitutes her character. For the hero, she incarnates the lie.

Albertine epitomizes deceit for several reasons. First, she is an excellent storyteller. Lying in the *Remembrance* is synonymous with narrative fabrication and hence is a means of exerting power. Other characters as well as the hero tell competing stories that cannot be adjudicated by reference to a veridical plot, and the stories they tell sometimes undermine his narrative authority. Second, Albertine's tales have a special status insofar as they systematically belie his version of her life. Complicating the matter is the fact that her stories are related by the same enamored hero for whom she is an inflated symptom of his own fears and desires. Her putative lies are thus transpositions of the lies he tells himself. Third, Albertine symbolizes discursive duplicity. As we have